Praise

The Redemption

"*The Redemption of Bobby Love* is the perfect title for a story that explores both redemption and love with such vital, fulsome heart. At once tender and brutal, the Love family's journey explores parenthood, marriage, the penal system, and the human condition of sustaining hope in the center of the storm. The systems that govern our most vulnerable are larger than one family, and yet this family's story encompasses those systems with a power that will shake you."

—Jeff Hobbs, author of *The Short and Tragic Life of Robert Peace*

"The full, astounding story of an unbelievable life and what it means for true love to endure above all else."

—*Newsweek*

"This book is more than a jailbreak/escapee story. Sure, there's lots of drama and tension, but in the hands of Bobby and his wife, Cheryl, faith and love take center stage in this well-paced book about forgiveness and revealing a person's true self."

—*Garden and Gun*

"In this moving story of struggle and forgiveness, an escaped convict reflects on his life in hiding alongside his wife of thirty-five plus years. . . . In parallel narratives from Bobby and Cheryl, those secrets are disclosed against the history of their unshakable love. . . . Readers will be awestruck by this inspiring account."

—*Publishers Weekly*

"A rumination on the justice system and the way that it can work in inequitable ways. . . . Coauthored in an alternating storyline by Bobby and his wife, Cheryl, the book sees the Loves rewind their love story and dissect Bobby's 'roadmap to destruction.' . . . Bobby writes honestly about his own self-reflection, the realities of growing up in North Carolina during Jim Crow, and the impact that incarceration had on his early life."

—*Booklist*

"A warmhearted story of an ex-con's long and winding road to an honest life."

—*Kirkus Reviews*

"In this captivating memoir, Bobby and Cheryl Love share the astounding secret Bobby had kept for over thirty-five years of their marriage: that Bobby wasn't his real name and that he had escaped from prison when he first met Cheryl. . . . The Loves's warmth, humor, and honesty shine from the pages."

—*Library Journal* (starred review)

The
Redemption
of
Bobby Love

The
Redemption
of
Bobby Love

A Story of Faith,
Family, and Justice

Bobby and
Cheryl Love

with Lori L. Tharps

MARINER BOOKS

New York   Boston

HarperCollins books may be purchased for educational, business, or sales promotional use. For information, please email the Special Markets Department at SPsales@harpercollins.com.

A hardcover edition of this book was published in 2021 by Houghton Mifflin Harcourt.

FIRST MARINER BOOKS PAPERBACK EDITION PUBLISHED 2022.

Book Design by THE COSMIC LION

Photographs courtesy of Bobby and Cheryl Love

The Library of Congress has cataloged a hardcover edition of this book as follows:

Names: Bobby Love and Cheryl Love, authors; with Lori L. Tharps.
Title: The redemption of Bobby Love / Bobby and Cheryl Love
Description: Boston : Houghton Mifflin Harcourt, 2021.
Identifiers: LCCN 2021010182 (print) | LCCN 2021010181 (ebook) |
ISBN 9780358566052 (hardcover) | ISBN 9780358566229 (ebook) |
9780358581703 (CD) | 9780358581871 (audio)
Subjects: LCSH: Broome, Brian. | Escaped prisoners—
New York (State)—New York—Biography.
Fugitives from justice—New York (State)—New York—Biography.
African American men—New York (State)—New York—Biography.
Prisoners' families—New York (State)—New York—Biography.
Classification: HV6248.L816 (print) | LCC HV6248.L816 A3 2021 (ebook) |
DDC 364.1092/27471
LC record available at https://lccn.loc.gov/2021010181
LC ebook record available at https://lccn.loc.gov/2021010182

ISBN 978-0-06-326907-1 (paperback)

22 23 24 25 26 LSC 10 9 8 7 6 5 4 3 2 1

For our parents:

Annie Miller &
James Edward Miller
(Bobby)

Reverend George Leon Williams &
Gertrude Williams
(Cheryl)

Jeremiah 29:11 "For I know the thoughts that I think toward you," says the LORD, "thoughts of peace and not of evil, to give you an expected end."

Romans 8:28 And we know that all things work together for good to them that love God, to them who are the called according to *his* purpose.

Contents

Authors' Note

The Redemption of Bobby Love is a memoir. The story you're about to read is true and is based on our memories and recollections of the events we lived. To protect the privacy of the people who did not agree to have their stories told in these pages, we have changed the names and identifying details of most of the people mentioned. In a few cases, to limit confusion, we have created characters who are an amalgamation of multiple people in our lives.

The
Redemption
of
Bobby Love

A Knock at the Door

CHERYL

It was still dark when I opened my eyes. Bobby was asleep next to me, but I could hear Jordan rattling around in the kitchen. It was Thursday. That meant Jordan had to catch the subway by 6:15 in order to make it to school for his 7:00 a.m. class. I gave thanks that the twins were so responsible that they didn't need reminding to get up for school and out the door on time. As high school juniors, they showed us every day their growing maturity. I peered at the clock on my nightstand and sure enough, it was 5:30 a.m.

I slipped out of bed, careful not to wake Bobby, grabbed my robe from the chair, and padded to the kitchen without bothering to put on my slippers. Even though our little Brooklyn apartment was cramped —Bobby and I slept in the living room, pretending it was a fourth bedroom—at least it was toasty warm. Even in January, my bare feet weren't cold on the linoleum floor.

Jordan was drinking the milk from his cereal bowl, standing at the sink. I made a face but didn't say anything. I knew he was rushing. Instead, I went to fill the kettle for my tea and Jordan dashed back to his room to collect his things. Before he could make it out the door, I stopped him. "Wait a minute, Jordan," I called, making my way over to my son. He knew what I wanted.

We bowed our heads together, and I reached for his hands. Normally I would have woken up Bobby to pray with us, but I decided to let him sleep.

"Father God, in the name of Jesus, I ask you to keep us safe and covered as we go about our day," I began. Jordan grew still as I prayed over him, as I did every day for all of my children before I allowed them out of the house. It was our regular ritual, no exceptions.

"Amen," I whispered and smiled up at my son, who was now several inches taller than my five-foot-seven frame.

Jordan bent over and kissed my cheek. "I love you, Ma," he said before he slipped out the door.

I tiptoed back to the kitchen as I heard the teakettle begin to whistle. I grabbed a peppermint tea bag out of the box in the cabinet and set my tea to steep. The sun hadn't yet come up, but I knew it was going to be a nice day. The weatherman had said it was going to be sunny and in the low forties, which was a blessing for a New York winter. I thought about how many layers I'd have to put on for my walk to work. After fourteen years walking to the same office, the same thirty-minute route, I knew exactly how to dress for my daily commute but still look appropriate for the office. As a nutrition coordinator, I didn't have to dress fancy, but I always wanted to look nice for the clients I was helping get back on their feet.

I glanced at the clock and saw that it was almost 6:30 a.m. I knew I'd have to check on Justin shortly. He had a different schedule than his brother and didn't have to be at school until 8:00, but his commute included two different subways, so he needed to be out the door in less than forty-five minutes. I picked up my teacup, took a sip of the warm liquid, and closed my eyes to savor the taste for just a minute.

A loud banging on the front door interrupted the moment.

My eyes flew open. Without thinking, I called out with my best Brooklyn attitude, "Who is it?"

I couldn't imagine who would be knocking at this early hour in the morning. I hoped the tone of my voice conveyed my annoyance and anger at whoever was on the other side of my door.

Apparently it didn't, because they knocked again. Louder this time. More insistent. Whoever it was had now woken up my husband. Bobby called out from our bed, "Go next door! This is apartment two A!" He too sounded annoyed at this unwanted early-morning intrusion.

If whoever was on the other side of our door was indeed looking for our neighbor in 2B, I was ready to go off. That woman was bad news. We were always seeing strange men coming in and out of her apartment. She cursed and hollered at her kids so much, we weren't surprised when Child Protective Services showed up the year before, threatening to take her children away. I started to make my way to the door to see if whoever it was needed to be set straight. As I walked past the living room, I noticed Bobby hardly seemed concerned and was still lying in bed, the blankets pulled up around his shoulders. Even though he'd have to get up in a few minutes anyway, I let him enjoy his last few moments of rest. I could handle whoever it was pounding on the door.

"Open up, this is the police, we want two A!"

I scrunched up my face in confusion. Did the police get another complaint about that woman? Did they need to talk to witnesses? I peeked through the peephole and saw the unmistakable blue of a police uniform. I nervously smoothed my hair down, pulled the edges of my robe tight, and slowly cracked open the door.

That's all it took.

A wave of police officers poured into our apartment. All men. At least ten of them. Maybe twelve. There were Black ones, white ones, and a few who looked Latino. They just pushed their way in, forcing me backward toward the kitchen so they could all get through the door.

My first thought was *Did the boys get into some sort of trouble?* But most of the officers went right into the living room and crowded around Bobby, who was still in our bed. I couldn't make my way over to him because the other officers were practically barricading me in the kitchen, but I managed to push around them enough so I could at least see what was going on. Bobby was still lying down. Police officers surrounded him. I could hear one of the officers barking at him: "What's your name?" Then a pause while Bobby answered.

"No, your real name!" the officer said.

I could see Bobby's lips were moving, but I couldn't hear a word he was saying because he was speaking so quietly.

"What's going on? What is this?" I cried to anyone and everyone, but mostly to Bobby. Nobody answered my questions, though. All the attention was on my husband.

"Are there any guns in the house?" one of the officers shouted at Bobby. I saw Bobby shake his head no, but two of the officers took off toward the back of the apartment anyway.

"Wait, my kids!" I shouted, now turning my attention away from the living room. Our apartment was a typical railroad apartment with a long hallway that led to the bedrooms and bathroom. We had given the twins and our daughter Jessica the bedrooms because we figured they needed more privacy than we did. Our eldest daughter, Jasmine, was married and had already moved out.

The two officers who were heading toward the bedrooms ignored my cries, but I couldn't ignore their guns. My heart leapt into my throat with fear. Every day there was another story on the news of an officer killing an unarmed Black man or woman. They shot first and asked questions later. I didn't want the boys or Jessica to be another statistic, so I kept hollering, "My kids are back there! They're sleeping! They're not doing anything!"

I tried to follow them down to the bedrooms, but an officer held me back. I heard Jessica give a frightened yelp when the officers entered her room, but I didn't hear a sound from Justin. My heart ached for my kids because I knew they must be as confused and as terrified as I was. I just prayed that neither Justin nor Jessica would make any sudden moves that would give these men the slightest justification to shoot.

Once they were satisfied that we weren't hiding any guns in our home, the two officers came rushing back toward the living room and announced that they had found no weapons. That's when Justin came and stood in the doorway of his bedroom, where he could observe everything that was going on, and Jessica tiptoed up to stand next to him. The two of them were frightened and looked at me for answers. I just shook my head at them and motioned for them both to be quiet.

Knowing the kids were safe for the time being, I turned my attention back to Bobby. When I looked over, I saw he was now sitting on the edge of the bed with his head hanging down. He was still talking so quietly I couldn't make out a single word he was saying to the officers. All I could see was that he was nodding his head yes to most of the questions he was being asked.

"You had a long run," I heard an officer say, and Bobby's head seemed to drop even further.

I couldn't take it anymore.

"Bobby, what happened? What did you do?" I screamed, pushing against the wall of bodies in front of me.

My questions weren't answered, and Bobby looked like a frightened little boy instead of my tall, proud husband. The officers crowding our apartment treated me like I was invisible, simply causing my panic to grow. My heart was pounding like crazy and I started to imagine the worst, and that's when I noticed that not all the men surrounding Bobby were police officers. My eyes got a little wider as I realized that half of these men were FBI agents. It said so on the back of their blue jackets.

With a burst of energy, I pushed past the officer blocking my path to the living room. I had to find out what was going on, but he grabbed me and pulled me roughly back toward the kitchen.

"Ma'am, stand back!" he shouted. "You don't know who this man is. You don't know what he's done!"

His chilling words had their intended effect. I stopped for a moment to try to take in what he was saying. The chaos all around me. FBI. Police. And a husband who refused to answer my questions.

"Bobby!" I shouted across the room. "What is this? What's going on? Did you kill someone?" The words just flew out of my mouth because I couldn't think of any other reason for the drama unfolding in our living room. But Bobby still didn't answer.

"Bobby, did you kill somebody?" I shrieked, my hands clenched in tight fists, wanting and not wanting to know the truth.

Finally, Bobby answered me. "No, Cheryl," he said, loud enough for me to hear this time, but still too quiet for my liking. "This happened before you. This was before the kids."

My mind went to a thousand places in less than a second. My emotions ricocheted from shock, to fear, to sadness, and then, of all things, to relief. But it was true. Some part of me felt a sense of relief because now I knew that I had been right all along. I knew my husband had a secret he had been hiding from me since the day we met, and it was all coming to a head right in front of my eyes. I didn't know what it was, but it was obviously something big. Of course, this wasn't how I'd imagined it would be revealed, but there was a part of me that understood that this moment was something I had been waiting for, for nearly thirty years. Finally, I was about to learn the truth.

That's when an officer turned to me and said calmly, "We're going to be taking your husband to jail."

Without even thinking, I shouted back at the officer, "You can't take him to jail!" I knew Bobby had obviously done something wrong, but I just couldn't fathom that it meant he needed to go to jail.

Everything was happening way too fast. I closed my eyes for just a second to try to gather my thoughts, and when I opened them, my vision landed on the refrigerator, where pictures of the kids grinning in places where we'd traveled together as a family hung from magnets bearing inspirational messages my friends from church had given me over the years. We weren't perfect, but we were a normal family. How could the secret Bobby had been keeping mean he was being arrested and taken to jail? It just didn't make sense.

It didn't matter what I thought though. The officers were growing impatient with my protests and insisted they were just following orders and had to take Bobby away.

"But he's a diabetic. He needs his medicine," I said. I don't know if I expected the officers to change their minds or if I just hoped to prolong the process. I was simply working on instinct. And my instinct told me to take care of Bobby. Even though he was always the one who took care of us, it was clear Bobby needed me to be the strong one at that moment. For the first time since we'd been together, Bobby looked his age. The twelve-year difference between us suddenly became apparent and I could see my husband needed me. I wasn't thinking about what he had done. I wasn't scared of his past. I just wanted to take care of him to the best of my ability.

The officers continued to ignore me and told Bobby to get dressed. Diabetic or not, he was being taken away.

One of the officers — it was hard to keep track of who was talking — said Bobby wasn't allowed to take any medication at the house, but he promised they'd get him his medicine en route to the jail. Jessica cautiously moved out of Justin's doorway then and pleaded with the officers to let her father take his medicine, but the officers were adamant.

I was so frustrated because it wouldn't have taken but a second to grab the bottle and give Bobby his pill. I wondered if they just wanted him to die.

Not on my watch, I decided. If they wouldn't let Bobby have his pill, at least I could get something sweet into him so he wouldn't pass out from low blood sugar.

I grabbed a handful of Bobby's favorite Chips Ahoy! chocolate chip cookies from the package on the kitchen counter, and then I pushed hard against the officer blocking my path. I forced my way over to Bobby.

"Here, Bobby, you gotta eat," I said, pretending we didn't have an audience of twelve police officers watching us. I handed him two cookies. I started to cry then, and Bobby's eyes were full of tears too. He didn't say anything to me, but the look on his face was one of pure shame. He took the cookies and shoved them in his mouth to make me happy but didn't say a word.

One officer tried to tell me I had to move away from Bobby, but now that I had broken free from the kitchen, I wasn't going back. Bobby's medicine was just inches from me now and I tried to give it to one of the officers, but they wouldn't take it. A chubby Latino-looking officer just repeated that he would get Bobby his medicine on the way to the jail. And then he told Bobby he had to get dressed.

I told myself if I didn't stop moving, somehow I could keep whatever was happening from happening. So I became a flurry of nervous activity.

I grabbed Bobby's clothes from the chair near the bed and handed them to him. He slid his pants on right over his long johns and then he put on a fleece sweater and his sneakers. The police tried to hustle him out of the apartment, but I shouted, "Wait, it's cold out. He needs a coat and a hat." I didn't even bother trying to control my tears at this point. I just kept wiping the sleeve of my robe across my face and wouldn't take my eyes off Bobby. I knew Justin and Jessica were crying too, but I couldn't even take a moment to comfort them.

I ran and got Bobby's warm leather coat from the closet and helped him put it on. I knew he didn't need my help getting dressed, but I wanted to be close to him for as long as I could. One officer kept telling me to stay away from Bobby, but I didn't pay him any mind. I didn't know what Bobby had done, but at that point I didn't care. I was doing what my heart told me to do, and my heart told me to make this moment last because I had no idea what was going to happen next.

Bobby let me help him, but he kept his head down the whole time, like he didn't want to look me in the eye. I knew I should be mad, but I couldn't pull up that emotion. He was so obviously filled with shame and what looked like fear.

"Let's go," one of the officers said brusquely, and Bobby quietly followed him out the door, leaving me standing there. When I saw him like that, my mind returned to the question "What did he do?"

The rest of the officers filed out of the apartment and had the decency to stay silent as they walked past the kids and me. The last officer to leave, the Latino officer from before, paused before he walked out the door. He called out to his team, "I'll be right there."

And then he went over to Justin, who was now standing in the living room, and said, "Your father's not a bad guy."

Justin stayed staring ahead stoically. It was pretty obvious he was trying not to cry, but the officer wanted Justin to hear what he had to say.

"Your father is not a bad guy. You need to know that," he repeated.

Justin turned to look at the officer then. He didn't say anything, but the officer seemed to think Justin was listening, so he kept talking.

"You stay in school. Stay on track, okay?"

Justin nodded but refused to speak. I knew he was hurting, and I don't know what the officer expected Justin to do. I wanted to say, "If you think Bobby is such a good guy, why are you arresting him?" But I kept my mouth shut.

"If you have any questions you can call me," the officer said, addressing all three of us then. He held out his card and Jessica took it. She mumbled "thank you," and the officer rushed out the door to catch up with the others. I followed him into the hallway, just in time to see Bobby, one flight down, being led out the front door of the building, his hands in handcuffs. "Bobby!" I cried out and he looked up.

"I love you, Cheryl," he said.

The pain tore through me then and I couldn't contain the sobs of grief that poured out of me. I rushed back into the apartment, raced past the kids, and ran down to Jessica's room, because her room was the only one where the windows looked out onto the front of the building. I just had to see this thing through. I had to see them take Bobby away because I still couldn't believe it was real. I kneeled on Jess's unmade bed and pushed the curtains open wide. The bright morning sun blinded me for a moment, and then I was able to focus on the scene unfolding below.

The cars were what brought all the people out into the street. At least six blue-and-white police vehicles and some unmarked black sedans were parked in front of our building, half of them on the sidewalk blocking any clear path in or out of the building. Even though it was only a little after seven in the morning, there were so many curious people trying to figure out what was going on. And when they saw that it was Bobby being led out of the building in handcuffs, I could see the confusion on their faces, because everybody in our neighborhood knew Bobby. I saw the Asian lady from the laundromat, her hand covering her mouth in shock. The workers from the CTown grocery store across the street weren't even pretending to sweep the pavement as they gawked at my husband. Most of our friends and neighbors all just stood there, mouths open, whispering and, I assumed, trying to guess what the man they knew as Mr. Bobby could have done to warrant not only police officers but FBI agents escorting him out of his own home. They were all wondering, just like I was, what it was Bobby had done.

BOBBY

An officer put me in the back seat of a police car and another officer slid in next to me and slammed the door, blocking out the sounds of my neighbors' cries of shock and wonder. I made note of the officer in the passenger seat and of course the driver. I was surrounded. My mind was moving a mile a minute.

I wanted to cry, but I was also trying to stay alert. I didn't know what was going to happen to me or where we were going. I turned my head away from the officer sitting next to me and kept my gaze focused out the window. We took off down Bedford Avenue and then we turned onto Flatbush. I could tell we were heading toward the bridge to cross over into Manhattan. I thought of asking about our final destination but realized I didn't really want to know. All I wanted was to be back home with Cheryl and the kids.

I looked down at my hands in handcuffs and pushed down a cry that wanted to escape. I couldn't believe after thirty-eight years, the life I had so carefully created was over. I knew someone must have turned me in, and I started to replay the last few weeks and months in my mind. Did I let my guard down? Had I gotten too confident? Probably.

I groaned inwardly. I always knew this was a possibility, but it had been such a long time. I guess I thought I really was free. Instead,

I had made a mess for my family. Visions of Cheryl having to face her friends at church knowing what I'd done tormented me. Then my mind jumped to the boys going to school and having to defend their father who was heading to jail. I hated that Justin had to witness my shame. I hated that everyone in the neighborhood had seen me getting carried off in handcuffs.

"Mr. Love," the officer riding shotgun interrupted my thoughts. "We just wanted you to know that we didn't want to arrest you."

I lifted my head to make sure I heard him right. "Excuse me?"

"Yeah," the officer next to me said. "We kept getting calls from Charlotte about your case. But it was from an incident so long ago, we just sat on it. But the calls kept coming."

"Really?" I said.

"Yeah," the guy in the front chimed in. "We've known about you since the day after Christmas. Of course, we had to investigate you to make sure that you were the right guy and that the things that they said you did, way back when, actually happened."

All I could do was nod my head. I couldn't believe these cops were telling me they hadn't wanted to arrest me.

They kept talking. "Man, we've been watching you for a month. We came over here and watched your every move. We saw you going into the store. We saw you walking down the street. We saw you all around this neighborhood. And we know you've been doing all the right things. It really seemed silly that we had to arrest you."

I did some quick calculations in my head and tried to figure out who had dimed me out. I thought about all of my family members who I'd just seen a few months prior at my brother's funeral and tried to imagine which one of them would do this to me. A bitter taste filled my mouth as I considered the betrayal. My hands curled into fists of their own accord, but the pinch of the handcuffs reminded me where I was and who was to blame for my current circumstances. And just like that, the anger receded, and I was back to thinking about my family. Guilt and shame festered in my stomach and I wondered if Cheryl would leave me once she found out what I had done.

A moment of silence passed, and then the cop driving the car spoke up again. He asked me about my kids. Their ages and where they went to school and stuff. It was small talk, but I was grateful because it kept me from thinking about what I knew I would be facing in a matter of time.

"My son Jordan plays football," I said proudly. "And he's hoping to get a scholarship to college."

"Man, that's great. Good for you," the officer sitting next to me responded.

"You know, when you have your chance to talk to your lawyer or the judge, make sure you let them know that stuff. Tell them about your boys wanting to go to college and all the things you've done to raise good kids. That's gotta help," he added.

All the officers had their own advice to share. They all had something to offer for my upcoming reckoning in front of a judge.

"You know, man, you could write a book with your story," the officer driving the car said.

"Yeah," the guy in the front seat agreed. "Your story is incredible."

I wasn't thinking about writing a book. This was my life. It might have sounded "incredible" to other people, but it was just my life, and I would have done anything to go back to it, flaws and all. I knew I wasn't the perfect husband or father. Our struggle was constant, but my kids had a better childhood than I did because they had two parents who loved them.

I answered any question the officers threw my way, but mostly I was silent as I watched New York pass by outside the car window. Soon enough we arrived at Bellevue Hospital, the city's largest public hospital, situated on First Avenue at 27th Street in Manhattan.

"We're stopping here to get you your medicine, Mr. Love," the officer in the front seat said.

They pulled the car up to the emergency entrance and I was taken into the building. Because Bellevue is the hospital where even the homeless won't get turned away, seeing a man in handcuffs didn't cause anyone to look at me twice. Still, I kept my head down as I was led through the hospital corridors until we came to a nurse's station that was already bustling with activity at this early hour. The officer who had escorted me in, the clean-shaven Latino guy with the curly hair, instructed me to tell the nurse what kind of medication I needed for my diabetes. After I did, the officer led me to a couple of nearby seats to wait.

We sat in the chairs in awkward silence for a moment, and then I decided to ask if I could get something to eat with my medication. I could hear Cheryl's voice in my head reminding me that I shouldn't take my medicine on an empty stomach. The officer agreed and came back a few minutes later with a Danish and a Styrofoam cup of orange juice. I didn't want to press my luck but I asked if he could remove the handcuffs so I could eat without making a mess on myself. To my relief, he agreed.

While I ate, the officer told me I could call him Hector. Then he cleared his throat and told me again how sorry he was that he had to arrest me.

"Listen, your story really is incredible," he repeated.

I grunted in response because my mouth was full, but he had my full attention.

Hector continued. "You know, they really just dropped this in our lap."

"They who?" I asked.

Hector wouldn't say, but he told me again that whoever it was had been calling two and sometimes three times a week, insisting the NYPD investigate me.

I let that sink in. And then it dawned on me. "Was there a reward out for me?"

Hector looked me dead in the eye. "Yeah."

"How much was it?" I asked.

"Two thousand dollars," he said quietly, but this time he didn't have the nerve to keep the eye contact. I'm sure he could feel the anger emanating off my body. Somebody turned me in for a measly two thousand dollars.

"It's not like you came out here and did other things and became a priority, or a number one person on the FBI's list or something like that," Hector said, trying to explain why my recapture was worth less than a big screen TV.

"I know," I said. "And it's nobody's fault but my own."

That's what I said out loud, but inside I was seething. Everything I'd built for myself and my family over the last thirty years was gone for two thousand dollars. I was pretty sure I knew who was responsible for calling the NYPD because I had a family member who worked in law enforcement in Charlotte. It didn't take much to put two and two together. I remembered that at my brother's funeral, one of my nieces had listed me as Bobby Love in the funeral program instead of using my real name. Most people didn't pay any attention to it, but a few of my relatives wanted to know why I was calling myself Bobby Love. I didn't have a ready excuse, so I simply said it was the name I used in New York and didn't elaborate. That was the end of the discussion, but obviously somebody wasn't satisfied with my answer. The thought that it was my own flesh and blood who had sent the cops to my door made the juice and the Danish I'd swallowed rise up in my throat. I was furious. But I didn't have time to sit with my anger, because Hector told me we had to go.

He was about to put the handcuffs back on when I quickly asked, "Could I just call my wife real fast to let her know I got my medicine?"

Hector paused for a second, but then he sighed and said yes. He arranged for me to call from one of the hospital phones.

Cheryl picked up on the first ring. I could hear the anxiety in her voice and it just killed me to know I had done that to her.

"Cheryl," I said, trying to keep my voice calm and steady, trying to sound like I had things under control, even though we both knew I didn't.

"Bobby!" she cried. "Where are you? Are you okay?"

I told her I was at the hospital and that I had been given my medicine.

"But where are they taking you? What's going to happen?"

"I don't know what's going to happen, Cheryl," I said. "But I'll be okay, and I'll let you know something when I can."

I didn't hear anything on the other end except Cheryl breathing.

Finally she spoke. "Well, I'm going to work, Bobby," she said. "If you have to call me, call me on my cell when you know something, okay?" Now she sounded like the calm one. She was the one sending me strength.

"I will," I promised.

"It's going to be okay, Bobby," Cheryl said. "I'm with you and I'm not going anywhere. Promise me you won't do anything crazy. You hear me? No crazy stuff."

"I promise, Cheryl," I whispered into the phone. And then I hung up.

Hector put the handcuffs back on me and led me out to the waiting car. Even with rush hour traffic in Manhattan, it only took about fifteen minutes for us to arrive at our final destination, One Hundred Centre Street. Central Booking for the New York City Police Department. Also known as The Tombs. The imposing granite building stretched across an entire city block with adjacent towers reaching up to the sky. Everyone in New York knew about The Tombs and did their best to avoid it. Now that I was here, a cold stone of dread settled in my stomach.

I was passed around from one officer to another, led through procedures, entered into the system. Pictures were taken. Fingertips got inked. They took my leather coat. They took my shoestrings and my belt. Anything I could use to hurt someone, including myself, was removed from my possession. Once I was officially processed, I was led down an endless winding staircase into the deep basement, where I was placed in an empty cell by myself. All around me were massive cages crowded with other men who were in various states of waiting. The sounds of their angry and insistent calls to be let out, to be moved, to eat, made me give thanks that I was alone in my misery.

I sat down on the one wooden bench, the only thing that could pass as furniture. It was so cold down in that section of the building, I couldn't even squeeze out a tear. Instead, I prayed I wouldn't be down there very long. I prayed for Cheryl and the kids. I prayed God would help me walk steadily down whatever path was put in front of me.

It was close to two hours before I was moved out of that frigid basement and up two floors to another holding area. I learned that there was some kind of order to this upward movement. At some point I would meet my court-appointed lawyer, and then I would stand before the judge who would decide my fate. I knew the system well enough to have hope that I would make bail and be able to go home sooner rather than later. So that meant all I had to do was figure out how to survive the waiting game.

Because I was deemed a medical risk, I was kept out of the crowded bullpens and was placed in another cell by myself. The tiny space was filthy and the stench from the toilet in the middle of the room permeated the air. I prayed I wouldn't have to use it because there was no privacy and no toilet paper. Since the other men were yelling and screaming, making demands, I decided to try my luck. I asked if I could get a blanket or my coat back because I was still so cold. None of the officers passing by or sitting at their nearby desks even looked my way. They acted like they didn't even hear me. Like everyone else down there, I was something less than human and deserving of zero sympathy. Even the lunch they offered — a sad-looking cheese sandwich and a carton of milk — told me I was a nothing. I didn't even try to eat that sandwich, but I drank the milk.

Time passed slowly. I wanted to yell. I wanted to kick the graffiti-scarred walls. I wanted to kick myself. I was so mad that I was back behind bars. The harsh sounds of the other men in the bullpens around me only added to my agitation. For hours I just paced around the tiny cell, pausing every now and again to lean against the bars and stare at the activity in front of and all around me. There was a constant stream of people being led in and out of different places. Some of them looked like they deserved to be in there. Others looked like scared little kids who should have been in school, not in a place like this.

I lost all track of time, but I knew hours had gone by and I was still waiting. I tried to stay calm and keep my focus on God, but I couldn't stop my thoughts from straying toward the worst-case scenario. My biggest fear was that I was going to end up on Rikers Island, the notorious overcrowded jail where I'd heard that gang violence was rampant. I didn't think I'd be able to survive that type of lockdown. I was a sixty-four-year-old diabetic who walked with a cane. The last time I was arrested and put behind bars, I was a spry twenty-year-old who knew how to fight.

"Walter Miller!" someone called out, and it took me a minute to remember that was my name. I stood up in my cell and called out "Here!"

I was pulled out of my cell then and lined up with a group of about five or six other guys.

"You're heading to court. Shut up or we'll drag your ass back down here," an officer in a pale-blue uniform told us. I think all of us were so happy to get out of our cells we didn't dare make a sound.

The officer led us up a yellow cinder block staircase to a small hallway with a couple of dingy-looking holding cells, where we were told we would meet with our court-appointed lawyers before we faced the judge. I was led to a chair and found myself facing an attractive brown-skinned woman with shiny black hair. She appeared to be in her late thirties or early forties. She looked tired and not exactly excited to be in a holding cell with me. I couldn't blame her, seeing as how it was long past 5:00 p.m.

"Hello, Mr. Miller. My name is Erica Valdez and I'm going to be your lawyer," she said, barely making eye contact as she shuffled through her papers.

She didn't waste any time with small talk. "So, you were arrested this morning for a prison escape?"

"That's correct," I said.

Erica looked down at the sheet of paper in front of her and a confused look came over her face. "Wait, this dates back to nineteen seventy-seven." She looked up at me for confirmation. "You escaped in nineteen seventy-seven?"

"Yeah," I said with a bittersweet smile.

She put her papers down and really looked at me then. "Wow," she said. "What have you been doing all this time?"

"I raised a family," I said, sitting up straighter. "I have four children. My twin sons are doing their thing in high school and they're both looking to go to college."

Erica started writing in her notepad as I talked. She interrupted me only when she had a question or needed clarification.

"Have you been working?" she asked.

"Working and paying taxes," I said and proceeded to tell her about all of the jobs I'd had over the past forty years.

When I finished sharing my story, Erica put her notepad down and just looked at me for a minute before saying anything. Finally, she spoke again.

"Mr. Miller, I've never heard of any case like this before," she said. She told me she'd done some preliminary research about other escaped prisoners who had been arrested, but almost all of them had committed other crimes while they were out.

"I don't have any precedents for how your case is going to be handled," she admitted. She also told me that there really wasn't a lot of information about my past crimes either.

"From what I understand, they don't even have records on you from way back in North Carolina," she said.

"Is that good or bad?" I asked.

"Actually, I think it's good because we can focus on all of the positive things you've done, and if we have evidence on that, we can build a better case."

I must have smiled or something because Erica frowned.

"Mr. Miller, they're still going to send you to Rikers."

"But what about bail?" I asked.

"You escaped from a state prison, Mr. Miller," she said, as if I'd asked a really stupid question. "They're not going to give you any kind of bail. They're not even going to consider that."

I felt the flicker of hope I'd been desperately holding on to vanish.

But Erica laid out the plan she thought we should follow. And that was to get me sent back to North Carolina as soon as possible and then work with the authorities and possibly the governor to seek clemency in light of my record of rehabilitation. She actually laid out a bunch of different scenarios of what could happen, but I stopped paying close attention after she said I would have to go to Rikers.

It was late. I was tired.

"Hey, Mr. Miller." Erica raised her voice to grab my attention. I lifted my head to look at her.

"You're going to do some more time, okay? But we're going to try to make it as short as possible."

That simple statement reignited my hope. Not a lot, but enough to face what I knew was coming. I reminded myself that I had survived prison before. I could do it again. At least I hoped that I could.

By the time I was loaded up into the van that would take me to Rikers — handcuffed, cold, and hungry — all I wanted to do was sleep. I wanted to sleep and forget everything that was happening to me. By this time it was well past midnight. Once we made it to the island prison complex, I was led directly into a tiny room and was told to strip. When I had all of my clothes off, I had to pass them through to a guard and submit to a full-body cavity search. Every single orifice on my body was invaded. The humiliation of that moment had me thinking back to the day I escaped. Planning. Running. Freedom. If only I had waited a few more months for my next chance at parole. If only I had sucked it up and hung around for a legal release. Instead, I had fled, and now here I was in this hellhole, having a stranger probe my naked body like I was a slave on an auction block.

Once it was determined that I hadn't smuggled any contraband into the jail, I was given a gray jumpsuit, slip-on shoes, and a pair of socks. They wouldn't allow me to keep my cane. I had to wait while someone located the linen for my bed, which turned out to be a sheet, a pillowcase, and a scratchy gray wool blanket. Then I was marched up several flights of stairs, my arms out in front of me, balancing my bed things like precious cargo. I limped the whole way. The guard didn't care and didn't say a word. He opened the door of my cell, watched me enter, then locked the door behind me.

I was alone. It was quiet. The cell was dark with only a sliver of light coming in from the hallway.

I looked at the filthy twin mattress on the metal bed frame and could only imagine what bodily fluids might be on it from the last occupant. With my last bit of strength, I flipped the mattress over before making up the bed. Then I lay down, looked up at the ceiling, and felt my tears make warm rivers down my cheeks, then pool in my ears. Out loud I whispered quietly, "God, please help me survive this." And then I asked myself, "How did I get here?"

As I started to review my life, trying to figure out how I had ended up in the place I swore I'd never return to, I fell into a merciful sleep.

chapter two

When We Were Young

BOBBY

A midwife brought me into this world on November 6, 1950. In those days, Greensboro, North Carolina, was still a city divided along the color line, including the hospitals. So when I made it known that I was ready to make my debut, my father, James Edward Miller, took my mother, Annie, to the midwife, who had a little place where she worked off Highway 421. That's where I was born.

I was my mother's seventh child, but my parents' second child together. As the story goes, my parents were each other's second chance. They had both been married before and both had children. When they decided to marry and start a family together, getting out of South Carolina was their first priority. They came north to Greensboro hoping for new beginnings. My father took starting over to an extreme and never spoke about his former wife and two children in South Carolina. I never met them and don't even know their names. My mother, on the other hand, refused to leave her five other children behind, and they became part of the new beginning.

In our house we didn't use words like "half-brother" and "half-sister." We were just a family. My eldest brother, Millard, was twenty-two when I was born; then came Leroy, Mildred, Raymond, and Irma. Jean came next. She was my sister closest in age, and we shared a father. Three years after I was born, my mother had my little brother, Melvin. And I was Walter. Walter Curtis Miller, Mama's lucky number seven. She named me Walter because she thought it was a name that sounded like somebody important. I hated the name Walter, though, so for as long as I can remember, everyone in my family called me Buddy.

My eldest brother and eldest sister were living on their own by the time I joined the family, but we were still eight people crowded under one roof. I didn't care. All I remember about that time in my life is being surrounded by love. My parents rented a small one-bedroom wooden house that was nothing to brag about. It was down on Wilmington Street on the east side of town. We didn't have many modern conveniences. No hot water. No real bathtub. When I was four or five years old, I can remember having to take our baths by the fire in the living room. My mother would have to heat the water on the stove and pour it into a big old tub she bought. Then Melvin and I would have our bath with everybody in the room watching us. I thought it was a whole lot of fun and I'd always ask my mother, "Mama, why doesn't Jean take a bath like us?" Jean was three years older than me and didn't think bathing in front of our entire family sounded anything like fun.

Our little house was the first one on the block, and at the end of our street was a lumberyard. We used to go down there and gather up leftover wood planks and then pretend they were horses and we were cowboys like the ones we watched on TV, like Wild Bill Hickok and the Lone Ranger. Right across the street from the house there was a dusty clay field where our whole family would go out and play baseball. As a child, I actually thought it was a real ball field. The other kids from the neighborhood would come out and play too. Especially in the summertime as the sun began to go down and it stopped being too hot to have fun.

The only person who wouldn't join us was my father. He would sit on the little porch in front of the house and watch. But he'd never play with us. That was his way.

I loved my father, but he was difficult to like. He was tall like I would eventually be. He had a dark complexion, and I always remember him with his steel-toe work boots on that he had to wear for his job at the steel mill. He rarely smiled.

"Daddy, can you read this book with me?" I'd ask him, excited to show off that Mama had taught me how to read before I'd even started school.

"No, boy," he'd answer and brush me aside.

When he came home from work, I'd say, "Hey, Daddy, how are you doing?" and ask to sit on his lap. The answer was always no.

I remember asking my mother, "Mama, why Daddy don't like me?" And she would say something like "Your daddy likes you, Buddy. But he don't know how to express himself or say things to you to tell you how he feels about you."

Sometimes my father would let me help him take off those heavy steel-toe boots and I would perform that task with honor. First I had to untie the laces, then pull those heavy things off his feet and place them dutifully by the door. When I'd come back, hoping for some kind of praise, or maybe just a smile and a thank you, my father would say, "I'm tired," and he'd head back to his room. Or maybe he'd go get a drink. I didn't know what it was called, but my father liked to drink a clear, colorless liquor that made him talk more, but the things that came out of his mouth weren't nice.

My mother, Annie, was the opposite. Like my father, she worked too. But for a Black woman in the South without much education, the options were limited. She did domestic work, like housecleaning and laundry services. She worked in a meatpacking company at one time and at a warehouse where she washed the linens for a local hospital. Sometimes my mother would even go back down to South Carolina and pick tobacco and cotton for a season and then come home with her earnings. I don't remember a single day my mother didn't get up to go to work. But she never made us kids feel bad or guilty for the work she had to do.

The only thing she asked of us in return was to love Jesus, be good, and focus on our education. She took us to church every Sunday and made sure we were up for school on Mondays.

By the time I was five years old, my parents had saved up enough money to move us out of our house on Wilmington Street to a bigger house just across the way. By this point another sibling had moved out, so it felt like we had more room to spread out, even though the house wasn't that big. We got a new couch and some bunk beds for Melvin and me. It wasn't much, but as a young child, I wasn't aware of the things we didn't have because most of the people who lived around us were poor and Black, just like we were.

Not having money didn't keep me from having a good time though. I was a curious child and found plenty of ways to keep myself happy and entertained. Mama said I asked too many questions. So did my teachers. But I kept on asking. Luckily, Jean was always there to help me find answers and to keep me abreast of all the things she thought I should know. She was the one who told me what all the bad words meant. She was also the one who told me, when I was six years old, that our parents were splitting up.

"Buddy, Daddy is going to move out," Jean said one day when we were sitting on the porch slurping popsicles. She said it real matter-of-factly, without much emotion.

"Why's Daddy gonna move?" I asked.

"Because Daddy and Mama is breaking up," she said, like it was obvious. My six-year-old brain couldn't compute.

"Why?" I asked again.

Jean was only nine so she didn't know much more than I did. She just shrugged her shoulders. "Because that's what's happening."

I tried to imagine what it was going to be like without my father around. Even though he barely showed me any affection, I still didn't want him to leave. We were a family. But even at six, I knew that daddies weren't supposed to do the things my daddy did. The yelling and screaming at Mama when there wasn't enough food for anyone to have seconds. Getting drunk most nights. And he beat my mama. She would come home from church feeling the spirit of the Lord, singing and all happy, then my father would start yelling at her for something he said she did wrong. If she tried to say anything, he would hit her. If she tried to stand up for herself, he would hit her more. I hated my father when he did that to Mama, and I didn't know what to do to make him stop.

But my brother Raymond did. One night after Daddy had hit Mama again, Raymond stood up to my father and said, "If I see you hit my mother one more time, I'm going to kill you."

Maybe that's why Daddy was leaving. He was afraid of Raymond. But Raymond was just a teenager. He wasn't that scary in my opinion.

I sat there thinking about the news Jean had given me. I wanted to ask if she thought Daddy was leaving because he didn't want to be our daddy anymore. I kept quiet, though. I didn't really want to hear the answer.

Mama acted like the fact she and my father were splitting up was no big deal. Daddy was going to move into a house by himself on Whitaker Street, she said, and we could visit him whenever we wanted. That was that.

I quickly calculated in my head. My aunt lived on Whitaker Street, and her house was close to my school. Daddy wouldn't be too far away. That gave me some relief, but it didn't stop my heart from breaking on the day he walked out of our front door.

"Daddy, don't go!" I cried, pulling on his arm. Tears and snot were running down my face but I didn't care.

My little brother Melvin was only three, but he too was begging my daddy not to go. Melvin pretty much did everything that I did.

My mother had no time for my tears. She snatched me up and took me to my room and told me to stay in there.

"Don't come out until your father is gone," she scolded me. "You're making this harder than it has to be, Buddy." Then she shut the door.

Mama kept her word and we saw Daddy on a regular basis. Jean, Melvin, and I used to go to his house on Friday after school, and we would come back home on Sunday. He would take us to this little restaurant for breakfast on Saturday mornings and we thought that was the greatest thing. Then, if we were good, we would go shopping at Blumenthal's for clothes or whatever else we needed at the time. My mother used to always tell us to tell Daddy to take us somewhere else besides Blumenthal's, some place nice like Belk's department store, where she liked to shop. But if we ever dared to relay messages to my father sent by my mother, Daddy would say, "Don't tell me a damn thing your mother said."

We quickly figured out that my mother's name and her wishes were off limits as far as my father was concerned. Their relationship had completely disintegrated. My father was angry almost all the time when it came to my mother. And likewise, Mama and the rest of my older siblings only had negative things to say about my father. Still, I wanted to see him and I knew I loved him, even if "I love you" wasn't something we ever said to each other.

After my father left, life went on, and the truth was, I didn't miss him all that much around the house. Things felt more peaceful. But now my mother had to figure out how to support us and pay the bills on her own because my father couldn't be counted on to pay for anything.

Miraculously, she still found ways to show us kids a good time. Mama would call on my eldest brother, Millard, to come drive us down to the amusement park in Burlington in the summer. Summertime also meant church picnics and taking a long bus ride to my uncle's farm in Rocky Mount, North Carolina. I didn't like being around all those animals, but I loved to see my mama happy visiting with her brother, so I made the best of it for her sake. Mama worked so hard, it was nice to see her happy and relaxed.

Back in Greensboro, I tried to make sure I didn't create any extra trouble for my mother. But for an inquisitive little Black boy in the Jim Crow South, that wasn't always easy. There were times I would do things just to see what would happen.

Like this one time when I was eight, my mother took me shopping with her downtown. We were in a store and I was thirsty, so I said to her, "Mama, I'm going to get some water." I went back to where the fountains were and discovered that nobody was at the colored fountain and nobody was at the white fountain. I was all alone, just me and my curiosity. *Is the white people's water colder than our water?* I wondered. I figured since white people always got the better stuff, then the water in the white fountain had to be colder. From years of observation, I had also noticed that the water shot up higher for the white people than it did for the Blacks, so they didn't have to lean over as far as we did. That water practically jumped right into their mouths.

I looked around again, just to be sure I was alone. And then I went over and quenched my thirst from that forbidden fountain. And just as I suspected, that white people's water was so cool and refreshing. As soon as I gulped down my last sip, I turned around and this white kid was standing there. He looked angry and mean. He yelled in my face, "Get away from there! You're not supposed to be doing that!"

And then he punched me in the face. I was stunned and scared and ran quickly to find my mother to tell her what had happened.

My mother pulled my hand off my face to make sure I wasn't bleeding, and then she looked at me like I was crazy. "You shouldn't have been over there drinking that water, Buddy. You know you're not supposed to be doing that." I don't know why I'd hoped that my mother would have marched over and found that little boy and stood up for me. That wasn't her way. When it came to the racial injustices that we endured every day, my mother never wanted to fight, and she certainly didn't want to see her children causing a ruckus either. "God will take care of it" is what my mother would tell us. "God will take care of it and take care of us."

My mother's faith in the Lord was unshakeable. He was her solution to every problem — personal, social, cultural, everything. Even when the adults in her church community weren't acting like good Christians, she would judge the people, not God. Like when Deacon Johnson threw his shoe at our minister in a fit of rage in the middle of his Sunday service because Deacon Johnson found out the minister was getting frisky with the young girls in the congregation. Mama yanked us out of that church real fast and condemned the behavior of the minister. A month later, she'd found a new church for us to attend and expected us to continue on with our love for the Lord. I was just a kid, so I did as I was told, but the hypocrisy I witnessed from churchgoers made me an early skeptic of religion, even though it was so important to Mama and to our community.

We moved again, this time into an apartment building instead of a house. I missed having a yard, but this new place was in a nicer neighborhood. And in our new apartment we were down to six people: Mama, my sister Mildred and her son Bodie, Jean, Melvin, and me. Raymond was also around, although he was getting ready to join the military. I was eight years old then and had started to play Little League Baseball. My mother also signed me up for the Boy Scouts, plus I had church every Sunday. Mama believed that if she kept me busy and occupied with extracurricular activities, then I wouldn't have any time to get into trouble.

My father was still taking Melvin, Jean, and me out for breakfast on the weekends, but I never saw him at my ball games. He never took us out to play. To compensate, because my elementary school was close to his house, sometimes after school I'd stop by and see my father, just to say hi and check on him. Sometimes I'd even sleep over. My mother didn't like it when I did that, but she didn't try to stop me either. I could tell it was going to be up to me to maintain a relationship with my father, so I did what I could.

One night in early November, right after I turned nine, the sound of my sister screaming and crying woke me up. I climbed out of my bed and found Jean and my mother sitting on the sofa in the living room bawling their eyes out.

"What happened? Mama, what's going on? What happened?" I asked, the panic rising in my voice.

"Buddy, we just got a call and they said your father's house is on fire. They think he's inside."

I shook my head. "But you don't know if he's dead or not?" I asked. "Don't say that if you don't know for sure," I insisted.

My mother reached for me, but I moved out of her grasp.

"Buddy," my mother tried again. "Nobody can find your dad."

That's when I started crying. "Shouldn't we go over there and see for ourselves?"

My mother reached for me again. This time I let her and I just sat there and cried. I cried myself to sleep and woke up the next morning still in my mother's arms. That's where Melvin found me. He'd slept through the whole night's ordeal. As soon as he saw me, he asked what was the matter. Melvin was only six, but I didn't think to spare his feelings. The words just tumbled out of my mouth.

I told Melvin about the fire, but unlike my mother and Jean, I refused to say that my father was dead. "We need to go over there and find out for sure," I told him.

Mama got up to go to the bathroom. "Y'all don't have to go to school today," she said to us. Then she shuffled out of the room.

I raced to get dressed. Melvin was on my heels. I just knew we were going to find out that my father was still alive. We had to hurry up and get over there. I told Melvin he'd better move faster if he wanted to come along, as I helped him pull his sweater over his head. In my mind, I considered all of the possibilities of what could have happened to my father. He could be any number of places other than in that house. But before I could share my ideas with my mother, the doorbell rang.

It was the police. I heard Mama let them in and I snuck into the living room to hear what they had to say.

"Are you Annie Miller?" one officer asked.

My mother said yes.

"We're sorry to tell you that your husband, James Miller, died in a fire at his residence last night."

Even though Mama had shed so many tears the night before, hearing the words coming out of the police officers' mouths set off another round of wailing.

I slumped down right where I was, because now it was official. My father was dead.

The next few hours passed by in a blur. People started coming over to our apartment, bringing food and sharing in our sorrow. At some point in the afternoon, my brother Millard came to drive us over to see what was left of my father's home. When we got there, all we saw were smoldering ashes. Everything was gone.

The funeral took place a few days later, but the undertaker told my mother that my father's body was so badly burned, they had to have a closed casket. When we heard that, we all cried some more. No matter how mean my mother claimed my father was, and even taking into consideration all of his faults, nobody deserved to die like that.

The Christmas after my father died, my mother bought Melvin and me our very first bicycles with the money she received from my father's pension. These were brand-new bicycles, not secondhand ones. My sister Jean got a stereo set, and her friends would come over and play records and dance. It was the best Christmas I ever had. That sounds terrible to say, considering how Mama came into the money, but that's how I remember it. In addition to my new bike, Mama also splurged and bought me new clothes. She said she was tired of seeing me in my old overalls and T-shirts.

"I'm going to buy you a suit for Christmas, Buddy," Mama told me proudly. And she took me down to Vanstory. Vanstory was a high-end fashion store in Greensboro, and you didn't go there unless you had some money. Mama bought me my first suit and a really nice trench coat. Having these new, fancy clothes made me feel important and like we were moving up in the world. And that's kind of what happened after my father died. We had more money. We weren't rich or anything, and nothing dramatic changed in our lives. My mother could simply afford to buy us the basic things we needed, like an extra pair of pants or new sneakers when the old ones pinched our toes.

After the initial shock of my father's death wore off, I told my mother that I didn't really miss him. I felt guilty for those feelings and wondered if that made me a bad person.

"I don't feel anything," I told Mama one Sunday while I was sitting in the kitchen watching her cook dinner. "How am I supposed to feel about Daddy dying?"

My mother stopped stirring the pot of grits at the stove and came and sat by me. She put her arms around me and said, "It's okay, Buddy. If you don't feel it now, you'll feel it later, when it's the right time for you. Grief doesn't have a schedule."

And then she went back to cooking. And I took that to mean that it was okay that I didn't miss my daddy. And that it was okay that I loved my new bicycle and my new clothes. And even that it was okay that even though I loved my father, I had already promised myself at nine years old that I would never grow up to be like him.

Later that summer, I started going out with my friend Ronny to mow lawns for money. White people would offer us two or three dollars to cut their grass. After doing it a few times, I realized we should have been charging five or six dollars for their big old lawns, but we didn't know any better. Ronny had a push mower, and the two of us would take turns pushing that thing across those lawns, collecting our pay and then moving on to the next house. It was a lot of work, but I loved having my own money in my pocket so I could go to the movies and buy myself some popcorn and soda while I was there.

One day my mother said to me, "I'm going to buy you a real lawn mower, Buddy." She had seen me going out with Ronny and wanted to support me so I could keep earning money. I didn't really believe it at first, because a gas-powered lawn mower was expensive. But Mama kept her promise. One day she told me to meet her downtown after she finished work so we could get the lawn mower. Mama knew exactly where to go to buy a sturdy machine that I could handle. I was so impressed that she knew all this and that we could walk into this store and purchase not just the lawn mower but the gas as well. Once again I had to give thanks to my father's pension.

With my new machine, I said goodbye to Ronny and struck out on my own. Saturday mornings, starting at 9:00, I'd be knocking on my neighbors' doors, offering to mow their lawns. I refused to take anything less than four dollars per lawn, not only because I knew my service was worth it, but also because I had to buy gas for my machine, and if I still wanted to go to the movies, I needed higher profits. I tried to work as fast as I could and earn at least twenty dollars a day. Then on Saturday nights, I'd take the bus to the movies and buy treats for me and my friends. I was only ten, but I had already figured out the art of the hustle. I knew what I wanted and I knew exactly how hard I'd have to work to get it.

I learned that from my mother, that and my work ethic. Mama would work three jobs if she had to, to make sure we had food on the table. Whether it was taking on an extra job or picking up seasonal work so she could earn more cash, my mother did what she had to do to support our family. She gave me all the inspiration I needed for the job I was doing. I wasn't afraid of hard work, and I wasn't dissuaded when people closed their door in my face or told me they weren't interested in my services, which I expanded to include leaf raking and, in the winter when North Carolina got a few inches, snow shoveling. I didn't get upset when I heard "No." I'd just go to the next house, whether it was across the street or down the block. I would try every house until I'd earned my twenty dollars for the day. I didn't get rich from mowing lawns, but I learned some valuable lessons about doing business. Most importantly, I learned that someone shutting the door in my face wasn't the end of the road. It was just an opportunity to try again.

I knew my mother was proud of me. Even though I was earning my own money, she still would buy me things she thought I needed or asked for. She was just happy that I was staying busy doing honest work and not getting caught up in the troubles my older brothers had fallen into. By the time I was eleven, I had baseball, football, my yard business, and I played the trombone in my elementary school marching band. In the summertime, if we didn't have an activity to attend,

Mama would make Melvin and me sing on the street corner just so we wouldn't be idle. That's how desperate she was to keep me safe and away from harm.

And for a while, it worked.

CHERYL

I was born in Brooklyn, New York, on March 28, 1963. But my story really begins down south with my parents, George and Gertrude Williams.

Mommy and Daddy were both born and raised in Henderson, North Carolina. They met down there, fell in love, and were high school sweethearts. But like a lot of other Black people at the time, they came north and started their lives in New York City. Brooklyn to be specific. Daddy found a job in a bottling factory, and Mommy did domestic work. Just a couple of years before I was born, they were lucky enough to get a three-bedroom apartment in a building that was right across the way from Daddy's job. The building was part of a new affordable housing project called the Pink Houses that the city had erected in 1959. These new projects had 1,500 apartment units spread across twenty-two eight-story buildings. My parents were thrilled with their home because not only was their three-bedroom apartment clean and new and spacious, but also there were plenty of play areas and green space on the property for children.

The only thing my parents were worried about was the fact that they would be one of only a handful of Black families in their building. When they moved in, four other Black families moved in at the same time — the Thompsons, the Bradfords, the Johnsons, and the Conroys — and the five families quickly became friends. As it turned out, the white people didn't have any problems with the Black people moving into the building. And soon enough, my parents were happily absorbed into the Pink Houses community.

By the time I entered the world, my brother George Jr. was fifteen, my sister Cynthia was twelve, and my brother Bruce was ten. Three years after I was born, my mother gave birth to my brother Don. Three years later came Scott. So we were six kids in all. Even though I was technically a middle child, I was the youngest girl and I loved my role in the family. I was a daddy's girl, but I also loved being a little mommy to my two little brothers. The whole family doted on me, so I had no complaints.

The love started with my parents. It was obvious to me, even as a small child, that my parents truly loved each other. They were always happy around each other and affectionate, even after all those years of marriage. When Daddy came home from work, the first thing he'd do was go find my mom and say, "Hey, Gert," and give her a big hug and kiss. Then he'd turn and hug on us kids. If it was a Friday night, we might get pizza for dinner and have ourselves our own little party right there in the apartment. Mommy would put the music on and we'd all just be singing and dancing and having a good time. Sometimes I'd make my little brothers put on a show with me, and Mommy and Daddy would be our audience and laugh at the songs and dances we made up.

Our house was just always full of fun and laughter. And it all started with my mom. Mommy was the sweetest person. Once she started having kids, she stopped working and took care of us children full-time. She cooked us delicious food, kept a perfectly clean house, and made sure we learned our Bible verses. When it was hot out, she'd make us Kool-Aid popsicles we could eat outside. When it was cold, we'd come home from school and get mugs of hot chocolate. But most importantly, Mommy took us to the library every single week so we could get new books. She made sure we had our own library cards before we could even read. She loved reading. You would never find her without a book. We had a floor-to-ceiling bookcase in our apartment with books crammed into every single crevice. Mommy always told me that if I needed to learn something, I could find it in a book.

Church was also really important to my parents. Growing up, we attended the First Baptist Church of Coney Island. And everybody, all of us kids, had to go. Daddy was a deacon, and both of my parents sang in the choir. Naturally it was expected that we children would participate in as many church activities as possible. As a result, we were always in church. If you sang in the choir, you had to go to rehearsal during the week, either Saturday or Thursday night. I was in the children's choir and on the junior usher board, so that meant I was at church at least two times a week, in addition to Sundays. I liked going to church. I liked singing, and Mommy would sign me up to be in the church plays, and one time I even got to participate in a fashion show. I loved performing. It was all fun for me, even when old Mrs. Johnson would squeeze my cheeks too hard and tell my mother how cute I was.

My father was just as sweet and kind as my mother, but of course, since he worked all day at the factory and then sometimes in the evenings and on the weekends selling seltzer and soda door-to-door as a side hustle, I didn't spend as much time with him. But when my father was home, he loved to play with me and watch me and my brothers put on our shows. But the special thing my father and I shared was our love for comedy.

My father would let me stay up late sometimes and watch *The Carol Burnett Show* with him. I knew I had to go to bed right after, but this was me and Daddy's special time. Scott and Don had to go to bed earlier than me, but Daddy and I would eat our ice cream and be cracking up at Carol Burnett. Sometimes I'd try to stay up a little later and beg my father to let me watch one more show, but he'd always shake his head. "No, Cheryl, you know the rules. You gotta get in the bed now." I never argued because I didn't want Daddy to be mad at me. And I certainly didn't want to lose our special time together.

My childhood at the Pink Houses felt idyllic to me. Despite the fact that America was in the middle of a civil rights nightmare and tangled up in a war in Vietnam, everyone in my world got along. I had playmates in my building who were white, Jewish, Italian, Latino. Mommy let me go play in their apartments, and sometimes they'd come to our apartment to play. Never once did I doubt that I was a beautiful little Black girl. The only time I remember a white person being mean to me was when we were taking one of our annual trips down south to visit relatives. We were driving down the highway and I saw a little white girl in the car next to ours, so I waved, but the little white girl stuck her tongue out at me. For no reason! Mommy told me to ignore her. Daddy told me to ignore her too. But I stuck out my tongue back at her and felt much better.

Going down south meant going to North Carolina and staying for a week or two. We'd visit Mommy's mother and sisters and then go see Daddy's sister, my Aunt Betsy, and her husband, Uncle Marvin. They had a farm, and I just loved being around all their animals. We also drove down south together when it was time to take my older sister, Cynthia, who I called Sis, to college. She went to college at Johnson C. Smith in North Carolina. The drive down there was familiar, but the excitement in the car felt different. I was only six years old when Sis left for school, but even I could tell this was a big deal. Mommy and Daddy hadn't gone to college and George Jr. didn't either, so Sis was something special in the family. I cried when we left her down there. Mommy told me not to cry because Sis would be back sooner rather than later.

Mommy was telling the truth about Sis coming back home, but not for the reason she thought.

I was nine years old and I remember I was sitting at the dining room table doing my homework. It was a Saturday in March. Too cold to go outside, but Mommy had told me earlier that if I finished my homework, I could watch cartoons when I was done. Bruce and

George Jr. were both home that day and so were my little brothers. Daddy was out working and Sis was still in North Carolina, finishing up her last year of college. Nothing seemed unusual or amiss, except that Mommy was lying down in her bedroom. She said she wasn't feeling well.

Then I heard Bruce call for George. George got up from the sofa in the living room and went running to Mommy and Daddy's bedroom in the back. Then the two of them carried Mommy out to the living room and laid her gently on the sofa. She was barely moving and her skin looked gray to me. I couldn't move, I was so scared. George told me to stay where I was and keep doing my homework.

I could only nod my head and stare at Mommy and wonder why she wasn't moving. Why she wasn't smiling. Why she wasn't telling me that everything was going to be okay.

"We're going to take Mommy to the hospital," Bruce said, and then he and George picked Mommy up and carried her out the door. I knew the hospital where I was born was just across the street, so that's where I figured they would carry her. My little brothers were still in their room and didn't even know what was happening and I didn't want to tell them. What must have been only ten minutes later, my godmother, who lived on the fourth floor, came up to sit with the boys and me while we waited for somebody to call with some news.

I don't know how much time passed, but I know I watched *The Jetsons* and *The Flintstones* without hearing anything about Mommy. Then Daddy came home. He was in his work clothes and he looked exhausted and sad. I flew into his arms and asked, "What happened to Mommy? Where is she? Is she okay?"

My father picked me up and said, "Cheryl, Mommy is in the hospital because she didn't feel good. But the doctors are going to take care of her. She'll be better soon."

I trusted my father and told myself that Mommy would be okay. But the look on my father's face wouldn't let me truly believe it. My father quickly changed his clothes and said he was going back over to the hospital. My godmother assured him that she would stay and take care of us kids.

The next morning I woke up in my bed and I talked to God. I said, "Dear God, please let Mommy get better soon." Then I jumped up and walked out of my room to see if I could find a grown-up to tell me what was happening with my mother.

I found my brother Bruce in the living room, looking out the window. He was just standing there, barely moving.

"Bruce, are you all right?" I whispered. He didn't answer, so I raised my voice. "Bruce? Bruce!"

He finally turned around to face me. "Cheryl, Mommy passed away."

"What do you mean?" I cried. "What does 'passed away' mean?"

"Mommy died. She had a stroke or something," he said and started to cry. "They said her blood pressure was too high."

None of it made any sense to me. I never heard anything about Mommy's blood pressure. And she was never sick. I ran to my parents' bedroom, hoping to find my mother there. But she wasn't. Neither was my father. I just threw myself on their bed and hugged my mother's pillow close. I could still smell her Jergens lotion and the oil she used on her hair.

On the day of my mother's funeral, the church was packed. All five of my mother's sisters were there, as were her two brothers, Uncle Carlisle and Uncle T. Sis was there too, of course. Everyone from the church community showed up as well. Everybody loved my mother. As I sat there, squashed between my godmother and Sis, I remember thinking how popular my mother was. I waved at my godsister across the aisle and didn't understand why she didn't wave back. People all around me were sniffling and sobbing, but I just knew that Mommy wasn't really gone. I told myself, "Mommy is going to get up. She's just sleeping in that thing up there. She's going to get up." I had decided my mother was only sleeping. *She's going to get up. She's going to get up* was the one thought running through my head.

It wasn't until we went to the cemetery and I watched them lower my mother's coffin into the ground that my mother's death seemed real. I looked at my father and my brothers and sister and saw the grief distorting their faces and I finally understood. My mother was truly gone. That's when I started to cry and couldn't stop.

The days following the funeral were filled with people in our house bringing food and making plans for us children. My sister wanted to drop out of school to take care of my little brothers and me but my father wouldn't hear of it.

"You're going back to school and you're going to graduate," he told her. "That's the one thing your mother wanted more than anything in this world," he said, tearing up. "To see you with your college diploma."

But that meant my father was left to decide what to do with us. He worked all day. He couldn't handle three little kids by himself. Scott was only three years old. He wasn't even in kindergarten yet.

I kept quiet and listened while the grown folks were trying to decide what to do.

"We'll take the kids, George," one of my aunts said in hushed tones in the living room, while I listened from the hallway.

"I'll take Cheryl," my mother's sister Aunt Jane said.

"And we'll take the little boys," my Aunt Alma offered.

"You can't handle these kids by yourself, George," someone else said. I couldn't make out who.

"No," my father said loudly. I could tell he was mad. "One of the last things Gert said to me in the hospital was 'Do not split my children up!' She told me if she didn't make it, I had to promise her that I would keep the children with me. And I made that promise." And then I heard my father start to cry. I was used to hearing that sound now and it hurt my heart.

My aunts were quiet for a moment and let my father collect himself.

"George, we're only trying to help and do what's best for those kids. And for you."

I realized I was holding my breath in the hallway as I waited to hear what my father would say. I loved all of my aunts, but I didn't want to leave my daddy or my brothers.

My father's voice was clear and firm when he opened his mouth to speak again. "I appreciate the offer, but the kids will stay here with me. I promised Gert, and I'm not going to let her down."

"But how will you manage, George?" Aunt Jane asked.

"I don't know," Daddy said. "I'll figure something out."

Daddy did the best that he could after Mommy died. And I did the best that I could not to make his life any harder than it had suddenly become, being a single working father of three little children. My godmother and godsisters helped out, as did the women from the church. But it wasn't enough. I wanted my mommy.

When she was alive, at the end of the school day I'd find my mother waiting outside the gates of PS 224, ready to walk me home. But now I was forced to wait for whomever my father could persuade to come and get me. They were usually late. It was never the same person, and sometimes I'd be left there waiting so long I'd think I'd been forgotten. I tried to keep my hurt and sorrow inside because I knew Daddy was trying his hardest. And I didn't want him to send us away because we were too much to handle.

One day later that spring, my father called me to him. He was sitting in the living room watching the evening news.

"Why are you walking funny, Cheryl?" he asked me, frowning.

I hobbled over to him but was afraid to tell him the truth. My sneakers were too small but I didn't want to cause my father any extra trouble.

"Cheryl," my father said again. "What's the matter, sweetie?"

My father always said I had to tell the truth, so I told him.

"Your shoes was hurting, and you didn't feel like you could tell me?" He looked at me with such sorrow in his eyes that I felt like I should comfort him. But he grabbed me up and held me close. Then my father shook his head and forced me to look him in the eye. "Cheryl Lynn Williams, you are never a burden to me. I am your father and my job is to take care of you."

"Okay, Daddy," I said, and sure enough, the very next day Daddy came home with a new pair of sneakers for me. They weren't the latest style like Mommy would have bought for me, but they were the right size and didn't pinch my toes. That was good enough.

As soon as Sis finished college in May, she came back to Brooklyn to help take care of us. It was wonderful to have Sis home again, and I thought she'd make things feel like Mommy did, but Sis wasn't Mommy.

I knew my sister was trying her best and I tried my best not to complain, but it was almost like the more she tried, the more glaringly obvious it was that Mommy was gone. I kept my observations to myself, but in my head I'd be watching my sister and thinking, *Oh, brother, this is not what Mommy would do.* Every little thing Sis did wrong made me miss Mommy more. One day Sis laid my clothes out for me to wear to school.

"I don't wear this sweater with this outfit. This doesn't go together," I told my sister, crossing my arms across my chest. She had put together an outfit that Mommy would never make me wear.

"Listen, you better wear this sweater," Sis said, getting angry.

"I don't want to wear that sweater," I said, tears springing to my eyes, thinking that Sis was getting it all wrong. And I just lay down on my bed and cried. Sis thought I was being stubborn about that stupid sweater, but I just missed my mother so much. I missed her big kisses and hugs. I missed her laughing at my jokes and silly performances. I missed her playfulness and that sensation when she made me feel like I was the most important thing in the world to her. But Sis wasn't doing any of that.

"Why are you so upset about a silly sweater?" Sis asked me. "I just thought you should wear it because it's still cool in the mornings. I don't want you to catch a cold."

I couldn't stop my tears, but I sat up and collected myself.

"It's just that . . . ," I started. "Nothing is right. Nothing feels right since Mommy died."

Sis sat down next to me on the bed. Now she had tears in her eyes too. She hugged me tight.

"You're going to be okay, Cheryl. It's all going to be okay," she said.

Sis knew all I wanted was my mother back, but she also knew she couldn't give that to me. I could see she was doing her best, though, trying to be strong and put on a brave face so she could keep things in order around the house. At the time, I didn't think about Sis needing comfort, but she was hurting too. Mommy was her best friend. They wrote letters to each other every week while Sis was away at college. Mommy's absence in our family was felt by us all.

One year after my mother died, Daddy figured out a better way to deal with us kids.

I was ten years old and I was sitting outside playing with my dolls by myself. My father came outside and found me. He told me he had something important to tell me.

"Cheryl, Estelle and I are getting married," he said.

Estelle went to our church, and lately Daddy had been taking us to her house over at the Red Hook projects for Sunday dinners. She was a good cook and I liked looking at all of her pictures of her own children, who were all grown up. But I had no idea she was about to marry my father.

"Okay, Daddy," I said with a shrug without looking up at him. I didn't know what else to say. I continued playing with my dolls as I tried to figure out how I felt about this big announcement.

"I already told Scott and Don," my father said, "and they're happy they're going to get a new mom. What about you, Cheryl?"

That got my attention. I looked up at my father and said slowly, "I guess it sounds good." It was almost a question.

"Will you call her Mom or Estelle?" my father wanted to know. "The boys already decided they are going to call her Mommy."

I scrunched up my face as I tried to figure out how to answer my father's question. Why would I call this new lady "Mom"? I wondered. But just as quickly, I felt a flicker of hope. I hadn't been able to call anyone Mommy in a year. I didn't just miss *my* mother. I missed having *a* mother. Daddy had picked Estelle to be his new wife, and so maybe things would be like before when Mommy was alive. As this idea formed in my head, I started to feel excited about Estelle and encouraged, too.

"I'll call her Mommy," I said, warming to the idea by the minute. That made Daddy smile and he bent down to hug me. I think we were both ready for some joy back in our lives.

Unfortunately, Estelle wasn't the person to bring the joy. She wasn't mean, but she wasn't playful. She was totally different from my mother. Where my mother would invite all of us kids to come watch our favorite TV shows together all snuggled up on my parents' bed,

Estelle put a lock on the bedroom door and told all of us kids we were forbidden to enter the room. She brought her own furniture and decorations into our apartment and told us that we were never to touch any of her things. I had never met a grown-up like that before. And I just knew my father was going to realize he made a mistake and send her packing. But he never did. I think he was just so grateful that there was a woman around to handle the household that he was willing to overlook Estelle's particular disposition. He even ignored the whispers from the people at church who said it was shameful that Daddy barely waited a year after Mommy passed to take a new wife.

I couldn't fault him, though. I wasn't a big fan of Estelle's, but I understood Daddy needed the help. Sis had found a job in Atlanta and moved down there once Estelle officially became part of the family. Before she left, Sis told me to give Estelle a chance. And it was true. Estelle wasn't all bad. She made us good meals and baked us cakes for our birthdays. She would take me to nice stores like Macy's and Gimbels to buy me clothes for school and special occasions. And even though she had a job as a nurse's aide and worked during the day, Estelle was around for me and my brothers after school and in the evenings.

Luckily, my godmother Katherine and her two daughters — my godsisters — did their very best to shower me with the affection I lost when Mommy died. So I didn't have to depend on Estelle's infrequent bursts of kindness. I loved Katherine so much and I knew she loved me. My parents had met her when they first moved into the Pink Houses. Our families grew close. Katherine's daughters were five and eight years older than me, and they spoiled me. I loved to go down to their apartment on the fourth floor and play. After Mommy died, I spent even more time with them.

Whatever I needed, Katherine stepped up to take care of it. If I needed my hair done, she'd take me to the beauty parlor. My father usually couldn't make it to my dance performances or musical concerts because he had to work during the day. So did Estelle. But Katherine would come. She worked the night shift as a nurse, so she would come home, get her snack and a nap, and then she would come out to support me. I was in the glee club and African dance, and I played the clarinet in the school band, so there was always something going on. Katherine would always be there so I could look out into the audience and see her cheering me on.

By the time I was twelve, we were in a new little rhythm as a family. Daddy finally let me walk to school by myself. Estelle brought a familiar and welcome routine back to our household. And things had returned to some sort of new normal. But I still missed Mommy a lot. I missed her sweetness and her joy. I missed seeing my father come home with a smile on his face looking for his "Gert" to squeeze and laugh with. He didn't squeeze Estelle. They didn't laugh together. We didn't dance together in the apartment anymore. But I had my godmother and my godsisters to fill in those empty spaces for me. And I continued to love on my little brothers, like Mommy used to love on me. I wanted them to know they were special and appreciated. So while Estelle was the new engine of the family, keeping everything running, I took it upon myself to be the heart.

Our family hummed along like that for a few years. Then I came home one day and Estelle was gone.

chapter three

Trouble

BOBBY

When I was five years old, my sister Mildred taught me how to gamble. Let me clarify. She didn't actually teach me, but I learned by watching her play cards with her friends in our living room. "Go back in your room, Buddy," she'd say over her shoulder when I would come lurk by the table. But I didn't listen. I wanted to see what these big kids were doing instead of going to school like they were supposed to.

By the time I was twelve, not only was I skipping classes to take part in the occasional game of cards with high school kids, but I was also skipping school on Fridays so I could work my new job at the golf course near our house.

I was tall for my age. That meant I was able to pass for sixteen and pick up extra money as a golf caddy. Even though the golf club was for white golfers, all the caddies were Black, so it was easy for me to blend in. All I had to do was show up in the parking lot on Friday and Saturday mornings and ask the white men who came to play if they wanted to hire me for the day. If they said yes, I'd enter the golf club as part of their group and spend the day chasing after balls, handing the golfers their clubs, and otherwise making myself available and useful. On a good day I could make twice what I made mowing lawns.

By the time I was thirteen years old, I'd been caddying for almost a year and had learned the intricacies of the game by keeping my eyes and ears open. Now I could tell the difference between an iron and a wedge and when was the best time to use what club for what shot. Sometimes these players would place a thousand-dollar bet on a game, and they'd tell me at the start that if I did a good job and helped them win, I'd leave with a generous tip in my pocket. I wanted those tips, so I learned the game inside and out, to the point where, when I found a discarded putter on the course — sometimes these men would get so mad while playing, they'd break their clubs or throw them away — rather than turn it in at the office, I took it home and used it to practice my swing in our front yard.

With the money from the golf course, I had a steady source of income to hang out with my friends, and to start buying my own clothes. In fact, the first thing of value I bought was an alpaca sweater, just like the ones I noticed the golfers wearing on the course. Once I wore that sweater to school and saw the attention it brought me, I was hooked. I started paying more attention to fashion in magazines and on TV and I began to focus on creating my own look. If I didn't have enough money to buy the clothes I wanted, then I'd put them on layaway and would work and save until I could bring the item home.

At this time Greensboro was bubbling with civil rights activities. Sit-ins, marches, and calls for integration were roiling the city. Things got really heated in 1960 with the four young men who refused to leave the Woolworth's lunch counter without being served. Their actions sparked a movement, not just in Greensboro but all across the South. Even though all of this was happening right downtown, we could only watch things unfold on the TV in our living room because Mama refused to let any of us kids go down there to participate. She wanted things to be different for Black people, but she was unwilling to sacrifice her children for the cause.

"It's too dangerous," she'd tell me whenever I asked if we could go downtown to march or protest.

I kept asking, but Mama didn't budge. "Buddy, you better not go anywhere near that madness or I'll send your brother to snatch you right up."

I knew she was serious.

Despite the fact that my mother tried to keep me from getting caught up in the civil rights movement, she couldn't keep the movement from coming for me.

The summer before I started eighth grade, a letter arrived in our mailbox informing my mother that the city was going to actually start enforcing its desegregation laws. That meant I was supposed to stop taking a one-hour bus ride to attend an all-Black school on the other side of town and start attending the junior high school that sat three blocks from my house.

Gillespie Park Junior High School had been an all-white school for seventh-, eighth-, and ninth-graders up until 1957, when four brave Black children had integrated the institution. Every year since then a few more Black students had enrolled in the school, but now the city government was getting involved, requiring all of us Black kids who lived in the district to start attending Gillespie whether we wanted to or not. When that letter arrived, my mind immediately flashed to all of the things that were happening in Greensboro — the sit-ins, the violence, the police dogs tearing at flesh. I was scared, but Mama said I had to go because it was the law now. Mama always followed the rules. To her, it kept us safe.

She tried to put a positive spin on it. "At least you'll be closer to home, Buddy."

"But what if they try to do something bad to us?" I asked.

Mama sighed before answering. "God will protect you," she said.

"Your job is to get your education and stay out of trouble. That's all you can do."

That was Mama's reply for a lot of things.

The good news was that I wouldn't be going to Gillespie by myself. I had friends from the neighborhood who had gotten the same letter as me. And we were all worried. At thirteen and fourteen years old, we weren't ready to lay down our lives just so we could go to school with white kids.

I remember the first day of school, my friends Spencer, Lewis, and Jesse were by my side as we walked the three blocks to Gillespie. My mother couldn't come with me because she had to work, and as she always reminded me, she didn't get paid if she didn't show up.

When we rounded the corner where the school was, we were met by a parking lot with a bunch of white people shouting at us. "Niggers, get away from here!" "Y'all not wanted here!" "This is our school!" This was different from seeing it on the TV screen. To me, these people looked like they wanted to use their bare hands to tear us apart. Even though there were now a significant number of Black students at Gillespie, the whites still felt it was their school and didn't want this influx of new Black bodies sent by the city.

We walked past the angry protestors and entered the school on the other side of the building. I could feel my heart pounding and the sweat running down my back. I didn't dare say a word, but I was grateful that I was with my friends. Once we made it inside, a man who introduced himself as Mr. Dean came out into the hallway. I thought he looked like Howdy Doody with his gap-toothed smile. It turned out he was the principal.

Mr. Dean didn't waste any time trying to make us feel welcome. He gave each of us a piece of paper with our schedules and told us to get to class.

I went to my assigned eighth-grade classroom and found myself for the first time in my life in a class with white children and a white teacher. I took a chair in the back of the room and prayed my way to lunchtime, when I'd get to meet up with my friends again.

At noon, when I made my way to the cafeteria, I kept my head down and tried not to attract the attention of any adults. But that was hard. Nearly every adult in the building was white — the teachers, the secretaries, and the principal of course. As I recall, there was only one Black teacher in the entire school, and she seemed as overwhelmed and out of place as we were.

"Yo, Curtis!" Spencer called out when he saw me. My friends called me by my middle name because I hated the name Walter.

I ran over to Spencer and breathed a sigh of relief. We'd made it halfway through the first day.

Jesse soon joined us, and the three of us got in line behind the few white kids already standing there. Despite the fact that I was still on guard, I was hungry and was happy we were close to the front of the line. But then the kid in front of us let his friend cut in and join him in the line. Then he did the same thing again and again with other kids. Pretty soon, instead of being at the head of the line for lunch, we were way at the back.

Spencer was the first to speak up. He tapped one of the white kids who'd skipped us on the shoulder and said, "Hey, y'all can't get in front of us."

The boy laughed and said, "You can't stop us," and went back to talking to his friends.

He didn't know those were fighting words.

Jesse, Spencer, and I muscled our way back to the head of the line, and that's all it took. A big fight broke out, right there in the lunchroom. Fists were flying as white kids hit us and we hit them back, but the only kids that got pulled into the principal's office were the Black ones.

When I went home defeated after that first day, I threw myself on the living room couch and wailed to my mother and sister, "Why do we have to go to that school with these white kids who hate us?" And my sister Jean looked at me and said, "I got two words for you: Thurgood Marshall."

I was confused. Mama explained who Thurgood Marshall was right then and there. She ended her little sermon with "It's for the best, Buddy. This is what all the people are fighting for and this is how you fight. By going to that school and showing those white folks that you deserve to be there."

For the next two weeks I tried to keep my mama's words in my head, but I dreaded going back to Gillespie, knowing that I would be fighting all the time. Whenever I tried to sit down, someone would say, "That's my seat." In the lunchroom we were pushed to the end of the line. The teachers never defended us, and the white students knew they could get away with bullying us. I think I got into at least one fight a day, and I spent more time in the principal's office than in the classroom.

Mr. Dean had no sympathy for me and my friends' situations. In fact, he told us Black kids that it was our job to be more understanding and sympathetic to the white students.

"You have to remember, Walter," Mr. Dean said to me one day when I was in his office, "This has been their school for a long time and now you're coming in here trying to change things."

I didn't know how I was going to survive the agony of going back to Gillespie for two more years.

Luckily, the problem resolved itself.

About three weeks into the school year, I found out that some of the white kids had left Gillespie and they weren't coming back. The next day a few more left. The following day even more failed to show up. By the end of the first semester, there were only a handful of white kids left in the entire school. The others had all found schools to attend where they wouldn't have to learn alongside Negroes. The white teachers and administrators, however, were still there and they didn't show us any love. There was one teacher in particular, Mr. Morgan. He taught civics and was a former marine. Mr. Morgan claimed he wasn't a racist and said he treated all his students equally, but in the same breath he would refer to us Black kids as "nigrunts."

"I don't have any problem with you nigrunts as long as you do as you're told," he regularly reminded us. I hated it when he called us that and I hated the way a lot of the white teachers were openly hostile to us, but at that point in my life, school was where I got to hang out with my friends and play basketball and baseball. And now that the white kids were mostly gone and I wasn't worried about getting into fights every day, I could also concentrate on learning. I liked math and art class. Going to Gillespie wasn't a positive experience like my former school had been, where all of the teachers had been Black, but I managed to make it through eighth grade without too much drama.

By the time summer arrived, I was ready for some fun. My friend Eddie Lee and I bought tickets to see the singer Sam Cooke at the Greensboro Coliseum. This was going to be my first live concert. The Coliseum was brand new and had brought some great musical acts to the city. But Sam Cooke was going to be one of the first performers that both Blacks and whites were coming to see together. Eddie and I could only afford the cheapest tickets in the nosebleed section, but I planned on sneaking down closer to the stage once the music started.

The night of the concert, I was so excited.

"You ready for this, man?" I said to Eddie as we entered the gleaming new building.

Eddie grinned at me. "You know I am."

We took the stairs two at a time up to our seats, and sure enough, they were so far away we could barely see the opening act. The sound in that place was fantastic, though, and the cool clothes cats were wearing were incredible. Between the fashion and the music, I was already in heaven.

I turned to Eddie. "Hey, as soon as Sam Cooke comes out and they turn the lights back down, let's go sneak down toward the stage."

"You sure?" Eddie said, looking around to see what kind of security was on duty.

Because this was an integrated concert, and because Sam Cooke had a reputation as a civil rights agitator, there were cops everywhere.

But I wasn't deterred. I loved Sam Cooke and I wanted to get as close to the music as possible.

"If you're too scared to come down there with me," I said to Eddie, "then just stay up here. I'll find you after the show."

Eddie slumped back in his chair and looked like he was trying to make up his mind.

"Ladies and gentlemen, please take your seats. The show is about to start," a voice announced and the lights went down.

"You coming?" I asked Eddie one last time.

"Naw, man, I'll watch from up here," he said.

I shrugged. "Suit yourself. I'll catch you later." And with that, I started making my way down to the stage area. As I was walking, doing my best to act like I was looking for my seat, Sam came onstage and started singing. People went crazy. They stood up, clapped, and screamed their approval. In all of the chaos, it was easy for me to blend in.

Then Sam started singing his second song, and the crowd was loving it. I was just feet away from the stage when he abruptly stopped singing.

"Ladies and gentlemen," he spoke into the microphone. "I'm going to have to ask you to please take your seats," he said. "I can't sing with so much commotion and noise. Please sit down or the show will be over."

People looked at each other with confusion. I was confused too. Why should we sit down? We were here to jam. A murmur of defiance started to spread across the Coliseum. But Sam was adamant. "Please sit down or I won't perform," he repeated.

Nobody sat down, so he walked off the stage and refused to come back. A few minutes later a voice announced that the show was over.

I was devastated. And angry. This was my first concert. I'd saved up fifteen dollars for the ticket and spent all of my leftover money on bus fare. All around me people were expressing their displeasure, and I fed off their anger. I ran up to the front of the stage and shouted as loud as my thirteen-year-old lungs could project, "Sam Cooke ain't shit!"

Before I could open my mouth to repeat it, I felt a firm hand on my shoulder.

"You're under arrest. Come with me," a voice growled in my ear. It was a cop.

I struggled to get out of his grasp, but he just grabbed me tighter.

"What did I do?" I cried as he pulled me through the crowd. I tried to find Eddie in the mass of people being forced out of the building, but it was useless.

"What did I do?" I asked again, trying to stay calm.

The officer didn't slow his pace, but he answered me. "You used profanity in a crowded area."

"That's a crime?" I asked.

"Yeah, it's a crime," the cop said as we approached a room behind the stage. He opened the door, threw me in a metal folding chair, and told me to stay put. And then he left. I was too terrified to move. This was my first time being in trouble with the law. I wondered where Eddie was. I wondered how I was going to get out of this mess. I knew Mama was going to kill me.

I didn't have to wait for long. The cop came back, and another white man accompanied him. I assumed he was a detective because he was wearing a suit.

The detective had a notepad in his hand and asked me my name, how old I was, and where I lived. I answered his questions and then asked again what I had done wrong.

He repeated what the other officer had said before. "You used profanity in a crowded area. And we're charging you with disorderly conduct. You could have incited a riot or something, boy, with all those people in here."

A riot? I thought to myself. With all the noise that was going on, nobody even heard me. These cops had to be kidding. But they weren't. They took their time writing up a citation and telling me that what I had done was very dangerous. I didn't try to argue with them because I was scared that they might do something to me and nobody would ever know what happened.

Finally the detective announced that he would drive me home. I tried to refuse the ride, but he said he had to drive me home on account of my age. That put the fear of God in me, but I climbed into his unmarked black sedan anyway and prayed I'd actually make it home safely. I also prayed that the detective wouldn't demand to see my mother when we got to my house. Thankfully, the Lord answered both of my prayers. When we pulled up in front of my house, the detective handed me a slip of paper.

"This is your citation with your court date. Make sure you show up in court on that day, boy. You hear me?"

I took the paper and nodded my head. "Yes, sir." And then I scrambled out of the car and ran up to the front door. I let myself in and watched his car pull away. I gave a sigh of relief and looked down at the paper in my hand. Before I went to my room, I ripped it up into little pieces and threw the shreds in the trash can in the kitchen under a pile of greasy napkins. I didn't want my mother to know anything about what happened to me at the concert. I had to destroy all of the evidence so I could put the whole miserable experience behind me.

About one month later I was sitting in Mr. Morgan's civics class. Ninth grade had started without incident or drama.

"Walter Curtis Miller, please come down to the principal's office." The voice of Mrs. Olsen, the school secretary, rang out over the intercom.

"O-h-h, Curtis, you're in trouble," somebody called out behind me. And then a few others joined in the chant.

"You nigrunts quiet down," Mr. Morgan said, standing up and demanding calm. "Mr. Miller." He turned to me. "Collect your stuff and go on downstairs."

"Yes, sir," I said, wondering what I had done. I racked my brain as I headed down the three flights of stairs to the first floor. Since it was only a few weeks into the school year, I couldn't imagine how I could already be in trouble.

A man in a uniform who looked like a police officer was now standing in my principal's office.

"Hello, Mr. Miller," he said to me. He then told me he was a probation officer.

I was too frightened to respond.

"Have a seat," he said.

I turned to the principal to see if he was going to intervene, but all he did was point to the chair in front of his desk. I sat down.

"You didn't show up for your court date," the officer said.

I didn't know if that was a question or a statement, so I just shrugged and said, "No, sir."

The man then turned to Mr. Dean and recounted what I had done at the concert the month before.

Mr. Dean listened to the detective and then turned to me and said, "Well, Walter, I hope you learned your lesson."

"Yes, sir, I did," I said. "And I won't ever do that again."

"Good," Mr. Dean said. "I know you know better."

"Can I go back to class now?" I asked the principal.

Mr. Dean leaned over on his desk. "Walter, this officer is going to tell you what happens next. This isn't school business so I'm not in charge here."

I turned to the man in uniform. "Can I go back to class now?"

"No, boy, I'm going to take you home and we're going to talk to your mother."

The officer's words scared me. I thought I had succeeded in keeping my mother from finding out about the whole Sam Cooke concert incident. And now it was all going to blow up in my face.

The probation officer drove me home and waited in the house with me until my mother made it home from work.

When Mama arrived and saw me sitting in the living room with a white man in a police uniform, she almost passed out from fright.

"Buddy, what's going on here?" she said.

The probation officer stood up and introduced himself. And then he launched right into the purpose of his visit. While he told my mother about my "outburst" at the concert, subsequent arrest, and then my failure to show up for the court date, I sat on the couch with my head hanging down, wishing I could just melt into the floor.

"Buddy, I hope you learned your lesson. I told you not to use that kind of language and now look what you've done," Mama said when the officer was done explaining.

"I'm sorry, Mama," I squeaked.

"You need to be saying sorry to the officer," she said.

"I'm sorry," I repeated, not looking up.

"Well, that's not really going to help now," the officer said. "Since you didn't show up for that court date, you have to serve your time for the crime you committed."

"You're not sending him to jail!" my mother shrieked.

"No, ma'am," the officer reassured her. "But he will be put on probation for the next two years."

My mother sat down next to me and started to cry.

I was only thirteen years old, but I knew this was an outsized punishment for the "crime." I glared at the man but didn't say anything. He left a slip of paper with instructions on the table and showed himself out the door.

As I expected, after the officer left, my mother had my brother whip me with a switch, but later that evening she told me I was too big to beat anymore. "I don't know what to do with you, Buddy," she said. "I tried to keep you out of trouble."

"I can stay out of trouble," I said, not liking the sound of resignation in her voice.

She shook her head like she didn't believe me. "Buddy, I don't want to see you end up like your brothers, but that's exactly how you're fixin' to end up."

"No I won't, Mama," I said. "You'll see."

"I hope so, Buddy," she said. "But I don't know what else to do. All I can do now is give you to God."

My probation officer's name was Mr. Allen. He was a middle-aged Black man who thought the way Black people were going to survive was to play by the white man's rules. When we met for the first time, he told me, "This is their world we're living in so follow their rules and don't make them mad."

Mr. Allen assured me that probation was no big deal. All I had to do was stay out of trouble.

"What do you mean stay out of trouble?" I asked.

"Three strikes and they'll send you to some kind of juvenile detention center," he said.

"What counts as a strike?" I wanted to know.

Mr. Allen narrowed his eyes and leaned in close. "Stay out of trouble, Walter. No trouble at school, no trouble with girls, no trouble with the law. Keep yourself clean. Don't give them a single reason to come find you."

"Okay," I said, thinking I had to stop cutting classes. Stop playing cards. Stay away from trouble. I knew I could do that. I wanted to prove my mother wrong about turning out like my older brothers. The last thing I wanted was to end up in jail.

Throughout ninth grade, I continued working at the golf course and cutting grass to earn money, and I played basketball whenever I could. My big brother Raymond told me if I kept it up, I might get a college scholarship. At school I did my best to avoid getting sent to the principal's office, but I wasn't able to manage that completely.

I got sent to the principal for telling Mr. Morgan to stop calling us nigrunts. For that incident I got a beating from the assistant principal and found myself officially one strike closer to being sent to a juvenile facility.

After that, I doubled down on following all of the rules and stayed out of trouble for several months. I even got a job washing dishes at K&W Cafeteria. It was a real job, so I had to apply for my working papers and my Social Security card before I could be hired. Even though I knew I could make more money hustling on the golf course than they paid me for washing dishes, I was trying to show my mother and my probation officer that I could do the right thing.

But then, one afternoon in the spring, I was sitting in my English class and the teacher, Mrs. Bell, was writing the day's assignment on the board.

"Hey, Cotton Foot," one of my friends called out to me. "Cotton Foot" was the nickname I'd picked up the past summer when I stepped on a rusty nail that pierced the sole of my foot right through my sneaker. "I don't have any money to take you to the doctor, Buddy," my mother had said to me when I showed her my red, swollen heel the next day.

Mama left me in my bed and came back with her medicine kit and a slab of fatback that she usually used to season the greens. As she dug around in her kit, I watched her get a bunch of cotton and douse it in white vinegar before cleaning off my foot. Then she took a copper penny and the fatback and wrapped the two things around my foot with another big wad of cotton. She told me I couldn't put any weight on my foot for a week. When my friends saw me sitting on the porch with my foot propped up covered in cotton, they started calling me Cotton Foot. The name stuck and I liked it. Because anything was better than Walter.

"Hey, Cotton Foot," my friend said again, a little louder.

I turned in my seat. "Yeah?"

Mrs. Bell turned around from the board and said, "Mr. Miller, you're talking out of turn. Get out of my classroom."

"I didn't say anything, Mrs. Bell," I said.

She pointed at the door. "I heard your voice and I don't like what you said," she insisted.

I didn't know what she thought she heard, so I pleaded my case. "Mrs. Bell, I didn't do nothing. My friend just called my name and I said 'Yeah?'"

"Do not argue with me, Walter. I know what I heard. Now go downstairs to the principal's office and he can deal with you."

She turned back to face the chalkboard and I gathered my things and slunk out of the classroom. "Sorry, Cotton Foot," my friend whispered as I walked past his desk.

Before I went to the principal's office, I left the school grounds and bought a soda at the store across the street. I knew I wasn't supposed to leave the building, but I was so mad I needed to cool off. I drank my soda and headed back to face the principal.

"Walter, why did you think you could go buy a soda in the middle of the school day?" the principal asked with a frown when I finally showed up in his office about fifteen minutes later and told him where I'd been.

I wanted to say "Because I was thirsty," but I just shrugged my shoulders, looked at Mr. Dean, and waited for him to tell me what my punishment was.

"Walter, you just can't stay out of trouble, can you?" Mr. Dean said.

Again, I didn't answer.

Mr. Dean pulled his eyes away from mine and turned his attention to a piece of paper. He signed the bottom and handed it to me.

"Walter Miller, you are suspended until the end of the school year. Don't come back."

He handed me the paper and told me I could leave his office. He had washed his hands of me.

I scanned the paper. Usually a suspension lasted a few days, but Mr. Dean had written that my suspension would last for six weeks, until the very last day of school.

That sounded crazy to me, but I just took the letter and headed out the school doors.

The school contacted my probation officer, Mr. Allen, and told him I had been suspended. When he heard the news, he called my mother and told her he would come by the house to talk to me.

On the day Mr. Allen arrived, I was nervous.

"What happened, Walter?" Mr. Allen asked me as we sat at the kitchen table.

My mother stood in the doorway and watched what was going on but didn't interrupt.

"I honestly didn't do anything wrong," I started to explain. "I wish you could go in there and ask all the other kids. I don't know what Mrs. Bell thought she heard."

"Walter, you're not being suspended because of what happened in the classroom. You're being suspended because you left the school grounds and bought you a soda. That's against school policy," Mr. Allen said.

"But Mrs. Bell didn't have the right to throw me out of the class!" I protested. "I didn't do nothing!"

Mr. Allen looked at me like I was stupid. "Didn't I tell you, son, that you have to play by their rules?"

"But their rules aren't fair," I said, scowling.

Mr. Allen sighed, and I watched him crack the joints in his neck.

"Walter, the sooner you learn how to do what you're told, the better off you'll be."

Then he pulled a paper out of his bag and told my mother she needed to sign it. She wrote her name on the line where he indicated and then went back to standing in the kitchen doorway.

"As for you, young man," Mr. Allen said, turning his attention back to me. "Your job now is to stay in this house during school hours. You cannot be out in the streets because you will be picked up for truancy and then it will be all over for you. You got that?" he said.

"I got it," I said, but I was still seething that I was in this situation.

Mr. Allen picked up on my mood and said, "Listen, Walter, don't let them beat you down. Just stay out of trouble. Remember, it will be all over before you know it."

"Okay," I said, but I didn't feel very confident.

More and more I was starting to feel that trouble was going to find me whether I went looking for it or not. Maybe it wasn't worth trying so hard to avoid it.

Word got out that I was stuck at home on suspension, so my old card-playing friends decided my house was the perfect place to gamble, drink beer, and party during the school day. I figured since I wasn't on the streets, like Mr. Allen said, I wasn't breaking any rules.

My reputation was starting to grow as a guy who knew how to make the good times roll, and I enjoyed the attention from the older kids, especially the girls.

I started sneaking out at night to go meet up with girls and to party with my friends. When I'd get home after midnight, Jean would yell at me, but she'd also open a window for me to sneak through so Mama wouldn't find out. I wasn't exactly avoiding trouble, but the fun I was having seemed harmless. Plus I was getting away with it.

Meanwhile, Gillespie Junior High gave me passing grades at the end of the year. Even though I was out of the classroom for the last six weeks of school, they allowed me to graduate without having to go to summer school. I wasn't a stellar student, but I wasn't failing, either. I got the idea that Gillespie just wanted to get rid of me and that's why I was passed. I didn't dwell on it, though. I was just happy to leave junior high behind and start a new chapter of my life in high school.

People assumed that after being a guinea pig in Greensboro's school desegregation experiment, I would want to go back to an all-Black high school. But there was a new option for us Black kids — a high school called Ben L. Smith. Formerly an all-white school, Smith was one of the latest schools to desegregate. Some of my friends were going to Smith, and I wanted to go too. Jean told me that I should go to Dudley, where she went, where I would be safe and surrounded by other Black kids and teachers, but I had made up my mind. If Smith was the new, better school where all the white kids were going to go, then I wanted to go there too. At that point in my life, I was interested in doing the things that nobody expected of me. My instinct very early on was not to be afraid to step into new experiences. I had a full-sized imagination and always wanted to push the limits of what was possible, even though the rules and laws of the time were meant to curtail my freedoms, right along with my imagination. My mother allowed those restrictions to rule her life. She was motivated by fear. But I was the opposite. If I knew something was off limits, I was even more determined to get a taste.

Technically Mama had the final word about where I attended high school, because she had to sign the registration forms for me, but she didn't have a strong opinion about where I went. She just said, "Wherever you decide to go, just go there and do your best."

For me, part of doing my best in high school was looking my best. The summer before the school year started, I began saving my money to put together a new wardrobe so I could start the year in style. I wanted to project a high-end look from day one, a look that would command respect and admiration. I wanted slacks from a store called The Slacks Shop. I wanted Italian shoes from Ralph Johns. And as an accessory, I wanted a London Fog hat. My goal was to have enough clothing combinations that I never had to repeat the same outfit in a week. My mother had bought me a new trench coat and I got "Cotton Foot" embroidered on the collar and that was going to be my signature piece. I was only fourteen years old, but I took fashion very seriously.

The problem was, my love of fashion was an expensive hobby, so I started looking for new ways to get money, because washing dishes, caddying, and mowing the occasional lawn didn't provide enough funding for the clothes I wanted. Playing cards for money was an option, but that was never a guaranteed payout. So I started stealing. At first I'd just take some cash from my sister's purse or off my mother's dresser. Then I moved on to stealing from people I didn't know. I knew what I was doing was wrong, but I justified it in my mind by telling myself that white people could afford to lose a few dollars. I didn't set out specifically to steal only from white people, but in my experience, white people were the ones who had money. And from where I sat, it was easy for them to get more. All my life I had witnessed white people being given the better version of everything — from water fountains to schools to neighborhoods — so stealing from them somehow felt justified in my teenage brain.

One night I rolled a drunk guy for almost three hundred dollars. I stole a lady's purse at the fairgrounds with more than five hundred dollars in it. Being that young with more than five hundred dollars in my pocket was exhilarating to me. I didn't tell anybody what I'd done. I just went downtown and bought myself a new velour sweater, some new shoes, and some records. And that's how the thief in me was born. Every time I stole something, I told myself that I had just taken advantage of an opportunity that had presented itself. I didn't plan on stealing. But if I saw some money unattended, I didn't resist grabbing it. My mama would ask me sometimes where I was getting the money to buy all my nice clothes, because she knew my little jobs couldn't be the source of such wealth. I would tell her I had just put things on layaway, and she'd leave me alone.

I quickly went from petty thievery to stealing cars. The first car I took without permission was my sister's, just joyriding. Jean threatened to call the police if I did it again. So I never stole *her* car again, but soon after, I did steal two other cars in a one-month period. By then I had given up any notion of being strictly law-abiding. It never seemed to get me anywhere, and I liked the thrill of breaking the rules and having fun. I didn't want to get caught, but I also didn't have any intention of curtailing my new habits.

My mother witnessed my increasingly bad behavior and became all but resigned to the fact that I was going to mess up. Without her riding me to do better, I felt no compulsion to do the right thing. Two of my older brothers were in jail, my aunt who'd lived across the street was incarcerated, and two of my sisters had babies as teenagers. In other words, there just wasn't anyone in my life modeling this "good behavior" I was supposed to exhibit. Except my mother, of course. And what good was it doing her, following the rules? She worked like a dog every single day and we were still poor. While I wanted to make my mother happy, I didn't see her logic when it came to "honest work." Working a legitimate job was no guarantee you'd have enough money in your pocket for the things you needed and wanted. The trick, I decided, was finding the right hustle and playing by my own rules. So I quit my dishwashing job, and hustling became my focus. I was getting better and better at it.

Going to high school with white kids provided endless opportunities for me to steal. When I started tenth grade at Ben L. Smith, I had no plans to rob my fellow classmates, but I noticed right away how many of them carried cash on them all the time. When we'd be in the locker room changing for gym class, I'd see their wallets hanging out of their pants pockets with ten- and twenty-dollar bills stuffed inside. I couldn't help but think how easy it would be for me to linger while everyone else hustled into the gym and then steal some of those bills before going to class myself.

Right before homecoming weekend, I spotted another "opportunity." My friend was in the band, and I tagged along with him to the band room while he got ready for practice. Everybody in that room was changing their clothes, getting their instruments ready, and then heading outside to rehearse for the big weekend performances. I noticed that a lot of the kids hadn't locked their lockers, so I made some excuse to hang back and then waited until everybody was gone. I quickly went to work and grabbed about sixty dollars from four or five different wallets, and then trotted out to the field to catch up with my friend.

Two days later I got greedy and returned to the band room after school to see if I could get lucky again. The thought of having extra money to spend on homecoming weekend spurred me on. I was dating a girl at the time and wanted to be able to take her out to a nice dinner before the football game on Saturday night.

I quickly got to work opening lockers that had been left unlocked and rustling through the backpacks sitting on the floor. I started to worry that I was going to get caught, so after pocketing about forty dollars, I scurried toward the door. Before I could open it, a voice shouted, "Freeze! Police! You're under arrest!"

My heart leapt into my throat. This was strike number three. I put my hands up in the air, and a police officer, who had been hiding in a closet in the band room the whole time, grabbed me by the arm and dragged me to the principal's office.

"We caught your thief!" he announced to everyone in the office.

The principal, his assistant, and the secretary all looked at me with thinly veiled disgust.

"Empty your pockets, boy," the officer said to me.

I pulled out the money I'd shoved in my pocket. The officer grabbed it from the table and showed the principal the markings he'd made. Apparently so many kids had complained about missing money at school, the principal had hired a detective to set up a sting operation. I'd fallen right into it.

I was so angry with myself. If I hadn't been so greedy, I'd be getting ready for homecoming instead of getting ready for a future at a juvenile jail.

"Goodbye, Mr. Miller," the principal said like he was just happy to see me go. And with that, the officer grabbed me again and led me out of the office.

When the officer stopped in front of my house, I knew Mama was home. She'd heard the car pull up, come to the door, and watched as the officer yanked me out of the back seat and then forced me up the steps in front of him.

"Buddy," my mother cried, opening the door. "What did you do now?"

"Are you his mother?" the officer asked.

"Yes, sir," my mother answered, her face careening between fear and rage.

"Your son was caught stealing in the school and is being arrested for theft. I understand he's already on probation, so we will be contacting his probation officer to handle the situation."

My mother went from looking at the officer with shame to looking down at me with disappointment.

"Thank you, officer," Mama said. "I'll be sure he's here when Mr. Allen comes for him."

The officer tipped his hat to Mama and then turned on his heels and left.

Mama then dragged me into the house. I could feel the heat rising off of her.

She barely waited for the door to close before she started hollering at me.

"When is it going to stop, Buddy? Why do you keep doing these things?"

"I'm sorry, Mama," I said, but she didn't want to hear any apology from me. She continued to yell at me until she had to sit down and catch her breath. I was afraid she was going to make herself sick. Over the summer Mama had lapsed into a diabetic coma. She had type 1 diabetes and had forgotten to take her insulin. The doctor told her she had to stop working so hard and try to relax more. And here I was making her worse.

"Mama, please calm down," I said. "I promise I won't do it again. I don't know why I did it. But I promise I'll be good. Please, just don't get yourself all upset."

Mama looked at me like she'd lost all hope. Like she didn't believe me.

"Buddy, there isn't going to be another chance for you if you don't stop doing these things."

"I know, Mama," I said.

"You're supposed to be my lucky number seven, Buddy," Mama reminded me. "You're not supposed to end up like your brothers."

She sounded so sad when she said that. I knew I'd let her down. Deep inside I knew that I could do better. I knew I could stop stealing if I wanted to. I just hadn't wanted to badly enough.

Mama sighed and hoisted herself up.

"Go on in your room, Buddy, and think about what you've done. When Mr. Allen gets here, you can try to tell him you're sorry, but I don't know if it's going to make a difference."

I didn't want to cause my mother any more stress, but I also didn't want go to jail. My mind started calculating my options. As I paced around my room, trying to figure out what I should do, I stopped for a moment and looked at my reflection in the mirror. I saw a scared kid staring back at me. A sheen of nervous sweat covered my face and made the pimples on my forehead stick out even more. I had a bad case of acne. Mama said it was because I was running the streets, living the fast life. "You've gotten away from God, Buddy," she told me when I complained about it. "Those marks on your face are the devil's handwork."

I turned away from the mirror and pushed my mother's warnings to the back of my mind. I decided I wasn't going to jail. I opened my sock drawer and grabbed the few dollars I'd saved, threw some clothes in my backpack, and hopped out my bedroom window. Without looking back, I hightailed it to the Greyhound bus station and bought myself a ticket to Washington, DC, where my older brother Raymond lived with his wife and three young sons. I figured I'd be long gone from Greensboro when Mr. Allen showed up at our house.

"Sorry, Mama," I whispered as the bus pulled out of the station.

Unfortunately for me, Raymond wasn't interested in helping me avoid my punishment. As soon as I showed up on his doorstep and told him what I was fleeing from, he called Mama and sent me back home.

A judge sentenced me to thirteen months at the Morrison Training School, a juvenile facility that was established in 1923 for young Black men who were in trouble with the law. I'd heard about Morrison, and the rumors about the place put a cold fear in my heart.

"Please, Mama, don't let them send me there," I pleaded with my mother after the hearing.

"Buddy, I've already told you that I don't know what else to do with you," Mama said. "You don't mind me. You don't do anything you're told."

"I promise I'll be good. I'm not a criminal. I don't need to go to jail," I pleaded. It hurt me that my mother wasn't willing to fight for me in this moment. I knew that what I had been doing was wrong, but deep down, I still felt like I was more good than bad. When I measured my thievery against all the rest of me, the tally wasn't all negative. I played sports. I knew how to work hard. I took care of my nieces and nephews and my little brother. I loved my family. I didn't think of myself as bad. But obviously others did.

Mama started pulling her gloves on. It was only October, but a chill was already coming to Greensboro. "Listen, Buddy," Mama said. "Mr. Allen tells me that the Morrison School isn't that bad. You can take high school classes and learn a trade. They got all kinds of programs up there for you. And maybe they'll knock some sense into you. Lord knows I've tried and it hasn't worked."

Mr. Allen walked over to us then. He greeted Mama and me.

"You ready to go, Walter?" he said.

"No, I'm not ready. Why do I have to go there?"

"You know what, Walter?" Mr. Allen said. "I think this is going to be exactly what you need. You haven't had a father figure around to teach you right from wrong, and you just won't obey your mama, so this is where we are. If you don't like it up there, play by the rules so you can get out and come be with your family."

I tried to take in what Mr. Allen was saying, but it was impossible to think positive about Morrison while also trying not to cry.

"I'll pray for you, Buddy. Just do your best" were the last words Mama said to me before she turned to head home.

CHERYL

When I turned thirteen, my father finally let me buy my own copies of *Right On!* magazine. I no longer had to borrow them from my friends and sneak down to my godmother Katherine's apartment to read them. Daddy had a lot of rules for me when I officially started turning into a young woman. No makeup, no high heels, no boys. If it weren't for Sis and my godmother standing up for me, Daddy would have kept me a baby forever.

But time wouldn't stand still, not even for Daddy.

By the time I turned fourteen and started high school, he let me wear lip gloss, and I would sometimes sneak a pair of high heels in my backpack and change into them at school. The thing was, Daddy had to leave the house before us kids, so he didn't really get to see what I looked like when I walked out the door. I wasn't trying to rebel, but now that I was in high school with a whole new crowd of kids, looking good mattered to me. I paid attention to the latest fashions, kept my hair nicely styled, and flashed my dimples whenever necessary.

My two best friends, Carla and Deena, and I had decided to attend August Martin High School in Jamaica, Queens. The only reason we chose to go to a school so far away from our homes in Brooklyn was that it was the only high school that all three of us had gotten into, and we refused to be separated. So we tolerated the one-hour ride on the Q7 bus at 7:00 in the morning and then again coming home in the afternoon.

Despite the commute, I really enjoyed high school. There were new kids to meet, and our teachers gave us more freedom as well. We could leave school grounds for lunch, and in between classes we could hang out and socialize. Plus, there were a lot of cute boys to talk to, and I was happy to discover that they wanted to talk to me too. The only downside about attending high school in Queens was that I didn't have time to join any of the after-school clubs and activities. Daddy didn't want me walking home from the bus stop after it got dark outside. But I still sang in the church choir and participated in other activities at church. Daddy was glad to see me in church as much as possible, so doing extracurricular stuff there helped to keep everyone happy. And that's how I liked things. I didn't want to cause any commotion, and I wanted Daddy to be proud of me. I kept my grades up in school, did my chores around the house, and that way I was allowed to go out with my friends. Daddy said no boys until I was fifteen — not even on the phone — but that didn't stop me from looking at boys and talking to them with Carla and Deena.

Everything was going great until one day I came home and found the kitchen table was missing from our apartment. So was Estelle.

Daddy wasn't home from work, and Scott and Don were just as confused as I was.

"Where's the table, Cheryl?" Scott asked me.

I looked at him and shared my confusion. "I don't know." I knocked on Daddy and Estelle's bedroom door, but there was no answer.

The three of us tried to solve the mystery of the missing kitchen table but had to wait until my father came home to tell us what happened.

"Estelle moved out," Daddy said when he got home that night. There was no explanation. He just said she moved out and then he went and changed out of his work clothes like he normally did. My brothers and I looked at each other like Daddy was crazy, but we didn't say anything to him about our stepmother. Not even when he dragged an old trunk into the kitchen for us to eat on. Or when he served us plates of franks and beans for dinner with no vegetables.

I knew the kitchen table was Estelle's because she brought it with her when she moved in, so if she was gone, I guess the table was gone too. I felt bad for my father because he obviously seemed upset that his new wife had left him, but secretly I didn't mourn her leaving. While I was grateful for Estelle's help around the house, she never became a good substitute for Mommy.

I didn't want Daddy to get overwhelmed, so I immediately started offering to cook dinner, and I cleaned up the kitchen after we ate, too. I tried to keep things neat and tidy in the apartment, and I made Don and Scott help out. They were eleven and eight, so they were old enough to pull their weight with chores. By the time Estelle had been gone for a month, we had a pretty good rhythm going and I knew we'd be okay. But then Estelle came back.

Oh, brother, I thought when I got home that day and saw the kitchen table back in its usual place. Daddy had never told me why he and Estelle had broken up, but I figured they must have patched things up if she and her table were back. Like my father, Estelle never said anything to me about why she left. She didn't apologize or reassure us that it would never happen again. She just made dinner and acted like she hadn't disappeared.

Scott, Don, and I sat down at the table and basically kept our mouths shut. But I for one was trying to figure out what was going on. Daddy didn't seem upset. He had on his typical happy face for us kids, and he told Estelle that the pot roast she'd made was delicious. I couldn't keep up with grown folks and their issues. I was only fourteen and had no interest in figuring out their problems.

But Estelle left again about a year later. This time Daddy said it was for good. I didn't need to ask why she'd left. There were definitely cracks in the relationship, and it appeared to me that Estelle just didn't want to raise us kids full-time. She acted like we were a burden and a nuisance. I knew she still loved my father, because Daddy continued to visit Estelle and stay over at her apartment, but she was done being a mother to us.

"I didn't need her stingy butt anyway," I complained to Deena and Carla one day on the bus ride after school.

"Yeah, Cheryl. You guys are better off without her. She was so mean," Carla reminded me.

"I know that's right," I said.

But now I had to take on all of the work of the house for real, including taking care of Don and Scott. I had to cook breakfast and dinner, do the cleaning, laundry, and grocery shopping. Daddy was so happy that I'd stepped up. He kept telling me how proud he was of me and how thankful, and so I didn't have the heart to tell him how all that work was wearing me out. But I had no problem telling my friends.

"Maybe she'll come back again," Deena offered.

I gave her a look. "I don't want her to come back," I said. "I just don't want to have to do everything."

And that was the truth. I didn't want Estelle to come back. I actually liked the idea that I got to choose what we would eat for dinner. And I liked that we could all go back to watching TV together on Mommy and Daddy's bed. I liked that we didn't have to tiptoe around Estelle and her strict rules. When she was around, we couldn't laugh too loud or talk too loud. What I didn't like was that taking care of my brothers, washing everybody's laundry and cooking and shopping meant I didn't have any time to do the things I wanted to do, like hang out with my friends or go to parties or even take a later bus home after school. I loved my little brothers and I loved my father, but I was quickly beginning to resent being the one responsible for running the house. But I kept my feelings to myself.

Daddy always taught us that what happened in our house stayed in our house. We weren't supposed to air our business out in public. That meant that we weren't supposed to tell anybody that he and Estelle had adjusted the rules of their marriage and that she lived in her own apartment. I didn't understand why we had to maintain the illusion that Daddy and Estelle were together. I just knew that we had to do it, especially at church, where Daddy was a deacon and Estelle was a deaconess. Estelle would drive herself to church, and we would meet in the parking lot and walk in together. This went on for years. I thought it was embarrassing and weird that we had to keep pretending, but I went along with it because that's what Daddy expected from us kids. Plus, I didn't mind Estelle being a part of our lives from a distance and showing up for events with my father, like a mother normally would.

"What do you guys want to eat for dinner?" I asked my brother Scott as he sat between my legs on a Sunday after church. I was braiding his hair so his Afro would stand up nice and tight for school on Monday. Don would be next, and then I had to start cooking. I wouldn't make anything elaborate like Mommy used to for Sunday dinner, but I at least wanted to make something my brothers would like.

"Can we have hamburgers, Cheryl?" Don asked from the sofa, where he was stretched out reading a comic book.

I did a review in my mind of what we had in the refrigerator. I knew we had ground beef and frozen fries in the freezer.

"Yeah, we can have burgers," I said to Don. "But you gotta go to the store and get some buns."

"Okay," Don said. I knew he wouldn't mind going to the store because he could buy himself some candy with the leftover change. Both Don and Scott had no problem stepping up in their own ways now that Estelle was no longer part of our household. They cleaned the bathroom and helped me haul all the dirty clothes over to the laundry. On Saturdays, they helped me mop the floors and change all the bedsheets. But it was on me to do everything else. I got up early to make sure they had breakfast and checked that they had lunch money for school. Sometimes in my efforts to get them out the door on time, I'd miss my own bus and get to school thirty minutes late. After a while, I stopped trying to make it to class on time and just decided that getting to class a few minutes late was okay. If I needed extra time to get to school, I decided that with all of the hard work I was doing, I deserved it.

Pretty soon, that extra hour I needed to get to school stretched into entire days that I needed to rest. I still didn't tell my father that taking Estelle's place was too much for me, but inside I was growing irritated, and skipping school became my own form of protest. Not only did I skip school, but also I'd have my friends over and we'd party in the apartment until it was time for my father to get home. I thought I was being careful, but there were eyes all around our building watching me. My godmother cornered me one day and said, "Cheryl, I didn't see you at the bus stop the other day. Is everything okay?" I hated to lie to my godmother, but I'd gotten good at it.

"Everything's fine," I assured her.

My godmother didn't look like she believed me, but she let it pass.

I don't know if my father ever suspected something wasn't right. He seemed content with the way things were going. He complimented me on my cooking, which was getting better every day because I had taken my simple recipes that I'd learned in home economics class and improved on them by reading some of my mother's old cookbooks. And while I resented the fact that I had to do so much work, I also felt proud that I could run a household and keep my brothers fed and looking sharp. The thing that made me mad, though, was that my father praised me for being mature enough to take care of things around the house, but he didn't think I was mature enough to go out with my friends and have fun like other kids my age. I didn't think it was fair.

"Daddy, you say I'm grown enough to do the shopping and to take care of everything around the house. How come I can't go to a party with my friends?" I would argue, being sure to keep my tone respectful.

"Cheryl, you know the rules: no partying when there's going to be boys there," Daddy would say.

Because I was feeling grown, one night I decided to sneak out to a party Daddy had strictly forbidden me to attend. The event was being held in the community center at the Pink Houses so it was easy to get to, and I knew I could sneak back home before Daddy returned from his deacons' meeting at church.

Deena and Carla were so excited to see me when I showed up at the party.

"I told you I'd be here," I said as I surveyed the room. The lights were down, a DJ was spinning records, and way in the back there was a table with punch and snacks.

"How'd you get your dad to let you come?" Carla shouted over the music.

I gave her a look. "He doesn't know I'm here. I just have to be home by ten p.m. before he gets back from church."

"Well, I'm glad you came because Deon has been asking all about you," Deena said, giggling.

I smiled at that because Deon had been trying to talk to me for a while. He was really cute but I wasn't sure if he really liked me or not. "Well, let's go dance," I said to my friends, and they followed me out to the dance floor.

I loved dancing. Deena, Carla, and I would often spend our free time making up steps and routines to the latest hits, and we showed off that night on the dance floor. I was glad I'd worn my sneakers instead of my heels with my culottes and red shirt that said "Foxy" on the back. Now I could keep dancing the whole time.

Carla and Deena weren't as practical as I was and had worn high-heeled sandals, so they were taking a break while I stayed on the dance floor. That's when Deon came up to me and asked if he could dance with me.

"Sure," I said, trying to play it cool, even though inside my heart leapt into my throat.

"You're a good dancer, Cheryl," Deon said.

"Thanks. You are too," I said back with a dimpled smile.

And just then, the DJ put on one of my favorite Michael Jackson songs. Deon and I were getting down when all of a sudden I felt someone tap me on my shoulder. I expected to find Deena or Carla, but when I whirled around, I was staring at my father.

"Daddy!" I shrieked.

I very rarely saw my father mad, but I knew I was in big trouble.

He didn't scream or yell, but one look at his face let me know the fun was over. I was so embarrassed. I said a quick goodbye to Deon, and then I scurried out of the community center and ran back to our building ahead of my father, who I knew would wait to yell at me in the privacy of our apartment.

After that incident, I didn't mention the word "party" to my father until I was sixteen. By the time I made it to my junior year in high school, even Daddy knew he had to allow me out to have some fun. Of course, he had no idea how much fun I had been having instead of going to school, but he knew that he couldn't keep me locked up inside the house every weekend. Still, he'd always grill me about where I was going and whom I was going with before he'd let me go anywhere. And sometimes he'd still say no if the party I wanted to go to was too far away.

Junior year was winding down, and those of us in the class of 1981 were instructed to meet with the guidance counselor at school, Mr.

Campbell, to make sure we'd have all the credits we needed to graduate on time.

During the few interactions I'd had with Mr. Campbell, he'd seemed nice, so I looked forward to our meeting.

When I got to his office, Mr. Campbell told me to sit down and then he asked me for my name and my grade.

"I came to see where I stand with my credits," I said. "I'm supposed to graduate next year, and I just want to make sure everything is in order."

"Well, let's take a look," he said, searching in folders and moving papers around his desk.

"My goodness, Ms. Williams," he said. "It looks like you've missed quite a bit of class."

I felt my cheeks flush. "I guess," I answered.

Mr. Campbell kept looking at his paperwork and then he glanced up at me and said, "You're basically failing two classes, and you've been absent so much you're not going to pass another class."

I knew I had messed up, but hearing it come out of Mr. Campbell's mouth made it sound so final.

I felt tears start to build, but I told myself to hold it together. "But if I do better now, I can still graduate with my class next year, right?"

Mr. Campbell took off his glasses and wiped them clean with his handkerchief before putting them back on again. "I'm sorry, Ms. Williams, but with all of these absences and these failing grades, there's no way you're going to graduate on time."

"But I have to graduate with my class," I wailed. "We're the class of nineteen eighty-one."

Mr. Campbell shook his head and showed me the paper he was looking at. "I'm sorry, but it's just not possible for you to make up all this work plus take all your credits for next year by next June."

I couldn't stop the tears now. I felt so bad, and worst of all, it was all my fault.

I pulled myself off the chair and left Mr. Campbell's office with my head hanging down.

When Deena and Carla saw me at the bus stop, they knew something was wrong. I told them about what Mr. Campbell said and burst into tears all over again.

"What are you going to do?" Carla asked me.

"I don't know," I said. "But I have to do something. I can't tell my father that I'm not going to graduate. And I can't tell him that I've been skipping class."

"I'm glad I'm not in your situation," Deena said, and Carla punched her on the shoulder.

"You're not helping," Carla said.

"Are you guys going to graduate on time?" I asked them. They'd been skipping classes too, and they partied more than I did because they didn't have fathers as strict as mine.

"Let's just say my grades aren't as good as they should be in math and history," Deena said. "But I'm going to walk and get my diploma."

"Me too," Carla echoed.

So it was just me in this awful situation.

By the time I'd gotten off the bus, I'd decided that I had to get out of New York. I was failing school. Deon and I had been seeing each other for almost a year, and he had just suddenly stopped calling me and disappeared. Nothing was going right in my life. I needed to start over. I needed to find a school where I could finish my senior year, graduate on time, and get my life together. And the only place I could think of, where I'd have a safe place to land and someone to help me get back on track, was Atlanta. I knew Sis would help me get out of this mess. She always talked about the importance of education, and I knew if there were some way I could graduate on time, she'd be able to help me figure it out.

As soon as I got home, I called my sister to tell her what I had done and to beg her for help. I cried when I told her because I was deeply ashamed of allowing things to get this bad. But Sis didn't yell at me. She just agreed to let me come down there and stay with her as long as I promised to work hard and focus on my education.

"But you have to ask Daddy," she told me. "You have to tell him what you did."

I sniffed. "I will," I promised, so grateful for my big sister, but also wary of telling my dad.

That night after dinner I waited for my father to sit down in the living room and get ready to watch his programs.

"Daddy, I gotta tell you something," I said as I perched on the edge of the sofa. "I want to go down south and live with Sis."

"What you want to go down south for?" he asked.

"I want to go and finish high school in Atlanta."

"Why?"

The tears started again. "Because I messed up, Daddy," I squeaked out. "I haven't been going to class."

"What do you mean you haven't been going to class?"

I told him everything. How I had started going to school late and how that turned into skipping entire classes because keeping the house in order and taking care of the boys had me worn out.

Daddy looked disappointed. "I've been thinking all the time you've been doing what you're supposed to do around here *and* keeping up in school," he said.

Part of me got angry when he said that. "Daddy, you have me running around doing all kinds of things. I gotta do all the cooking and cleaning and shopping. You even have me paying the bills sometimes."

"It doesn't take all day to pay a bill, Cheryl."

"I know," I said. "And I know I didn't do the right thing, but I want to make it better. I want to walk with my class and graduate next year, so can I please go down and live with Sis?"

"Bring me the phone," Daddy said. "Let me talk to your sister."

I did as I was told and then sat on the couch and listened to Daddy talk to Sis. I couldn't hear what she was saying, but I could tell he was listening. I saw his face go from angry to resigned to what looked like sad. I didn't find out until much later, but apparently Sis had called my godmother and my godmother told Sis that I needed to get out of New York. She said she could tell I needed a change of scenery.

But Daddy didn't tell me any of that. He just hung up the phone and said, "I'm going to let you go, but when you get down there, I want you to go to class and do what you need to do to graduate. Okay?"

I ran over to hug my father. "I will, Daddy. I promise. I'm going to make you proud of me."

"I know you will, Cheryl," Daddy said. And then he made me look him in the eye. "I'm proud of you right now, Cheryl. You've kept this family together."

That made me cry again.

Daddy gave me a big hug and then asked if I wanted to watch Carol Burnett with him. Of course I did.

One month later, I was in a car heading south to Atlanta.

chapter four

Broken Promises

BOBBY

I cried when I saw my mother. It had been six weeks of misery at the Morrison Training School — fights with the other kids, threats from the counselors, and endless drudgery working on the campus farm. It was not what Mr. Allen had promised. It was everything I'd feared. So just seeing my mother unleashed all of the emotions I'd been holding in since arriving at the facility.

Mama had told me in one of her letters that she was going to come visit me, but she hadn't been specific with a date.

But here she was on a Sunday afternoon in early December, beaming at me as we sat together at a table in the dormitory where I was assigned.

"I brought you something to eat," she said as she started unpacking her bag. She took out small containers filled with fried chicken, potato salad, string beans, and candied yams. My mouth started watering just looking at Mama's food. Compared to the "shit on a shingle" that they had served us for breakfast that morning, this food looked like heaven.

"Thank you, Mama," I said as I dove into those dishes.

She laughed as she watched me inhale all that food. "Don't hurt yourself, Buddy," she said.

I grinned in between mouthfuls. "I won't."

When I was done eating, Mama asked me how I was doing, concern causing the wrinkles over her eyebrows to show.

I shrugged my shoulders. "I'm okay, I guess," I said, not wanting to tell her about the fights. I had already caused her enough grief. I didn't want to make her sick worrying about me up here.

My mother lowered her voice. "Keep your head up, Buddy. Do what they tell you to do and stay out of trouble," she said.

I nodded. "I know, Mama."

Mama looked around and then leaned in close. "I know these other boys in here are going to show you how gifted they are with their fists, but you just stay away from them. You hear me?"

"Don't worry, Mama, I can take care of myself," I said.

Mama sat back and looked me over and then said, "I know you can, Buddy, but you stay out of trouble."

I wanted to tell Mama that that was almost impossible to do when other boys started something. I had two choices in those moments: get beaten down and get a reputation for being weak, or defend myself and hope to avoid future fights. I was fifteen years old and trying to figure out how to survive in a place that had no real rulebook. But of course I didn't explain any of that to Mama. Instead, I changed the subject.

"You remember Buster Fleming?" I asked her. "He's here."

"Really? This is where he ended up?" Mama said. "I know his father can't be too happy about that."

Mama knew Buster's father from church.

"Probably not," I said.

We kept talking. Mama told me all about what was happening back in Greensboro with my sisters and brothers and all my cousins.

She filled me in on what she knew about my friends. Soon enough the sun started to go down and Mama had to head back. Before she left, she gave me a few dollars so I would have some spending money to use at the canteen.

"I'll try to come back again before Christmas," she said. "But in the meantime, I want you to start praying, Buddy. Ask God to help you get through this. Ask God to help you do better."

I said I would.

"Do they have church services for you here?" she asked.

"Yeah," I said.

"Well, you need to start going," she told me sternly. "God will help you. You just have to do your part."

I promised my mother I would go to church even though I knew I wouldn't. I still believed that church was for hypocrites and sinners, like the ones I'd seen over the years at all the different churches we'd been to as a family. As Mama started to gather her things to go, my tears started up again and she pulled me in close for a hug.

"You're going to be okay, Buddy," she said.

I didn't want my mother to think I couldn't handle myself, so I composed myself quickly and pulled away from her embrace.

"I know, Mama," I said. "I'm going to be okay."

The thing was, I wasn't okay. I'd been in three fights in only six weeks. It was a miracle that I hadn't been sent to the hole yet. My friend Buster was telling me I needed to come with him to the gym and start lifting weights so I could bulk up my skinny teenage body and be ready for the next fight. But I didn't want to get ready. I wanted to get out of there. I was tired of having to watch my back. I was tired of the counselors' threats. I was tired of the horrible food.

Mama's advice to turn to God for help seemed silly. But I decided that if I wasn't going to go to church, I could at least pray. When I was growing up in Greensboro, everybody prayed, either out of desperation or to keep good things going. So that very night I lay in my bunk and prayed to God to help me get out of Morrison. The next morning I woke up knowing I was going to escape. The idea just sprouted in my brain. Mama had always said that God answers our prayers even if it's not exactly in the form we asked for. I prayed for a way to get out of Morrison, and I woke up with a clear mind and the audacity to figure out how to break free.

Plotting my escape became my focus. Instead of buying snacks and toiletries at the canteen, I decided I would save the money Mama gave me and buy myself a bus ticket back to Greensboro. And instead of trying to figure out how to avoid getting into fights, I spent all of my mental energy on figuring out how to sneak off the Morrison campus without getting caught. I remembered that there were train tracks somewhere near the campus, from when Mr. Allen first drove me there. And I always heard the train whistles piercing the silence as I lay in bed at night. I figured if I could make it off the grounds of the facility, get to the woods, and then find the train tracks, I could follow those tracks all the way to the next town of Hamlet and then find the bus station.

Christmas came and went, but escaping was all I thought about. I started to fantasize about where I would go once I made it back home. I knew I couldn't stay in Greensboro because somebody would surely recognize me and I'd get sent back to Morrison. I dreamed about going to New York City because I knew a person could disappear in a big, crowded place like that. But I didn't know anybody in New York, so I crossed it off my list. I decided I'd go back to Washington, DC, and prayed I'd be able to convince my brother Raymond to give me another chance. If he didn't, I was prepared to live on the streets and make my own way if necessary.

By February I was ready to put my plan in action. I wasn't scared. That sounds ridiculous now, but I wasn't thinking about the potential consequences of my actions or what would happen to me if I got caught. Fear simply wasn't part of my mindset at age fifteen. Instead, I was excited to see if I could pull off this daring escape. I thought I was smarter than all of the other kids who had tried to escape and had gotten caught. I had the same thrill of anticipation as I did when I stole a car or when I walked into a school full of white kids and convinced them that I had the same right to be there that they did.

While I waited for the perfect moment to leave, I reviewed and replayed every step of my plan. I knew the dormitory counselor's schedule. I knew how far I had to run to get to the school gates. I knew that as soon as I was off the property, I had to head for the woods and find those train tracks. And I knew if I timed everything properly, I'd have at least an hour before the counselors would even notice I was gone.

My chance came on a Tuesday night. I knew after the call for lights out, the one counselor on duty would come to check that we were all in our beds, and then he wouldn't be back for close to two hours while he checked the other dorms. After that second visit, there wouldn't be another check until the morning counselor took over. So right after lights out, I slipped into the bathroom and put my street clothes on. If anybody asked me why I was lying in my bed fully dressed, my plan was to say I was cold. But nobody asked. I waited there in my bed until about 2:00 a.m., when the counselor came back for his second round of checks. When he left, I got up, looked around, pretended to yawn, and walked toward the bathroom. I looked around again, then slipped on my sneakers, grabbed my jacket, and headed toward the side door. I took nothing with me except the money for my bus ticket.

At that time there were no alarms on the door, so it was easy to just sneak out of the building. Once I was outside, and the chilly February air hit me, I started to run. I ran right off the premises and up the street the way I was brought in. I could see headlights coming toward me, so I crouched down on the side of the road until the car passed. Then I headed into the woods. Adrenaline and excitement flowed through my veins, pushing me forward even though it was pitch black out there. I knew the woods were full of poisonous snakes, but I didn't have time to let my fear slow me down. I just prayed I wouldn't step on anything that slithered and kept on running, looking for those train tracks. At some point, my mind played tricks on me and I imagined I heard the dogs they used to send after escaped slaves barking on my trail, which made me run faster.

After what felt like an hour, I finally found the tracks and I wanted to shout for joy, but I didn't. I stuck to my plan and followed the tracks — running and walking and running again — until they led me to an intersection where two roads crossed. The sun was starting to show itself, which meant I must have been in those woods for close to three hours. Up ahead I could make out the outlines of the town of Hamlet. I started walking toward what looked like the town center. Hamlet was so small I easily found the bus depot, bought a ticket back to Greensboro, and waited outside for about thirty minutes until they announced my bus was boarding. I hopped aboard and tried to stay awake and alert, but after the adventure I'd just had, I fell asleep almost instantly. When I woke up two hours later, we were back in Greensboro.

When I stepped off the bus, I knew I couldn't go to my house. I didn't know if they'd started looking for me or not, but I didn't want to take the chance and walk into a trap. Instead, I went to my friend Eric's house. Eric was a couple of years older than me and had already graduated from high school. He lived with his grandfather in a nice house on Warren Street. His mother had passed away, but the whole family had always been kind to me; plus, they had money. My hope was that

Eric would let me stay at his house for a few days while I figured out what to do next.

"Cotton Foot! Where'd you come from?" Eric said when he saw me on his porch. He was still in his pajamas.

"Can I come in?" I whispered, afraid someone would see me.

Eric ushered me in and we went straight up to his room. I told him what I had done and asked if I could lay low at his house for a few days while I made plans for my next move. He said yes, but he told me I couldn't stay there during the day because his grandfather might see me.

"No worries, man," I said. "But can I just catch a nap real quick, and then I'll make myself scarce. I promise your grandfather won't see me."

Eric told me as long as I was quiet and left the house before 10:30, when his grandfather usually woke up, it would be okay. Eric set his alarm clock to wake me up at 10:00. I breathed a sigh of relief and felt my shoulders truly relax for the first time since leaving Morrison.

I lay down on Eric's twin bed and watched him as he started picking out his clothes and getting ready for work. We agreed to meet back at his house at 5:00 p.m. I promised Eric I'd be careful when I left, even offering to climb out the window if I had to. Eric told me I could use the front door. "Just be quiet," he said.

Even though I only slept for about two hours, I was full of energy when I tiptoed out of Eric's house. I wanted to go over to Gillespie and catch up on everything I'd missed since being away at Morrison. I had more friends in that area of town and knew more kids at Gillespie than at Ben L. Smith. Since I wasn't in a hurry, I stopped and bought myself some snacks and a sandwich and killed more time walking around town, being careful not to go into any stores that I knew my mother liked to frequent.

By the time I made it to the park across the street from Gillespie in the afternoon, I had to wait just a short while before the final bell rang. While I waited, I started to make a mental list of friends I could visit who might be willing to let me stay with them or who could loan me some money so I could get out of town. But I still didn't know where I should go. Other than Washington, DC, I couldn't think of anywhere else where I'd have a safe place to stay. Before I could come up with any answers, school let out and kids started crossing the street and heading my way. I immediately saw my friend Wayne, who lived near us. Wayne was really my little brother Melvin's friend, but we all played ball together. I called his name and he turned toward the sound of my voice and headed my way when he saw me.

"Yo, Cotton Foot!" he said when he got close to me. "What are you doing here?"

I started to explain, since Wayne knew I'd been sent away to Morrison. But he interrupted me before I could finish my story.

"Man, there were cops all over your house this morning," he said. "I already knew you'd escaped."

"For real?" I said, beginning to sweat.

"Yeah, man," he said. "Melvin told me that they told your mama that if she sees you, she has to call them right away. Unless you're trying to get caught, I'd get out of here fast."

"You're right, I gotta get out of here," I said to Wayne, as cold panic flooded my veins. Greensboro wasn't that big. It was only a matter of time before somebody recognized me. Maybe somebody already had and had called the police on me, or worse, called my mother.

"I won't tell anybody I saw you," Wayne said, looking over his shoulder.

"Thanks, man," I said as I took off running toward the bus stop. I had to get back to Eric's house to lay low, get some cash, and get out of the city. I had planned to stop by my house and let my mother know that I was okay, but now that Wayne had warned me about the cops, I made the painful decision to leave without saying goodbye to her.

When I got back to Eric's house, it was only 4:30. I waited outside and tried to stay out of sight. As soon as I saw Eric, I ran up to him and told him what Wayne had told me.

"I gotta get out of Greensboro now!" I said. Eric agreed. We ran into the house. Eric changed his clothes, got some money from his grandfather, and we went down to the bus station together. Eric paid for my ticket to Washington, DC. Right before I got on the bus, he said to me, "Cotton Foot, be careful up there."

When I got to Washington, it was the middle of the night. I called Raymond from a pay phone at the station and begged him to come get me. Thankfully, he agreed.

As soon as I got in his car, though, Raymond lit into me.

"What have you done, Buddy?" he started.

"Raymond, I couldn't stay at that place," I said, pleading my case. "Every day I was in a fight. I was scared for my life to stay there."

Raymond looked over at me in the passenger seat. He didn't say anything. We drove the rest of the way to his apartment in silence.

The next morning Raymond woke me up and told me I could stay, but I had to get a job.

"You're not going to be here living off me and Marie," Raymond warned, lecturing me before I'd even had time to wipe the sleep out of my eyes. "You gotta pay your own way and you gotta stay out of trouble."

"What about school?" I asked.

"I thought about that," Raymond said, "but if you go to school, you're going to have to get your records from Greensboro. And once you let people from Greensboro know you're here, they'll probably send the cops to come get you. Besides, you'll be sixteen next fall and you won't have to be in school after that anyway."

I wanted to go to school, but I wasn't about to argue with my brother. He was the only thing standing between me and living on the streets. So that day, after breakfast, I went and registered at an employment agency. When I filled out all of the paperwork, I used my real name and Social Security number, but I said I was eighteen instead of fifteen. Since I was tall, nobody questioned me.

Meanwhile, Raymond called my mother and let her know that I was safe, working and living with him and his wife, Marie. When Mama heard the news, she was happy to know that I was okay and sent some money to my brother to help with my upkeep. She didn't want me to be a burden. Mama also informed Raymond that she had been told that as long as I stayed out of North Carolina, nobody from Morrison would be looking for me. I don't know who told her that, but it proved to be true. I stayed away from the state of North Carolina for a good long while and I never heard from anyone at Morrison again.

It only took one week to be assigned my first job from the employment agency. I was hired to be a janitor at Georgetown University.

And it only took me three weeks to lose that job. On the day I received my first paycheck, the other janitors invited me to an alcohol-fueled celebration during our lunch break. I had no business trying to party with grown men, drinking hard liquor, trying to act like a grown-up. When my boss found me passed out drunk on the job, she fired me immediately. Then when the employment agency found out about why I was fired, they refused to send me out for any more jobs. Undaunted, I hit the streets on my own and found a job at a fancy candy store on F Street. I worked as a janitor and stock boy. The white lady that owned the store was really nice to me, as was the Black lady who worked behind the counter, who would sneak me free samples of the chocolates. I liked working there and I felt important when I'd take my lunch break and go across the street and order a tuna sandwich at the lunch counter. But that job only lasted for about three months before the thief in me decided to come back to life.

I had noticed that the owner always left the safe open in the back of the shop. She'd put receipts and cash in there all day long and then lock it up at night. One day I just kept thinking, *Try it.* But I knew better. I walked past that safe three times before I finally opened it up and grabbed a handful of cash. By the time I got home to my brother's house that night, the owner had already called my brother and told him what I'd done. "Why did you do it, Buddy?" Raymond said to me when I walked in the door. And the very next day he made me go back to the candy store and return the money.

I was really ashamed of myself because that lady trusted me. And I liked working at the store. When I walked into the shop, I was afraid of what she was going to do to me. But all she said was "I gave you a chance, Walter. A chance a lot of other people wouldn't have given a boy like you."

"Yes, ma'am," I said.

"I hope you don't go through life like this, Walter. Let this be a lesson. And don't ever do something like this again."

"Yes, ma'am," I said. "I won't."

And then she fired me.

I wish I could say this is when I finally learned my lesson and got my act together. But it's not. I didn't take that woman's advice. In fact, I did quite the opposite. I kept stealing and robbing people like it was going out of style.

Within a year, Raymond and Marie kicked me out of their apartment after I stole Raymond's car for a night of joyriding with my friends. I was just about to turn sixteen. From his house, I went to go live with my older sister Irma, who also lived in Washington, DC. Unlike Raymond, Irma thought school was where I belonged, and she promptly got me enrolled at the high school closest to her apartment, Eastern High School. When I had to provide the name of the last high school I had attended, I said Ben L. Smith, and no questions were asked about my missing year of education. Because I had never finished tenth grade at Smith, I entered Eastern as a sophomore and started that year over again. But Eastern High School wasn't an institution that inspired learning. The way I saw it, the teachers and administrators couldn't care less whether or not students showed up or did any work. Kids spent more time in the hallways smoking and getting into fights than they did in the classrooms. The only good thing that came out of my experience at Eastern was learning about a special program that allowed high school kids to work in government offices for twenty hours a week and get paid. I applied and was given a job at the Pentagon, working four days a week.

At the Pentagon I was a file clerk, and I enjoyed the work, filing papers and running errands for the generals and secretaries in the office. I was good at my job, but I couldn't get promoted because when they tried to get me security clearances that would allow me to go into different parts of the Pentagon and take on more work, they found out I had a record. "I see you had some trouble in your life," my boss, Ms. McDonnell, said to me on the afternoon the information came through. I thought she was going to fire me, but she didn't. Ms. McDonnell was a very kind lady, and she told me that I could continue to work in her office. She never held my background against me. For that I was grateful.

I transferred out of Eastern High as soon as I could. Eastern's reputation as a "funhouse" wasn't what I was looking for. On my own, I enrolled at a nearby school called McKinley, where some of my friends went. Unlike Eastern, McKinley was known as an excellent institution for Black students. All of the teachers were Black, I'd heard they had the highest graduation rate in the city, and supposedly the principal had been named Principal of the Year several times. I wanted that for myself. The teachers at McKinley would tell us about how bad things were when they were coming up and that it was our responsibility to get our education and do important things in the world. They had high expectations for all of us and made us believe that we could do anything we put our minds to. It reminded me of my teachers at my first junior high school back in Greensboro, before I'd been forced to integrate Gillespie. While I was in the school building at McKinley, I wanted to perform well for the teachers, I wanted to believe in the vision they had for us. I wanted to be a good student. I even tried out for the basketball team but was cut in the second round. McKinley was a good place for me, but on the weekends, all I could think about was having fun and getting wild.

Two of my friends had cars, and we'd go all over DC to parties and clubs. It didn't matter that we were underage. As long as we had money, they'd let us in. Sometimes we'd rent a hotel room, invite girls, and have our own parties there. The only problem was that all of this fun cost money, and the money I was making at the Pentagon wasn't enough to cover my portion of the partying. So I got a second job at a topless bar called Clive's not too far from my sister's apartment. I was probably the only high school student in the District working at the Pentagon and a topless bar at the same time. I worked at Clive's during the week until 2:00 a.m. washing dishes, packing beer, taking the garbage out, and I had to clean the kitchen and bathrooms. It wasn't glamorous work, but my friends thought I was the luckiest cat around, having a job where seeing topless women was a regular occurrence.

All the kids I hung around with were Black. Some of them came from good families, and most of them went to some of the best high schools in DC for Black students, like Dunbar and McKinley. Dunbar had always been a school for Black Washington's finest families and was a feeder school for Howard University. But my friends and I weren't thinking about college. We were intoxicated with the untamed energy of the time, when lawlessness and criminal activity, the street life, and civil rights were all creating a sort of electricity in the air. Sam Cooke had been murdered in a seedy hotel. *Bonnie and Clyde* opened in the movie theaters. Malcolm X had been assassinated. Then so was Martin Luther King Jr. The Nation of Islam was telling brothers to use "any means necessary" to protect themselves. It was a dangerous time to be young and Black in America, but for me and my friends, it was an exciting time. We felt like we had permission to make our own rules for survival, even when our rules were against the law.

Little by little, I started to go to school less and less. Soon enough my sister Irma kicked me out of her home too. Raymond found a tiny apartment for me to live in by myself, and so I was on my own by the time I was seventeen. I was still going to school, as long as I didn't have something more exciting to do. And I was still working at the Pentagon and at Clive's. I was making enough money to cover my rent and my expenses, but I still wanted more. I always wanted more. And then the opportunity to get more made itself known.

One of my friends, Jack, pulled an armed robbery with some guys I didn't know. When he told me about it, I wanted in on the action. I didn't even pause to consider the consequences. By this point, taking one more step into criminal activity didn't faze me. Robberies of all kinds were taking place across DC at the time, and it didn't seem that big a deal to get involved. I told myself that as long as I wasn't physically hurting anybody, then it was okay. I didn't consider that taking someone's money was a form of inflicting pain, and that's how I absolved myself from feeling guilty about what I was getting into.

Jack told me he could introduce me to the two guys in charge, Davone and Rudy. They were brothers, one short, one tall. One dark, one light. People said they had different mothers but the same father, and he was in jail. Fashioning themselves after Bonnie and Clyde, the two brothers were robbing grocery stores and other mom-and-pop shops around DC. When I heard about all of their capers, I wanted some of that fast money they were making. It sounded dangerous and exciting. And easy.

Davone and Rudy weren't looking for another member of their crew, though. And they weren't impressed by my eagerness.

"You got a gun?" Davone asked me when I met him at Jack's house one night.

"No," I said.

Davone turned away from me like he had no use for a kid with my limited credentials.

"But I can get a gun," I added quickly, bluffing.

Davone turned back toward me and smiled real slowly. "You get a gun and then we can talk."

"All right," I said, not immediately knowing how I was going to get a gun, but also knowing that I wasn't going to let this chance slip away from me. I knew I could figure it out.

It turned out, getting my hands on a gun wasn't hard or complicated. Working at a topless bar, I'd met plenty of people who I knew could help me solve this problem. Clive's was the site of any number of illegal transactions. In fact, I was selling knockoff designer clothes and jewelry in there on the weekends, and I was doing a brisk business. It was actually that business that led to me getting my first gun. It turned out the bouncer Sam, who was this big white guy in his early twenties, liked the sweaters I was selling. I knew he had a gun and so I offered him a trade.

"If you let me borrow your gun for two weeks," I said, "I'll give you two of these sweaters."

Sam thought it was a great deal and he loaned me his gun, and I gave him the sweaters. But then Sam got fired. He never came back to Clive's, and so I kept his gun.

Davone eventually kept his word and I started riding with him, his brother, and another kid. On the weekends we'd pick a neighborhood to hit up on the other side of the city, where we wouldn't be recognized. Davone and Rudy were the ones who planned where we were going to go, and I helped grab the money and run. The whole time that we were robbing and stealing, though, I was still in school and still working at the Pentagon. One day my English teacher pulled me aside and said, "Curtis, you're not keeping up with your work. What's wrong? I know you can do better."

I didn't have an answer for her because at that point I wanted to say, "I am doing better. I got my own apartment. I got money. I got girls." Of course I didn't say that to her because I knew the life I was living was nothing to brag about to a Black woman who had sacrificed so much for her education and was now trying to lift up my generation. I promised I'd work harder on my assignments and for a few days I did try, but the pull of my criminal pursuits was too strong.

I felt invincible and my behavior grew bolder. I stole checks from the Pentagon, cashed them right there on the premises, and never got caught. Sometimes I stole just because I could. I wasn't starving, and all of my needs were met. It was almost like I looked at stealing as a challenge. Just like I figured out the game of golf so I could be a better caddy, or how I figured out how to break out of Morrison, I liked to figure out how to get more fast money. It was all exciting to me, and my friends were all right there with me. Like most teenagers, I didn't think about consequences or the future. I was just living day by day, taking advantage of every opportunity that came my way.

On the night of Richard Nixon's inauguration in January 1969, I was eighteen years old and a senior in high school. It was also the day I got shot by police after trying to rob a pharmacy with Davone, Rudy, and one other guy from their crew. Rudy told us it was going to be a quick job. We were going to rob a pharmacy in Southeast Washington, DC, since he figured the entire police force would be preoccupied with Nixon's inauguration festivities.

He was wrong. By the time the four of us had collected the money from the register and the safe in the back, we could hear the sirens wailing.

"Let's get out of here!" Rudy shouted, and we all headed for the door. In front of the pharmacy there was a big parking lot. Our getaway driver had disappeared, so I ran between two cars in the lot, trying to stay low and remain out of sight, all the while keeping my gun up for protection. I was wearing black slacks and a navy-blue peacoat and hoped I wouldn't be seen in the dark night. I looked both ways before I started to scoot over to the next car, but before I made it, I felt a burning pain rip through my leg. I'd been shot.

As I fell to the ground and dropped my gun, I looked behind me and saw a cop with his gun still drawn walking toward me. As he got closer, I had the nerve to ask him, "Why'd you shoot me?"

The doctors told me I was lucky because the bullet went through my right butt cheek and exited out the front of my leg. Still, they had to do surgery to repair the damage. When I woke up, I couldn't even feel my leg, and I spent almost a month in the hospital doing physical therapy so I could walk again. Once they decided I was healthy enough, a hospital orderly wheeled me right across the street to the DC jail.

I spent almost six months in jail awaiting sentencing. None of my family members were willing or able to post bail for me. In frustration, I watched other people who had done far worse crimes come in and get out of jail in a matter of days because they had good lawyers working on their behalf. I soon found out from other prisoners, though, that I could petition for my release by writing my own writ of habeas corpus. I had no idea what that meant, but I kept listening and asking questions and eventually figured it out. There was a law library at the jail, where I would go to find examples of what a successful writ looked like, and I copied those, substituting the details of my case for the ones in the examples I was using. Basically, I was just asking to be released on my own recognizance until my sentence was determined. The first writ I wrote was denied, so I submitted another one, and another one, and another one, until finally a judge accepted my request.

During the few months when I was free and awaiting my sentencing for robbing that pharmacy, I lived with a friend because I couldn't afford to get my own place. I got a job at a fast-food restaurant and did my best to stay out of trouble. I hoped that by living right, I might catch a break and avoid going to prison. I was trying to show the courts that I had learned my lesson. It didn't work. Even though nobody from Morrison had ever come looking for me, I still had a record from there. It wasn't supposed to factor into the judge's decision, but he said he was denying my request for "leniency" because I'd been in trouble with the law before. But because I was only eighteen at the time of the crime, and because I had shown that I *could* stay out of trouble those last few months, instead of being sent to an adult prison, I was sentenced to thirteen months at a facility in Lorton, Virginia, for juvenile offenders.

Compared to the danger and the grittiness I'd experienced at the DC jail, Lorton looked like a summer camp. The inmates were all twenty-one or younger. We slept in dormitories, not cells, and we had time to play sports and watch TV if we wanted. Still, it wasn't the place where I was going to repent and change my ways. A lot of the guys in there just sat around bragging about the crimes they'd committed and talked about the crimes they were going to commit when they got out. Fights were common, and I lost a pair of shoes and even a pair of underwear to theft. I kept to myself and showed up for my assigned job in the kitchen and tried to be invisible. When I wasn't on work duty, I was either in my bed or watching TV, just passing the time, waiting for my sentence to be over. At this point I wasn't planning on returning to a life of crime. But I also had no specific ideas about continuing my education or starting a career. I didn't even know what that would entail. I basically kept my head down and focused on getting out as soon as possible. I knew I'd come up with something when I had to. I always did.

When I was released after thirteen months, I had no family members willing to take me in anymore, so I was remanded to a halfway house, where I was told I had to find a job. I found one at another fast-food restaurant, and within a few weeks I had enough money saved to leave the halfway house and rent a room from an old friend named Ulysses Love. I stayed away from anyone from Davone and Rudy's crew and tried to keep focused on living right. I earned my GED so I could finally be done with high school. I spent time with Raymond and called my mother on Sundays and promised her I would come visit soon. I tried to play it straight. And for about six months, I did.

But as I started to hang with my old crew of high school friends again, talk turned to stealing. I kept telling myself, "I can do this. I can stay out of trouble. I know I am better than that." But everything we wanted to do — party, show our girlfriends a good time, buy nice clothes — required money we didn't have.

"What if we could pull off just one big heist?" my friend Jack said, and everyone nodded. We told ourselves if we could just make one big score and get enough cash, we wouldn't have to steal again. In maybe the worst mistake of my life, I started plotting with them.

We all agreed that DC was too full of cops, and Maryland and Virginia were out of the question for the same reason. I suggested Greensboro. I knew the layout of the city and I knew where the high-end businesses were. And so Greensboro became our target.

Right away, my friend Dan and I got busy planning our first heist. The only problem was that neither Dan nor I had a car. But that wasn't going to stop us. I could always find a way to work around a problem. It was kind of my superpower and my downfall. Once my brain started working on how to pull off a caper, I couldn't stop thinking about it. My first agenda item to work out, before worrying about transportation, was deciding on the best places to hit. I knew banks offered the biggest possible return, but I also knew there was too much security and surveillance. That's when I decided we should try credit unions. They had money, but they didn't have the same level of security as a bank. I knew Greensboro had plenty of credit unions right in the downtown area, and I knew for a fact that they didn't have anywhere near the same type of security as a bank or even the credit unions in DC.

Dan and I ended up taking a bus down to North Carolina on a Friday night, and we arrived in Greensboro on Saturday morning. Once we got off the bus, we found a credit union right down the block from the bus station. Without hesitation or any further discussion, we walked right in and announced, "This is a stickup!"

I ran behind the counter and got what money they had there. Dan watched the door and kept the people down on the floor. Then we ran out. It was fast and easy, just how I'd hoped.

Dan and I stopped running as soon as we rounded the corner so as not to draw attention to ourselves. We were just two cats strolling through the city on a Saturday. From downtown, we took a city bus to the North Carolina A&T campus. I had a friend who went there, so we looked him up and met him at his dormitory. I didn't tell him what we'd done, but I offered him a wad of cash if he could find someone to drive us out of town. His eyes grew wide when I showed him the money, but he didn't ask any questions. He found a guy named Dennis to drive us to the town of Reidsville about twenty miles north of Greensboro. Needless to say, I gave Dennis a nice tip.

Dan and I didn't breathe easy until we were back at his house in DC, after taking a ten-hour bus ride back to the city. We ran into his bedroom, locked the door behind us, and counted our loot. We had stolen close to eight thousand dollars! This was the biggest haul we'd ever made. Dan and I looked at each other and just laughed like little kids.

"We did it, man!" Dan said, grinning like a fool.

"Yeah, man, we did," I said. "Now let's go celebrate."

The celebration after that robbery was epic. We hit up the clubs. We had girls. We had beer. We had reefer. I bought myself a new seven-hundred-dollar leather coat that I'd been eyeing for a while. And I loaned some money to my friend Al, who needed it to help his mother pay her rent. I quit my job at the fast-food restaurant and started thinking about the next caper. It was as if I had never considered going straight. I was back in business.

My reputation as a thief grew, and more and more guys wanted in on the action. It looked easy to them because I made it look easy and fun. I went down to Greensboro a few more times and took different cats with me, choosing the kids who had a skill or asset that I needed, like their own car. But Dan was my true partner. In fact, he got mad when I went to Greensboro once without him, so I promised him the next time I planned a heist down south, I'd let him know.

That next time came a few months later, in June of 1971. I had promised two younger guys — Keith was sixteen and Vern was seventeen — that they could come with Dan and me to Greensboro. With the two extra guys, I decided to try tying up the people in the credit union so they couldn't get to a phone to call the police as soon as we were out the door. It would give us more time to get away. I put Vern and Keith in charge of tying everybody up because I didn't trust them to handle a gun. I was getting more ambitious and brazen as a thief.

Vern and Keith agreed to their roles, so the only thing I had to figure out was transportation, because nobody in our newly assembled crew owned a car. I had a solution for that, of course. The morning of the robbery, I stole a 1968 Dodge Charger from a DC parking lot. Then I picked up Dan, swung around and picked up Keith and Vern, and we were on our way to Greensboro. I was feeling lucky, and the mood in the car was upbeat.

When we got to Greensboro, I knew which credit union I wanted to hit up. This particular one was on Elm Street, near Vanstory, the fancy clothing store where my mother used to take me shopping for special occasions. We parked the car on a side street behind the building. I walked in first, then Dan came in behind me. Keith and Vern followed after. I did a quick look around and saw only three employees in the place, two men and a woman. I pulled out my gun and said, "This is a stickup. You know what to do." Without wasting a minute, we hustled the three people into a back room and forced them to tell us where the money was. I kept my gun out to let them know we were serious. I didn't hesitate when I barked out my orders. And I didn't pause when the woman looked at me with fear in her eyes. "Hey," I said to Keith and Vern. "Get over here and tie these people up."

Keith and Vern got busy, and Jack and I went to collect the money. We moved quickly, and I stayed focused on the time, but I was pissed that there was less than one thousand dollars behind the counter. Jack and I ran back to the room where the employees were now all tied up.

"Where's the rest of the money?" I yelled.

"There is no more," one man mumbled, his face down in the carpet.

"Well, empty your pockets then," I said, and we collected a couple hundred more dollars, a watch, and a ring.

"That's all they got, man!" Dan said, pulling on my arm. "Let's get out of here!"

The four of us hustled out the back door of the building and ran around the block to the car.

We jumped in the car, but I had a bad feeling. Nothing felt right about this job. All I was thinking was that I needed to get us out of Greensboro. Just get to the next city, where we could lay low and hide.

"Don't speed," Dan warned me. "We don't want to draw any extra attention to ourselves."

"I know, man," I snapped back. I kept telling myself over and over again to stay cool. To pay attention to the traffic signals. Don't get caught.

I was heading for the highway and I kept my foot on the gas but was careful not to overdo it. It was about twenty miles to the next town, and that was all I needed to know. Once we made it to the highway, I knew I could pick up the speed and put some real distance between us and the scene of the crime.

"There's a cop behind us!" Vern cried out.

I checked in my rearview mirror and sure enough, a Greensboro police car was now on my tail, but his roof lights weren't on. He just followed me for a few blocks. I kept my pace right at the speed limit and told myself, "Don't panic."

Then I saw another police car coming at us from the opposite direction. They were going to box me in. Suddenly their lights and sirens came on at the same time.

I pulled the car over and quickly reached for my gun.

"Man, put that gun down! Are you crazy? They'll kill you!" Dan hollered at me.

"I'm not stupid, man," I said as I hid the gun under the seat.

I turned around and looked at Keith and Vern. These cats were just kids. "Y'all be cool, okay? And don't say nothing," I warned them.

They both nodded back at me. They looked terrified.

One of the cops got out of his vehicle with his gun drawn and he came over to our car and ordered, "Put your hands out of the car!" Then another cop came from the back and opened my door and told me to step out. He looked in the back and said, "All of you, move out!"

They lined us up against the car. Then they patted us down and asked us if we had weapons. I said that I didn't have anything on me, but they started searching the car and found my gun. It was at that point that another officer back in the other car announced, "This car is stolen, too!" They moved us away from the car then and continued searching the vehicle. A few minutes later, another police car pulled up and the three employees from the credit union stepped out. One of the cops asked them if we were the people who had robbed them at gunpoint. They all said yes, and I knew what was coming next.

"You're under arrest for robbery. You have the right to remain silent. Anything you say can and will be used against you in a court of law."

As I listened to the officer read me my rights, I didn't feel an ounce of regret for what I had done. I just kept replaying the whole incident in my mind, trying to figure out what had gone wrong. What I could have done better. On the ride to the jail and up through my sentencing, I replayed the robbery in my mind over and over again and kept finding the flaws that I should have fixed. I wasn't the least bit remorseful. I was angry.

Vern, Keith, Dan, and I were each given court-appointed lawyers, but we were tried all together that August. Once the trial started, it all went very fast. Jury selection was one day, and our trial followed for four days after that. Nobody testified on our behalf, but there were six witnesses who identified us as the thieves — the three employees from the bank and three other eyewitnesses who had seen us on the street, jumping into the getaway car after the robbery. The jury deliberated for only thirty minutes. We were found guilty and sentenced all on the same day. Dan and I were sentenced to twenty-five to thirty years. Keith and Vern, who were treated as youthful offenders, got off with a shorter sentence and were sent to a juvenile facility.

I remember when I heard my sentence, twenty-five to thirty years, I laughed. It was a loud and obscene laugh that probably made the judge and everybody else in that courtroom think they'd done the right thing in sending me away. But they didn't know that I laughed because I had to. It was the only option as I contemplated spending the next twenty-five years of my life behind bars. That meant I wouldn't get out until my late forties at the earliest. If I didn't laugh, what was my other option?

When they put me back in my cell at the jail, my laughter turned to tears. I started crying and couldn't stop. All I wanted was to wake up from the nightmare I had made of my life. I knew I had done this to myself.

When I woke up the next morning and the guards were calling breakfast, I refused to get up and didn't want to eat. I stayed in my bunk and slept for the next few days, trying to sleep away the pain. I didn't clean myself. I didn't move. I couldn't bring myself to do anything except lie in my bed and try to imagine how I would survive twenty-five years in prison. And for the first time in my life, my big imagination showed me nothing but darkness.

CHERYL

The summer before I was to officially start my senior year at Columbia High School in suburban Atlanta, I spent my days relaxing and having fun. Sis and her husband, Jerry, had a nice three-bedroom house, and they made me feel right at home. Sis's son Corey was just three years old, and I loved him like he was my own little brother. I had my own room, and Sis didn't make me feel bad that the reason I was there was that I'd messed up so badly in New York. But she was very clear that I had to take my schoolwork seriously.

Before the semester started, Sis took me over to the high school to register me and to show me around. Columbia High was a big school surrounded by massive green fields for sports and recreation. In addition to the football field, there was a full-sized track circling another field as well. Columbia catered to the mostly Black students in the neighborhood, and I'd be just one more walking through those doors on the first day, thanks to all of Sis's hard work getting my transcripts and records forwarded from New York.

I was nervous on my first day, but I was determined to do whatever it took to graduate. I had let so many people down with my behavior, I just wanted to make it right. Plus, my pride was at stake. Back home, we made fun of the kids who got held back or had to repeat a grade. "You're not a dummy, Cheryl," I told myself as I checked my hair one last time before heading out the door. "You're going to graduate."

At first the kids at Columbia called me "New York" and made fun of my accent and my clothes.

"Those sure are some ugly shoes," one girl said to me that first week.

I looked down at my suede sandals with the sling backs and thought this girl simply had no taste. She didn't know what was fashionable in New York.

I wanted to say something back to her in her face, but I didn't. I just kept walking because I wasn't there to start any fights. I had to graduate. That's what I continued to remind myself.

Thankfully, as time went on, the kids stopped making fun of me and I slowly started making friends. I became close with a girl named Karen, who loved to hear all my stories about life in New York. She hooked me up with all of her friends and she even convinced me to join the soccer team.

When she first asked me, I said, "But I don't know how to play soccer." Karen assured me I'd learn, and sure enough I did.

I almost didn't recognize myself. My life very quickly felt different from the one I'd left behind. For one, I was exercising, not only playing soccer but also running on the track to stay in shape. I was going to pep rallies and all kinds of extracurricular activities. I could throw myself entirely into my school community now that I was no longer burdened with running a household. I was free to be a regular teenager. And my grades showed the difference too. Soon, I wasn't just thinking about graduating, I was thinking about excelling. It was like a revelation to me. I thought to myself, *If only I'd gone to class and done my work, I could have done so much better in school.* In Atlanta, I was loving my classes, loving doing the work, and I loved getting good grades.

Sis kept a close eye on me and wouldn't let me goof off if I had work to do. I felt her watchful gaze, just like when Mommy used to tell me she had eyes in the back of her head. But the truth was, it felt good to be watched, to know somebody cared about my well-being. And I wanted to make my sister proud of me. Sis's dream for me was to finish high school and then attend Spelman College, the prestigious all-Black women's college there in Atlanta. Sometimes she would drive me by the campus and say, "See, Cheryl, that's Spelman. And across the way is Morehouse, where all the successful Black men go. That's where you're going to end up too."

But Sis wasn't always about school and the future. She knew how to have fun, too. We were always talking and laughing, and every Friday we'd have what I called "sister time." We'd go to the beauty salon and get our hair done for church on Sunday, then we'd go out for dinner, just the two of us, and we'd be laughing and joking the whole time.

But as the calendar year came to a close, and the winter holidays approached, I started to get homesick. I talked with my father and little brothers almost every day on the phone and with my girlfriends almost as often, but I still couldn't keep myself from missing my life back in New York. And then I got some upsetting news from the guidance counselor at my school.

Right before Christmas vacation, she called me into her office to make sure I understood that when school started up again in January, I was to report to Open Campus, not Columbia High School.

"What do you mean?" I asked.

"Well, based on your transcripts from your former school, you have quite a few credits to make up if you want to graduate on time, and that is what you want to do, isn't it, Ms. Williams?"

"Yes," I said warily.

"Well, for students in your predicament," she started, "we send them to Open Campus, where you can double up on certain courses in an accelerated format so that you can finish school on time. And it looks like you need to do that for a few courses, particularly in math."

I rolled my eyes. I hated math and had never been good at it. Now I was going to have to make up all the math I'd skipped in New York.

"So does that mean I'm not going to graduate from Columbia?" I asked for clarification.

"No, no, dear. You will still be a Columbia student. You can still come to all the Columbia functions and participate in the clubs and sports and dances. You just have to go to Open Campus for your classes."

"Will I graduate on time?"

The woman smiled. "Yes, Ms. Williams. If you do everything you need to do at Open Campus, you will graduate from Columbia with your classmates."

I must have frowned because the woman added, "It's going to be okay. You'll like Open Campus. It's very nice."

"Open Campus? That's where the dummies go!" my friend Karen said when I told her what the guidance counselor said.

"Stone Mountain?" Sis said when she found out where Open Campus was located. "That's where the Ku Klux Klan holds their meetings."

Now I was really upset. I had to leave my new friends and start all over at a school for dumb kids where I might also run into the Ku Klux Klan! This was not what I signed up for.

Sis was equally worried. But she was more concerned with how

I was going to get to Open Campus, considering it was a good hour from her house. She called my guidance counselor and found out that there was a city bus that stopped close to the school.

"I'll drive you to the bus stop," Sis promised, "but you're going to have to get the rest of the way there yourself."

Luckily, just one week into the semester I met a girl named Yvette who lived close to my sister's house. Her father drove her to Open Campus each day. She asked him if he could pick me up too, and thankfully he agreed.

Open Campus wasn't that bad. It felt like just another school, but there were fewer kids in each class because these were all kids like me, who for one reason or another needed an alternative path to graduation. I met a few girls who were pregnant or who already had kids. Some, like me, had fallen behind with their credits. School started at 8:00 a.m., and we weren't finished until 4:00 p.m. There was no time for fun or socializing. I just kept reminding myself why I was there and what I had to do. It also helped that my godsister had promised me that if I graduated on time, she was going to take me on a girls' trip to Los Angeles to see all of our favorite celebrities and then go to Disneyland. That was a real added incentive for me.

As the semester progressed, I would regularly go check the board where the teachers posted who was on track to graduate at the end of the year. I saw my name and was determined to keep it on the board. Sis continued to talk to me about college, and I really started to think about my future after high school. Now that graduation seemed like a certainty, I could actually consider what would come next for me. Sis took me to a college fair at Columbia one evening, and I collected a handful of glossy college brochures and went home that night imagining myself as a college student. Sis always said education was the key to success, and judging from my other siblings, I knew she was right. Sis was the only one who had gone to college. George Jr. joined the military and then had come home and gotten addicted to drugs.

My brother Bruce had already done time in jail. Meanwhile, Sis had a stable, well-paying government job and a nice house with her husband. She had the life I wanted, so I kept working and planning.

True to her word, my godsister took me on that trip to Los Angeles, because I kept my word and graduated on time. My father, stepmom Estelle, and my godmother Katherine all came down for my graduation ceremony, and I have to admit I was so proud of myself, I practically strutted across the stage to collect my diploma. I felt like I had really accomplished something important, and I felt like I had truly earned that trip. I felt so grateful to have a godsister who would spend so much time and effort planning such a magical vacation for me. On the plane ride back, I thanked God over and over for letting me have such a wonderful experience.

When I returned to Atlanta, I found a job at a summer camp, and Sis helped me get ready to start college. I wasn't prepared for Spelman quite yet, but I was set to begin at the local community college. Sis said I could start there and then transfer to Spelman when I felt it was time. Sis took me shopping so we could build out my college wardrobe, and then I decided I should get a job so I could pay for more of my expenses. I was still homesick, but I was excited about opening this new chapter of my life.

I lasted one full semester at community college. I liked it, but I was too homesick to stay. I couldn't deny it anymore. I had tried to be happy doing my classes and planning for a future in Atlanta, but I couldn't stop yearning for my friends, family, and my life back in Brooklyn. We were sitting in Sis's dining room one afternoon and I told her in a quiet voice that I had something important to tell her. I wanted to sound mature, but I just blurted out, "Sis, I want to go home!" And then I waited for her reaction. I knew she was going to be mad.

Instead she laughed. "Dag, Cheryl, I thought you was going to say you were pregnant or something."

"No way!" I said. "I just want to go home."

Sis paused and then reached for my hand across the table. "Well, I can't keep you if you don't want to stay. If you want to go, you can go."

"I'm sorry, Sis," I said, getting choked up. I didn't want to let her down.

"You don't have to be sorry," she said. "But is everything okay, though? You feel comfortable here, don't you?"

"Of course," I said, wanting to reassure my sister. "I had a lot of fun. I love being here. I just want to go home. I miss New York. I miss Daddy. I miss my friends. I miss Don and Scott." It all just came tumbling out. I was a teary mess.

"Don't worry, Cheryl," Sis said. "I'll send you home."

And she did.

It felt so good to be back. Back in New York. Back to Brooklyn. Back to the Pink Houses. Back to our apartment. The first thing I did when I got home was jump into my bed and just luxuriate in the comfort of something so familiar. I called my friends then, and they had me out at our favorite Chinese restaurant that very same night. Within a week, it felt like I had never left. Scott and Don were better at cleaning up and keeping the house straight, but I quickly slipped back into my role as head of household. By then, I didn't mind. My friends and I continued our social life, going to clubs, dancing and partying, and I went back to church and reclaimed my place in the choir.

But I had promised Sis that if I went back to New York, I'd continue with my education, so I made sure to find a community college where I could start pursuing my dream of becoming a nurse. Daddy couldn't really help me navigate the higher education system in New York, so I was pretty much on my own, but I knew if things got too complicated, I could ask my godmother or any of my friends for help.

I ended up enrolling in Kingsborough Community College because they had a pre-nursing program and because it was just blocks away from our church. That was convenient. I could go to class and then make it to choir practice on Thursday nights. I let Sis know that I had followed up on my promise and was keeping up with my studies. Daddy was happy that I was in college too. For a nineteen-year-old, I thought I was doing pretty well.

One day, when I came home from class, I checked the mail and found a letter addressed to me from a prison in upstate New York. I couldn't imagine who it might be from. I tore open the envelope in the elevator on the way up to the apartment and almost fell over. It was from Deon, my boyfriend from the eleventh grade who had disappeared without a trace. All this time I'd thought he'd just gotten with another girl and dumped me, when in fact he'd been caught dealing drugs and was sent to prison.

Deon explained all of this in a letter, begging me to forgive him and asking me to take him back. I laughed and showed the letter to my girlfriends later that night. I honestly hadn't thought about Deon for over a year. And then he just showed up in my mailbox. I crumpled up the letter and threw it away, thinking that would be the end of it.

But Deon's letters kept coming, pleading for forgiveness and telling me he'd changed. In one letter he sent a picture of himself and I had to admit he looked good. I'd always thought he was cute, but during the two years since I'd last seen him, he'd matured and gotten cuter. I kept that picture in my purse and I started writing him back, telling him to come find me when he got out. And that's exactly what he did.

Deon's mother had always liked me, and she drove Deon to see me on the day he got out of jail. He hugged me so tightly and swore that thinking of me was the only thing that had kept him sane while he was in prison. I was a little overwhelmed by the whole thing, and I talked to my friends that night to ask them what they thought I should do. Deena told me to give him a chance, but Carla told me to let him go.

Although I didn't fall into his arms right away, I waited and watched as Deon got his life together. He got a job at the Wonder Bread factory in Queens and enrolled in community college. He still lived with his mother in Queens, but we managed to see each other quite often. Slowly but surely, I fell back in love with Deon, and our lives were a combination of college classes, work, and clubbing on the weekends. My friends gave us their approval after a while, and I felt like I was living the life I'd always wanted.

One day, when we were at Deon's mother's house just hanging around watching TV, all of sudden he told me he had something for me. I thought it was going to be one of my favorite chocolate bars or something, but he pulled a blue velvet box out of his pants pocket and got down on his knee. He opened the little box to reveal an engagement ring with a tiny diamond.

"Let's get married, Cheryl," Deon said. "I want everyone to know that we're together forever."

I looked at the ring and I looked at Deon and I yelled out "Okay!" We kissed and snuggled for a bit and talked about our wedding and the kids we'd one day have, but then I looked at the clock and realized my father would kill me if I was late getting home.

I showed off my ring to my family and friends right away. They all made fun of me because I was so excited.

"Y'all don't even have a wedding date," Deena liked to point out.

"I know," I said, "but we're engaged and that's what's important."

Now when I rode the bus to my classes at the community college, I'd look at bridal magazines, already planning for my future.

A couple of months later though, Deon started acting funny every time we were together. One Saturday I was at his house and we were watching TV in his basement. Deon kept getting up and fidgeting around with things.

"What's wrong?" I finally asked, exasperated.

"Nothing," he answered, but he wouldn't look at me.

"There's obviously something wrong," I pressed. "You can tell me."

Then he came and sat next to me on the couch but he kept his head down and avoided looking me in the eye.

"Cheryl, you know I like you a lot," he started.

The hairs on the back of my neck stood up. Those words never led to anything positive.

Deon looked pained, but he continued with his speech. "It's nothing you did, Cheryl. It's me. I'm just not ready for all of this."

"What do you mean 'all of this'?" I said, my voice cracking.

He shrugged. "Us getting married and stuff."

"You asked me to marry you, remember?" I said. "I didn't ask for all this. I was okay with the way things were."

Deon shrugged. "Yeah, I know. I just think we should take a break, that's all."

"So it's not just that you don't want to marry me, you don't want to be with me?" I said as I did the calculations in my head. I just knew Deon had another girl somewhere. He'd always been a big flirt.

I took off my ring, threw it in Deon's face, and stormed out of his house toward the bus stop.

"Cheryl, wait!" Deon called, chasing me down the street, trying to talk nice.

I let him apologize and say nice things, but I wouldn't even look at him. When the bus came and opened its doors, I climbed up the steps and didn't even look back. I cried all the way to Brooklyn.

I kept crying for several days after that. My heart was broken. And I had been so excited about getting married. My friends told me to forget about Deon and just get back into our New York life. And that's what I tried to do. We went out clubbing again. I still had school and choir practice at church. But my body and my mind weren't really in it. I would go out with my friends, but I just didn't seem to have the energy to keep up. If we went out, I'd find myself falling asleep in class the next day. The only thing I wanted to do to forget about Deon was eat and sleep.

Eat and sleep.

And that's when it hit me. I took a test to be sure. I wasn't eating and sleeping because I was depressed. I was eating and sleeping because I was pregnant.

chapter five

Prison

BOBBY

Before I left Greensboro for Central Prison in Raleigh, North Carolina, my court-appointed lawyer told me that he was going to appeal my case on a technicality. There wasn't a large part of me that believed I'd be set free on appeal, but still, I maintained hope. Dan was sentenced to the same facility I was, which was a relief, so I didn't have to face what was coming alone.

At Central Prison, all of us who were waiting on appeal were separated from the general population, which gave me time to get used to life behind bars. I walked around in fear for the first few weeks because nothing — not jail in DC or my stints in juvenile detention centers — could prepare me for the world of prison. The facility itself was massive and overwhelming, with multiple salmon-colored three-story buildings surrounded by razor-wired walls and gun towers everywhere I looked.

I was housed with three other men in a large cell with two bunk beds, a sink, and a toilet smack in the middle of the room. If we weren't at a meal or pulling fresh air into our lungs during our designated minutes of recreation time, we were in that cell, trying not to choke on the stench that comes from living in a single room with an open toilet and three other men.

Dan and I were on the same floor but not in the same cell. We were able to eat together and play basketball when it was our turn for recreation time. We stuck together for protection, and we made no attempts to befriend anybody else. We just tried to be patient and lay low while we waited for the results of our appeal. We didn't want to attract the attention of any of the inmates who were looking for fresh meat to exploit, and we didn't want to attract the attention of the guards, who were only too happy to show us who was in charge.

Dan and I watched a guard turn a water hose on a fellow inmate as punishment for some infraction. He aimed it straight into the man's cell. That water came out so fast and cold, I was sure it would rip the skin right off his body. Watching him try to escape the piercing spray by scrambling under his bed like a cornered cockroach convinced me that I had better be on my best behavior.

It took nine months before we were told our appeal had been denied. After that, Dan was sent off to another prison, and I was given a new uniform — a brown one — and taken over to the general population section of the prison. My so-called honeymoon was over.

Once I was settled in, I was taken for diagnostic testing to see what skills I had that could be utilized in the prison system. The state of North Carolina had to get some use out of its ever-increasing prison population and tried to give every inmate a job based on his abilities.

I apparently scored high enough on the test to be assigned to the prison hospital.

"They're going to teach you how to care for the inmates there in the hospital," the warden told me. "You okay with that assignment? Because if not, we can send you out to the road camp."

I didn't have to consider my options.

"The hospital sounds fine," I said.

"Good, you'll start tomorrow."

Working in the hospital turned out to have quite a few benefits, the best one being that I didn't have to live with the general population in a cell. All hospital workers slept in a special dormitory so we could be on hand for work at odd hours. I learned how to take vital signs, like temperature, pulse, and respiration. I also learned how to do physical therapy with inmates who had been shot or seriously injured.

Getting into the rhythm of work helped me take my mind off the twenty-five-year sentence looming in front of me. Although I had it in my head that if I did my job well and didn't cause any trouble, I could possibly be out in six years on parole. The other inmates had told me that if you keep a clean record, you only have to serve about one-third of your sentence. But if you mess up, then you have to do the whole thing. I didn't know if that was actually true or not, but I chose to believe it because serving six years sounded manageable. Twenty-five years did not.

"Miller, you have a visitor!" the guard shouted.

"I got a what?" I said, sitting up on my bunk. It was Sunday, and I had nothing special planned for the day. Even though I'd filled out a visitors' form with every family member I could think of, I had no expectations that anyone would actually want to see me.

"You got a visitor," the guard repeated. "Hurry up and get out to the visiting room."

I slid my shoes on my feet and hustled to the visitors' room and tried to imagine which one of my siblings might have made the seventy-mile drive from Greensboro to the prison in Raleigh.

When I got to the room, I saw that it wasn't one of my siblings. It was my mother, sitting primly in a wooden visitor's chair, dressed in one of her Sunday dresses.

The tears started to fall before they even took off my handcuffs.

"Mama," I said, my voice trembling as the tears continued to flow. "What are you doing here?"

My mother patted me on the shoulder and told me not cry, which only made me cry more. I hung my head down in my lap and tried to keep my blubbering to myself.

"Buddy," Mama repeated. "Don't cry now. It's okay."

"I'm so sorry, Mama," I said without looking up. "I promise I'm going to get out of here."

My mother forced me to look at her and she fixed me with her sternest gaze. "Are you done with this criminal life, Buddy? I mean really done?"

At that point I didn't honestly know if I was done with the criminal life. I knew I wanted to get out of jail more than anything. But I didn't feel any different about my chances on the outside. I still had no image of myself leading an honest life. I had no idea what that would look like, much less if it was possible. Would I turn away from an opportunity to steal or to rob someone if I had the chance? How could I know that until I was tested? That's what I thought when my mother posed the question to me. I'd been a thief for almost ten years. Could I say that part of me was truly dead?

"You'll see, I'm going to make you proud" was all I could think to say.

She gave me a look and then said, "I hope this is the end of it for you."

"Me too, Mama," I said.

My mother told me she'd brought me a whole bunch of my favorite foods, but the prison didn't allow visitors to bring food from the outside into the building. She had to leave it all in the car. So instead of giving me a taste of home, Mama regaled me with all of the family news and gossip from back in Greensboro. By the time visiting hours were over, I was laughing instead of crying and Mama had a smile on her face too. Before she left, she offered me her usual words of advice. "Stay out of trouble, Buddy. And ask God to help you."

"I will," I said.

"I'm always praying for you," she said, before hugging me and walking out the door. My mother didn't make it back to the prison, but we continued to write letters to each other after that so I could let her know what I was doing and how I was surviving. In every reply, she always reminded me to pray and to ask God for help and guidance.

"Hey, Miller, you want to come to the meeting with the Jaycees?"

I peeled my eyes away from the football game on the television in the common room and looked at this inmate everybody called Big Mike. Among the inmates, he was the guy everyone wanted to know. He was always full of useful information and seemed to like to help the new guys get acquainted with how things operated. And he wasn't one of those cats who expected something in return. I trusted him.

"What kind of meeting is it?" I asked.

"The Jaycees teach you about the Bible and Jesus and stuff. It's like Bible study," Big Mike explained.

"Naw, man, I'm good," I said, turning my attention back to the television. Despite my mother's best efforts, I continued to stay away from church and talk of God. My thoughts were so twisted on the matter. I felt like I kept failing God and therefore I didn't deserve Him or belong in His house. I didn't believe He had time for someone like me.

Big Mike moved his chair closer to mine. "Yo, Miller," he said. "You gotta think about getting out of here."

"What do you mean?" I said.

"I mean, people are always watching what you're up to. And the busier you stay trying to 'get rehabilitated,' the better it looks when you go up for parole. You feel me?"

"What do you mean?" I asked again, the football game completely forgotten.

"What I mean is that parole works like a point system. The more good things you do, activities you join, positive write-ups you get, the more points you're going to accumulate, which will lead you to parole. Plus, you need people from the outside to vouch for your character."

I frowned. "Vouch for my character?"

"You need people who will say good things about you, man. And I'm guessing there probably aren't a lot of cats on the outside who have nice things to say about *you* now, is there?"

Every family member I'd stolen from or betrayed flashed through my mind. I shook my head.

Big Mike leaned in closer. "That's why you gotta come to these meetings. Show them you're trying to repent for your sins and all that. And let them get to know you, so when you're up for parole, one of them can write you a letter of support."

"I see what you're saying," I said, nodding. Everything about prison life was calculated. And if I needed to get my religion on to ease my way out, I was more than happy to do so.

I stood up and looked at Big Mike. "Come on," I said. "Let's go find Jesus."

I took Big Mike's advice to heart and, from then on, made sure to stay busy doing positive things. In addition to my hospital job, I became one of the people to show movies to the other inmates. We showed films twice a week, on Saturday mornings and on Tuesday nights, and I learned how to use the projector from a fellow inmate named Ralph. Ralph got out on parole after a recommendation from one of the Jaycees. Big Mike was right. I just had to keep showing that I was trying to rehabilitate myself.

All of the extra activities weren't just for show. They helped the time go by faster, and after a while, I really started to enjoy going to the Jaycees meetings. They made me remember the good things I liked about church, like our summer picnics and seeing my mother so full of joy. They also made me feel better about myself, as they constantly reminded us that God loved all of His creations, even those in prison.

One day in early 1973, a little less than two years into my sentence, I was in my room in the hospital dormitory when my boss, Mr. Rice, came to the door. "Miller," he said from the doorway. "I'm sorry to have to tell you this, but I have some bad news." He paused before he continued. "Your mother has passed away."

"What?" I cried, sitting up. "When? What happened?"

"I'm sorry," Mr. Rice repeated. "I only just now got word that she passed away last night. I'm unaware of the cause of death."

I was stunned. No words came to my mouth.

Mr. Rice stood there for one more moment and then he said, "I'm sorry about your loss, Miller. The warden has decided to allow you to attend your mother's funeral, which we understand will occur sometime next week." And with that, he walked away.

I curled up in the fetal position on my bed and started to wail. I couldn't believe my mother was dead. I was devastated. A mixture of guilt, grief, and sadness roiled around in my gut and forced big wracking sobs through my body.

"Miller, shut up!" the guy in the next room called out.

I turned my face into my pillow to muffle the sounds of my sobs.

I knew the first rule of prison life was to never let people see you cry lest you get marked as soft. But I couldn't hold in the tears for my mother. The one person who I knew I could always go home to was gone.

On the morning of Mama's funeral, a guard woke me up and gave me a pair of dress slacks and a shirt to wear. I put them on, and then I was led out of the prison to an unmarked car. Two guards were waiting for me. I recognized one of them—Gaines. He was one of the guys who enjoyed telling the inmates that we were worthless and we'd never get out of prison. The other one didn't look familiar. But I didn't care. The only thing I cared about was saying goodbye to my mother.

"You ready, Miller?" the driver said.

"Yes, sir," I said, and we were off.

I spent the entire one-hour ride from Raleigh to Greensboro, handcuffed in the back seat, thinking about my mother and all of the good times we had together and the love she poured into me. I thought about how hard she worked to raise me and keep me out of trouble. How I'd watch her cook in the kitchen, making miracles out of nothing. How she taught me to iron my own shirts when I was just ten years old because she said she wasn't going to do it for me anymore but she wanted me to know how to present myself nicely. And how proud she was of me when I started mowing lawns and hustling for work. She supported everything I did as long as it was on the right side of the law.

Then I started thinking about all the things I'd never be able to share with my mother. She'd never see me get married. She'd never see the kids I hoped to have one day. Family was so important to her, and even when we messed up, which all of us kids did, she never stopped loving us.

By the time we arrived at Brown's Funeral Home, my eyes were already wet with unshed tears.

"Listen, Miller," Gaines said as he unlocked my handcuffs, "you get forty-five minutes in there with your family. Not a minute more. You try any funny stuff and I'll shoot you. Understand?"

"I got it," I said.

As soon as I stepped into the funeral home, I was assailed by a memory from my childhood. Brown's was the same place we'd laid my father to rest when I was nine. I was twenty-two now, and the pain was even worse.

"Hey, Buddy," the owner, Mr. Brown, came over and engulfed me in a hug. "It's good to see you, son."

"Thank you," I said, returning his embrace.

When I pulled away, I saw all of my siblings standing around the open casket at the front of the room.

Mr. Brown saw me looking.

"Go on over there with your family, Buddy. The viewing goes on for an hour, and then we're going to start the service."

The guards told me I only had forty-five minutes, so that meant I wasn't actually going to be able to stay for the funeral, just the viewing. That smarted, but I knew I couldn't argue.

"Buddy!" My sister Jean noticed me and called out my name.

I shuffled over to my siblings and received love from each and every one of them. They asked how I was doing and told me I looked good, but I didn't want their attention. I just wanted to know what had happened to Mama.

"Mama didn't suffer, Buddy," Jean assured me. "She had a heart attack, but I was with her the whole time she was in the hospital. She was in and out of a coma for a while, and her diabetes just made it worse. She just couldn't fight anymore."

Hearing that made me cry even more. My poor mother. All of us stood around the coffin crying and lost in our thoughts while more and more people entered the funeral home to pay their respects. It seemed like only a few minutes had passed, but suddenly Gaines was in my ear telling me it was time to go. Just then, Mr. Brown announced that the funeral service was about to start.

I wanted to stay longer, but Gaines was hovering right behind me, and his earlier threat lingered in the back of my mind. My feelings quickly shifted from anger at having to leave to guilt as, once again, I felt like I was letting my mother down. Even in death I couldn't be there for her.

I said goodbye to my family, and everyone told me they would pray for me. My brother Raymond told me to stay strong and I said I would. Then I walked over toward the door while everyone else headed to another room for the service. "I'm ready, let's go," I said to Gaines. He was kind enough to wait until we were outside before he put my handcuffs back on.

It took me a week or so to get back into my routine again at the prison. I was grateful that my boss and the other nurses were sympathetic and let me mourn. "I'm sorry to hear about your mother," one of the other inmates who worked at the hospital said to me. "But at least you got to go to her funeral. I didn't even know you could do that." Even though I knew that was true, hearing other guys say it made me feel more grateful that I'd gotten to see Mama one last time. Not to mention, seeing my siblings had been a gift to my soul as well. I now felt more determined than ever to do whatever it took to get out of prison so I could finally show my mother that she raised a good son. Even if she'd have to witness my accomplishments from heaven.

It took two more years before my good behavior was finally rewarded. In a meeting with my counselor, I was informed that I had earned the right to be transferred away from Central Prison to a minimum security prison somewhere else in North Carolina.

"Where do you want to go?" my counselor asked me.

I shrugged. "I just want to be someplace close to Greensboro so my family can come visit me."

My counselor looked down at his list and said, "All right, we'll send you to Asheboro, then. That's only twenty-five miles from Greensboro."

"Sounds good to me," I said, trying not to show all my emotions. But inside I was ecstatic. Being transferred to a minimum security prison meant a lot more freedom. I'd heard of cats who were in minimum security prisons and held jobs on a work-release program. They got to go to their job on the outside and just come back to the prison to check in and sleep. That's what I was looking forward to, that kind of freedom.

Before I left, my superiors at the hospital all congratulated me on my transfer.

"Good for you, Miller," my boss said, clapping me on the back. "I'm really proud of you. You earned this."

As I packed my few possessions from the dorm, Big Mike came by to say he'd heard I was being transferred.

"Don't forget what I told you," he said. "Keep doing what you're doing. This move is proof that you're going to come up for parole sooner rather than later."

"I hope so, man," I said with conviction. And then, "And thanks for everything."

"You're welcome," he said. "But you did all the work."

I thought about what Big Mike said while I was on the bus heading toward Asheboro. I *had* done all the work. I had spent the last four years working alongside doctors and nurses, helping to take care of patients. I had helped a prisoner learn to walk again after being paralyzed from a gunshot wound, and that felt amazing. Doing good work, I realized, was truly satisfying. In the beginning, I was just signing up for things like Big Mike advised, to make it clear that I was doing the right things to make parole. But some major things changed along the way. For one, I stopped avoiding church and started listening to the inspiring words the preacher shared. Those sermons lifted my spirits. And then there was the work itself. I liked having a job to go to every day. I liked the rhythm of my workday. And slowly but surely, I started daydreaming about living and working outside those prison walls.

I started to think, *If I can work every day in here for a dollar a day, I can work on the outside for a real salary and have a regular life.* So I made a conscious effort to stop talking and listening to the inmates whose only language was crime. Those guys were young, with very little education, and hadn't learned anything about life other than what they had discovered in the streets. And I wasn't any different. At first. But my mindset had changed. I realized I was capable of learning and executing new skills in a professional setting. I read books and magazines about successful Black men and imagined myself in their place. I started to see myself with a wife and a family and being an important businessman. Maybe for the first time in my life, I saw that Walter Curtis Miller had the potential to be a real somebody in the world. Basically, I was growing up and I liked who I was becoming.

One of the first things I did when I got to Asheboro was call Jean and let her know that I had been moved and that I was much closer to home. She was happy to hear the news and promised to come visit. Asheboro was a world of difference from what I'd just left. We were allowed to go in and out of our dormitory without supervision. We could play basketball whenever we wanted to, and there was even a tennis court. Even the food was better than it had been at Central Prison. What I appreciated most of all, though, was the freedom. There were far fewer restrictions on your movements. But you had to earn those freedoms, I soon figured out.

For the first three months I was in Asheboro, I enjoyed the slower pace of life. I played cards, played basketball, and otherwise tried to

lay low and keep out of trouble. I wanted to see how things worked, so
I asked questions and observed. I noticed that some of the guys were
allowed to actually leave the facility and go into town. They could go
shopping or to the movies or meet up with old friends.

"How do you get that privilege?" I asked one of the other inmates
on the basketball court one day.

"You have to get an Honor Grade," he told me. "If you earn the
Honor Grade rank, you get more privileges." Apparently I hadn't
earned that privilege, as I was soon to find out.

"Why didn't I get the Honor Grade?" I asked my new counselor,
a stern-looking middle-aged Black man who didn't like to smile. His
name was Mr. Grady.

He leaned over his desk and said, "Miller, what have you done
since you've been here?"

"What do you mean what have I done?" I repeated back. "It's only
been three months. I'm just trying to get situated. I've been staying
out of trouble."

"Miller, you haven't done nothing but sit at that table playing
them cards and playing basketball, and you think we're just going to
give you an Honor Grade?"

Big Mike's words flashed through my mind. I realized that I hadn't
been following his advice. It didn't matter that I had a good record
coming from Central. I had to start over here at Asheboro to prove I
deserved more privileges. I shook my head as I realized I wasn't going
to get anything for free.

"No, sir," I responded to Mr. Grady.

"Well, then, if you want to make Honor Grade, I suggest you find
a way to prove it," he said.

"Yes, sir," I said and left his office.

Within two weeks I'd discovered the perfect way to prove to the
administration that I was worthy of an Honor Grade. I signed up for

a cooking class that they were offering to the inmates. Felix, the old cook who ran the prison kitchen, was teaching the class. He was a civilian who had been working at the prison for years. Most of the guys loved Felix because he had a great sense of humor. He told us that by the end of his five-week class, we'd be able to make a seven-course gourmet meal for our girlfriends and wives.

The thing was, before we got to the cooking lessons, we had to work in the kitchen. They put me on pots and pans, and I scrubbed pots for five hours a day. Then we would sit down for our lesson around a table in the cafeteria. Felix didn't exactly teach us how to make a gourmet meal, but he did teach us how to follow a recipe and then how to double and triple that recipe if we had to feed five hundred hungry inmates. He taught us how to make fried chicken, gravy, and macaroni and cheese.

"There are a lot of different ways to make macaroni and cheese," Felix said. "Some people grate the cheese and then they throw that on the macaroni," he explained. "Fancy people make a sauce with butter and flour and cheese," he told us. "But here at the prison, we got to use what we have here. And what we have here is canned cheese."

I hated that canned cheese, and I hated the macaroni and cheese we made with it, but I enjoyed Felix's lessons and learned a lot. And the next time I was up for Honor Grade, I got it. But I never got to enjoy it, because for reasons I still don't understand, I was transferred away from Asheboro, farther away from my family to a facility three hours away in Asheville, North Carolina.

The experience at Asheville was shocking to me. For the first time in my prison experience, I was at a facility with more white prisoners than Black. Fights between the races broke out almost every day. I'd never seen anything like it. Thankfully I didn't have to stay there long, but for the better part of a year, I continued to get transferred around North Carolina until I ended up back in Raleigh, back at Central

Prison, right where I started. Only this time I was down the hill in the minimum security facility instead of maximum. It had been a tumultuous year, moving all around, my family often not knowing where I was, so I was happy to be back in a familiar place, even if it was far from home. I prayed I wouldn't get moved again. The only good thing that happened during that year is that I built up my reputation as a good cook, and everyone seemed to know it. When I returned to Raleigh, I was immediately assigned to work in the canteen.

That made me happy. But I was only there for two weeks before I was called into the office and told that I was being given a new job assignment.

"Why?" I asked, retracing my steps in the kitchen. I'd done nothing but follow orders from the two white guys who I cooked with.

Captain Moore, the man in charge, sighed and said, "Look, Miller, you didn't do anything wrong. Don't worry about it. We're going to send you up the hill to work in the office. You'll like it. It's easy work."

I wanted to argue because I liked working in the kitchen, but what was the point? I knew once a decision was made, it was made.

I didn't find out until later that night when we were eating dinner why I was transferred.

"I know what happened," a guy named Rick who washed dishes told me. "Derek, the dude that cuts himself, told Captain Moore if they didn't get rid of you, he was going to start cutting himself again."

"What?" I sputtered. I knew Derek was a crazy low-down dog serving a life sentence. He'd called me a nigger to my face and didn't care about anything or anybody. At 250 pounds and six feet three inches, he was someone most guys were afraid of. I wasn't afraid of him, but I didn't want to make him my enemy either.

"Yeah, he was probably intimated by you," Rick said. "'Cause everybody was talking about you being a good cook and all. They said you make the best fried chicken."

My chicken was good, but it wasn't worth getting on Derek's bad side. So I reported for duty at the office the next day and found that the work was pretty easy, just like Captain Moore had said.

For the most part I was an office assistant. I was pretty much doing the same work I'd done at the Pentagon: filing papers, running errands, even going off the premises to purchase supplies for people. In the mornings, it was also my job to pick up the newspapers from the front gate and bring them to the office for everybody to read. If nobody needed me, I had a little room I sat in with a television, where I'd keep the coffee pot full and watch whatever shows I liked. My day would be over by 3:30, and then I was free.

I was on a good ride at this time in my life. I was eligible to leave the prison grounds once every six weeks with a sponsor and get a taste of regular life. I got to go to a concert. I got to go shopping to buy myself some regular clothes, and I even signed up to take some college courses. Shaw University, a historically Black institution in Raleigh, had a program where inmates could enroll and study toward a degree. I already had a prison radio show that I started with the help of some volunteers from the college, and now I was going to officially start studying communications when the new semester began the following fall. One of my fellow inmates even introduced me to a lady, and we often made plans to rendezvous when I was on leave. Yes, I was in my mid-twenties, and yes, I was officially inmate number 0283128, but I was living an honest life and I could finally see what a future for myself could look like on the outside.

That summer — the summer of 1977 — I made my way to the gate to pick up the newspapers for the office but there were no newspapers waiting for me. This wasn't the first time it had happened. When I got up to the office, I told one of my supervisors that the papers hadn't been delivered. He was one of the civilians who worked at the office and he was always the first person who wanted his paper. His name was Mr. Avery.

"That's strange," Mr. Avery said. "But don't bother with them anymore."

"What do you mean?" I asked.

"I mean it's always something. Don't bother bringing up those papers anymore until we figure out why they can't get here consistently. I'll look into it."

"Yes, sir," I said and went about my day.

The next morning, before I headed to up to the office, the guard at the gate called me.

"Hey, Miller, come get these newspapers to take up to the office!"

I turned toward the gate and yelled back, "They told me not to bring the papers up there anymore!"

And then I went on my way. I had a regular day at the office, but when I got back to my dormitory that afternoon, I was informed that I had been written up.

Once again, I found myself in Captain Moore's office.

"Miller, you disobeyed a direct order," Captain Moore said.

"For what?" I said, not even bothering to hide my confusion.

"The guard by the gate said he told you to take the newspapers up to the office but you disobeyed."

"I wasn't disobeying," I began to explain. "Mr. Avery up in the office told me not to bring the newspapers up to the office anymore until he figured out why they were always missing. I was just doing what I was told."

Captain Moore shook his head like I should have known better. "Miller, Mr. Avery is a civilian. The guard outranks him. Your job is to follow the orders of the men who guard and protect this facility. Is that clear?"

"Yes, sir," I said. And then I knew what was coming next.

Every time a prisoner got written up, they got a hearing where it was decided what kind of punishment they would receive. My punishment was that I was going to be removed from my cushy office job. And instead I was sent to work in the kitchen!

I don't know who was making those decisions, but being sent back to the kitchen didn't feel like a punishment at all. All I had to do was keep my head down and stay out of trouble. And luckily, Derek had been moved to another job, so I didn't have to worry about him anymore.

I worked in the kitchen for nearly a month before I allowed myself to let my guard down. During that month I felt I had proven myself to my superiors by staying out of trouble and doing all of the extras I could manage. In addition to my radio show, I was still going to all of the Christian church activities that were offered. I hadn't had to bother God with any problems for a while because things were going so well, but when I got written up for the newspapers, I returned to Him asking for help.

"God, I need you to keep me from doing dumb stuff and to keep me straight, with no write-ups, so I won't have any setbacks." That became my constant prayer. Even when things seemed to be okay, being in prison always meant living in fear. You never knew when something bad could happen that you had no control over. Another prisoner could pick a fight, or a guard having a bad day might decide to take it out on you. I tried to stay focused on my routine: working in the kitchen, watching TV during my free time, and making the tapes for my radio show on the weekends. I also made sure to stay away from any inmates who were doing drugs or any other illegal activities that would ruin my chances for parole.

"Miller, you got written up again," a guard said to me early one afternoon when I was finishing up my shift in the kitchen. "Report to Moore's office in thirty minutes."

"What?" I said, turning toward the guard. "What for?"

The guard shrugged and simply repeated that I was to be in the captain's office in thirty minutes.

I said "Okay," but inside I was fuming. Why did this keep happening? As I finished putting away my cooking utensils, I went over everything that had happened in the previous twenty-four hours. I wracked my brain trying to figure out what I had done wrong but couldn't come up with anything that made sense. Rather than trying to guess, I took myself to face the music.

"Come in!" Captain Moore bellowed as I knocked on his door.

I entered the office and took a seat in what was now a familiar chair.

Captain Moore didn't beat around the bush. "Hozart wrote you up, Miller."

"For what?" I said, trying to remember the last time I'd seen the guard named Hozart, whom we all hated because of his attitude. He always wanted to make sure we knew he had power over us and liked to humiliate us whenever possible.

"Did you say something to Hozart this morning?" the captain asked.

"I didn't even see Hozart this morning," I replied.

"Well, he says he was walking across the yard this morning and he heard you call out 'Hozart is a punk ass!'"

Now, deep inside I would have loved to say that to Hozart's face, but I never would have been stupid enough to yell that out in the early morning hours across the entire yard.

"I didn't say anything to anybody," I said. "I was in my room and then I went to the kitchen."

Captain Moore sighed. "Well, you know how this goes, Miller. You'll have a hearing and we'll see what happens."

I couldn't believe it. This would be my second hearing in a relatively short amount of time. I felt like I was in high school again with two strikes against me. Only this time, the punishment would mean being sent back to maximum security prison and my chance for parole disappearing into thin air.

I gritted my teeth and thanked Captain Moore. Then I prayed that justice would be served at my hearing.

Of course it wasn't. The prison system always takes the word of a guard over a prisoner. Hozart himself was at the hearing, and he reiterated his accusation that I had shouted that he was "a punk ass."

"Why would Mr. Miller say that?" Captain Moore asked.

"I don't know why he would say that." Hozart shrugged, looking angry. "I just know it was him. I recognized his voice."

"I did not say that," I said, when it was my turn to talk. "I would never do that."

"See, I recognize his voice there," Hozart said again. "I know it was him."

Captain Moore rolled his eyes like he was having a hard time believing what Hozart said, but he still took the guard's word over mine.

"Miller, you're going to be moved out of the kitchen and onto the road crew," Captain Moore told me the next day. And he reminded me, although I already knew, that if I didn't shape up, I'd be going back up the hill to maximum security.

The road crew meant spending the entire day cleaning up North Carolina's roads. Picking up garbage, pulling weeds, and doing any other demeaning task given to you. It was the worst work assignment and everyone knew it.

As soon as Captain Moore demoted me, I went to see my counselor, Marcie. She liked me and had been the one advocating for me to try the college program. She was working to get me into a job-training program as well. Marcie had already seen the report and knew what I had been accused of and the punishment I'd been given.

"Can't you do something so I don't have to do road crew?" I begged Marcie as I sat in her office.

"Listen, Miller," she said, "my hands are tied. I can't get you reassigned right now, but I promise you if you do your best and stay out of trouble, I'll see what I can do to get you out of there. But in the meantime, they've taken away all of your Honor Grade privileges."

"What? They can't do that!" I said. "I didn't do anything wrong." I then tried to tell Marcie my side of the story. When I was done, she sighed.

"Look, Miller," she started. "You'll have a new hearing in ninety days. At that time, as long as you've stayed clean, we can revisit your situation."

"Ninety days?" I said aloud but didn't expect a response.

"I'm sure it will pass quickly," Marcie said.

For her it might, I thought. *But not for me.*

Working on the road gang meant being at the front gate at 7:30 in the morning, then being driven out to a depot on the highway, where we were given a burlap potato bag and a stick with a nail in it to pick up trash. Dirty trucks meant for hauling hay would drop us off on some desolate area of the highway where we'd spend the day working and avoiding the garbage thrown at us by our fellow citizens.

I wanted to take Marcie at her word and assume that if I picked up trash like a good little soldier, then things would go back to the way they were. But those last few months made me feel like it didn't matter what I did. Something or someone would find a way to drag me back under. I tried to play sick after the first few days on the road crew, but the guards took my temperature and sent me on my way. Once a week I would go bother Marcie and ask her if she could get me off the roads, and every week she would tell me that she was working on it. But nothing changed except the weather.

Fall came creeping in and it started getting cold in Raleigh. The prison officials gave us warm coats to wear, but by the time the afternoon sun hit, those coats felt oppressive. I began bringing a bag to put my coat in so I wouldn't have to carry it or wear it on the way back. One morning, just to see, instead of wearing my coat, I put it in my bag and walked onto the bus with it like that. Nobody seemed to notice. Nobody seemed to care. Nobody asked what I had in my bag.

chapter six

Escape

Every morning when I woke up, the same refrain played in my mind. "I hate this. I hate this. I hate this." To say that I was teetering on the edge of desperation would be an accurate statement.

But that bag gave me hope. That bag sparked something in my brain. That bag opened up a window of possibility. That bag was an opportunity. Nobody checked what was in my bag when I got on the bus every morning, so that meant I could potentially put other things in that bag. Things I might need outside the prison walls. Things I might need to escape.

And that's all it took for my mind to start calculating. I began to pay attention to everything with a whole new mindset. I was looking for flaws in the system. Now, instead of always saying "I hate it here," I had a new refrain: "I can get out of here." I had done it before, I could do it again. Of course, this time the stakes were higher. This wasn't a juvenile facility like the Morrison Training School. But I didn't care. I knew if I got caught I'd be sent back to maximum security, and I still didn't care. The way things were going for me, I could get sent back there anyway. All it would take was one more write-up. As I looked at it, going back to maximum security because I tried to reclaim my freedom was better than going back because a disgruntled guard or a revengeful inmate had it in for me.

So I began to formulate a plan.

Everything had to be perfectly executed. I knew I needed at least a hundred dollars saved up before I left. We were paid five dollars a week for working on the road, so I stopped buying things in the canteen and saved my paltry little salary. I also started playing in the evening poker games. If I won a little money, I'd get right up and leave.

"Man, aren't you going to give us a chance to win our money back?" the guys would ask me. And I'd say "no" without hesitation. I knew if I stuck around, I might be tempted to play another hand and lose everything.

Little by little, I also started emptying out my locker. I didn't want them to find any old letters from friends or family members with phone numbers and addresses that might lead them to me. I destroyed anything with personal information on it. When I walked out of this place, I didn't want to leave behind a single scrap of evidence that I'd ever been there.

As I went over my plan, I considered the stories I'd heard about other inmates who'd tried to escape and how they'd failed. There was the one Black guy who made it back to his home state of Pennsylvania. At some point he went to apply for a driver's license. He used his real name, and two days later they busted him and brought him back to North Carolina. Another inmate, a white guy, escaped off the road camp. He got all the way up to New York City but didn't know where to go or what to do. The cops started questioning him since he seemed so out of place, as a white guy hanging around at the bus terminal. The cops took his picture and ran it through the system. Somebody identified him and he was sent back to prison.

So those were two things I knew I couldn't do once I got out: use my real name or get my picture taken. I didn't know what name I was going to use, but I wasn't worried about it either. I hadn't used my given name, Walter, for my entire life. I was Buddy, Curtis, Curt, Cotton Foot, or Miller, depending on whom you asked. I knew I would have no problem saying goodbye to Walter Miller.

Even though I was confident that I could escape, I couldn't bring my stress level down. Time seemed to pass like cold molasses, and every day felt like a week as I waited for the best opportunity to leave. I didn't tell anybody what I was attempting to do, but I felt uneasy all the time, like any minute someone would say, "I know what you're planning." I had to keep telling myself, "Be cool. Don't blow it."

A week before Halloween, Marcie, my counselor, called me to her office as soon as I came in from work one evening. She asked me how it was going.

"Things could be better," I admitted.

"That sounds about right," she said and then went on to tell me that she'd been given a report about my job performance. "You're not doing a good job, Miller," she started. "Your attitude sucks, you're slow getting to the bus in the mornings, and you're not picking up much trash. This has to change. You have to do better."

As Marcie was talking, my mind drifted off and I saw myself handcuffed, being dragged back to maximum security. I shook the image out of my mind and realized Marcie was waiting for me to say something.

"Marcie, I don't want to be out there, but you're right, I can do better." That's what I said out loud, but in my mind, I told myself that it was time to go.

It only took me a few more days to finish collecting a hundred dollars. And my locker was wiped clean. I was ready. Now it was just a waiting game of looking out for the right day.

That day came early in November of 1977. My nephew's birthday was on November 8, two days after mine, so I simply made up my mind to make his birthday my special day too.

The night before, I couldn't sleep. I was restless and uneasy. As

I was lying there in my bed, I prayed that I hadn't missed any signs telling me not to go. I whispered to God, "It's not too late if you want to tell me not to do this." I fell asleep waiting for His answer.

The next morning I woke up knowing that that day was the day. I waited for everyone to go to breakfast, and then I snuck into the shower area to get dressed where nobody would see me put on two layers of clothes. I put my street clothes on first and then put my prison uniform over them. I had to roll up the legs of my jeans so they wouldn't show under my pants legs. I grabbed my plastic grocery bag where I'd been carrying my prison coat and stuffed it full with my brown leather coat and my one pair of leather shoes I'd bought on one of my shopping trips in the city.

Once I was ready, I heard the intercom announcement blare, "Attention! Attention! All the inmates working on the road crew, come to the front gate!" I went right out and just stood by the gate until 7:30, when the guard called my name. I hopped on the bus and headed for an empty seat a couple of rows from the back. As usual, except for the driver, there were no other prison personnel on the bus. My heart was pounding in my chest, but I played it cool. This was just another day of road crew. When the bus started to pull away from the prison, I felt my spirits soar in anticipation.

Only about fifteen minutes passed until we approached the street where I planned to jump off the bus. I scanned the area and saw no other cars on the street. The bus approached an intersection with a stop sign and came to a halt. "This is it," I said to myself. The driver slowly accelerated into the intersection, getting ready to make a right turn, and I began to move. I quietly got out of my seat, staying low so as not to attract the driver's attention. And then as soon as the bus started turning, I pushed open the back door of the bus and jumped out. I landed on my feet and sprinted toward the woods, the shrill sound of the bus alarm ringing in my ears.

I knew the driver was probably yelling at the other thirty inmates on the bus to close the door. He was probably agonizing over what to do. But I knew protocol dictated that he was to continue to the depot and report what I had done. He'd already lost one inmate; he couldn't afford to lose any more. That meant I had approximately thirty minutes of head start. Even then, he would have to call in the escape, and the guards would have to mobilize back at the prison and then send a team out to find me. It wasn't a lot of time, but I wasn't going to think about getting caught. I was only thinking about getting free.

As soon as I hit the woods, where nobody could see me, I started peeling off my top layer of prison clothing — the shirt, the pants, my prison sneakers. I just left it all there in the dirt, like shedding the skin of someone I used to be. I slid my feet into my own shoes, put on my leather coat, and exited out the other side of the woods. Just like Clark Kent in a phone booth. In the blink of an eye, I went from convict to civilian.

Of course, I wasn't Clark Kent calm on the inside. The clock was ticking, and I had no idea where I was going. I just kept heading in the opposite direction from where the bus had gone. I had been in the city of Raleigh several times, but I didn't really know how to get there on foot. I just kept walking and running until the rural road led me to a neighborhood with actual sidewalks. My plan was simply to find somebody and ask where the Greyhound station was, but I didn't see anybody on the streets. I figured it was too early for folks to be out, so I just kept walking. I was walking fast, but not too fast. I just wanted to look like anybody else walking to work or maybe to the bus stop.

When I eventually saw a white man on the street, I asked him for directions to the bus station. He looked at me funny and told me the bus station was a long way from there. He said to keep walking in the direction I was going. Then about thirty minutes later, I came to what looked like a Black neighborhood and I breathed a sigh of relief. I went up to the first brother I saw and asked him about the bus station. This brother gave me directions, but like the white man before him, he said it was still a good distance away. I didn't care. I just kept walking. When there was no traffic around, I'd pick up my pace and run. For over three hours I walked and ran, until at last I saw signs that said the downtown area was just ahead.

When I finally spotted the bus station, I wiped the sweat off my face, tucked my shirt in, and made sure I didn't look suspicious before crossing the street and heading toward the building. I thought I was playing it cool, but this older Black man came over to me before I made it to the bus station. He reminded me of one of the elders from my mother's church. "Are you okay, son?" he asked me out of the blue. "Do you need some help?"

"Yes, sir, I could use some help," I said without hesitating. "Could you spare a few dollars?"

The man looked me over and said, "I hope you ain't in no trouble."

I didn't want to lie, so I didn't say anything. I just held his gaze and he must have seen something because he reached into his breast pocket and pulled out his wallet. Then he handed me thirty dollars. "You look like you need this more than I do," he said.

"Thank you, man," I said, getting ready to tell him how much I appreciated it, but he just walked away. I don't know what that man saw in me, but I was so grateful. I didn't know how long the hundred dollars shoved in my pocket was going to last me.

With that extra thirty, I could buy my ticket and keep the hundred I'd saved for whatever awaited me in New York. I hustled over to the depot, but right before I pulled open the door, I stopped. What if they had cameras in the station? Or what if the police came with my picture and asked if anybody had seen me? I had to rethink this. I moved away from the door and stood off to the side of the building. Before I could lose my courage, I stopped a young brother on the street and asked him to buy me a one-way ticket to New York City. He agreed, so I gave him a twenty-dollar bill and told him I'd wait for him across the street.

The whole time I waited, I wondered if he was going to come back out and actually give me my ticket. I started to beat myself up for my stupidity. *This dude could be half a mile away with my money,* I thought. But then I saw him, and he waved as he jogged over to where I was standing.

"Here you go, man," he said, handing me the ticket and my change.

"Thanks, man," I said. I was so grateful that he had come back, I told him to keep the change.

"Thanks," he said. "And have a nice trip."

Things were looking good, but I still wasn't out of danger. I went back over to the station and found the area where the buses loaded up. I checked the sign and saw I had about twenty minutes to wait. I didn't want to join the line of people waiting for the bus, so I hung back and tried not to let my fears get the best of me. I started singing some of my favorite songs to myself to help me settle my nerves. Stevie Wonder's "Living for the City" came to mind and I sang that song over and over again.

Right on schedule, the bus began boarding. When they announced the last call for New York, I slunk forward and got on the bus. I found a seat toward the back and prayed that we could get out of the state without incident. My heart was still beating furiously in my chest, the sound echoing in my ears. I was so close to being free, but I was so scared that I wouldn't make it to the finish line. I didn't dare fall asleep or even close my eyes because I had to stay alert. At every stop I was waiting for a cop to board the bus and haul me back to prison.

When we finally left the state of North Carolina and crossed over into Virginia, I felt like I had crossed a major barrier, and I started to relax just a little bit.

"Do you mind if I sit here?" a young sister asked me after a stop in Virginia.

"I don't mind," I said, turning my body toward the window, hoping the woman would get the hint that I didn't want to talk. But she didn't. As soon as she sat down she started talking, telling me all about her no-good boyfriend who had lured her down to Virginia. I wanted to ignore her, but listening to her actually helped pass the time.

"So, what's your name?" she asked me at one point.

"My name?" I repeated.

"Yeah, I'm telling you my whole life story, I figured I should at least know your name," she said, smiling.

"Oh, okay," I said, trying to seem calm as I racked my brain for a name to use. "My name is Bobby. Bobby Love."

Bobby Love was the name of my friend Ulysses's son who had passed away.

"Well, Bobby Love, thank you for listening to me," she said.

"No problem," I said.

And she kept talking. And I kept listening all the way to Philadelphia, where she got off. Before she left, she smiled at me. "Thank you, Bobby Love," she said. "I feel a lot better now than I did when I got on this bus."

I did too, because now I had my new name.

Two hours later, the bus pulled into the lower level of the Port Authority Bus Terminal in midtown Manhattan. It was close to midnight, but there was still a throng of people waiting to greet the folks coming off our bus. I scanned the crowd looking for cops but didn't see anyone who looked suspicious, so I stepped off the bus, pulled in a deep breath of the foul New York air, and smiled as I said aloud, "Thank you, God, Bobby Love has arrived!"

After six years in prison, the first thing I wanted to do when I set foot in New York was get high and get laid. I headed straight for Times Square. In 1977, Times Square was a one-stop shop for sex, drugs, and rock and roll. I wanted them all.

The walk from the Port Authority Bus Terminal to Times Square was a short one, and when I got to 42nd Street, I felt like a kid in a candy store. Even though it was well after midnight, the lights of Times Square were bright. Peep shows, strip clubs, and XXX movie theaters beckoned people in with cheap prices and illicit promises. And it was all out in the open.

On a street corner I bought five dollars' worth of Panama Red marijuana, rolled me a joint, and enjoyed that high after so many years without. "I'm out here, baby," I announced to no one and everyone passing by. Feeling good, I ducked into one of the adult movie theaters to use the restroom, but when I was about to leave, a woman came in and asked if I'd like to try her services. Ten minutes and five dollars later, I left the restroom feeling like a new man.

Now that I was satisfied, I just started walking the streets of Manhattan. I walked and roamed until the sun came up. Every so often I looked up to the sky in awe and said aloud, "I'm going to live in this city!" Once the city started to come alive, I bought myself a hot dog, smoked another joint, and decided I had to find someplace to sleep.

I'd heard about the Bowery on the Lower East Side. I knew it was an entire area where homeless people could go and get a place to sleep and maybe a free meal. So I made my way down to that part of Manhattan. But when I got there, I was shocked. There were so many homeless people all over the streets. I couldn't believe that so many people could be this down on their luck in a city like New York. Coming from Greensboro, I thought New York was the type of place where anyone could find a job and a place to live if they hustled. The level of poverty and despair I was seeing was depressing, but all I wanted to do at that point was find a place to fall asleep and forget everything.

Seeing that everyone else was doing it, I collapsed on a bench and drifted off. I couldn't sleep deeply out in the open like that, but I got enough of a nap to keep from collapsing. Once it started to get dark again, I figured I'd try to find a hotel. I had seen signs for hotels in Times Square that you could stay in for less than ten dollars a night. Even though my cash was tight, I decided to spend the money for a bed in a room with a door. I made my way back to midtown and found a hotel between 41st and 42nd Streets where I rented a room for eight dollars. That eight dollars got me a bed, but there was no heat and no place to shower. I tried to get my money back, thinking I'd find another place, but the owner refused. So I shivered my way through the night under a thin, dirty white sheet.

The next day, after my breakfast of a hot dog and a soda, I counted my cash and realized I had to find a job or I'd be down in the Bowery with the rest of the homeless people. With winter approaching, I couldn't imagine being out on the streets. The day was chilly, but the sun was shining brightly. I started heading away from Times Square, paying attention to every store and restaurant I passed, hoping to see a "Help Wanted" sign. Before I had gone more than three blocks, however, I passed by a Social Security office. I stopped walking, turned around, and strolled inside like I belonged there. I wanted to see if I could apply for a Social Security card with my new name. Of all the things I could've done less than two days after escaping from prison, showing my face to try to get a Social Security card with a fake name ranks as one of the riskiest. But I knew if it worked, I'd be able to get a real job and not just some hustle. I decided to take the chance, before I could chicken out.

When I walked into the building, I saw an older Black woman standing behind the counter, but nobody else was in there. I walked right up to the window and said, "Hello, I'd like to put in an application to get a Social Security card."

She looked at me for a minute. "How old are you?" she asked.

"I'm twenty-seven," I said.

"You've never had a job?" she asked, looking me over.

I didn't hesitate. "No, ma'am," I said.

"So you never had a Social Security card?" she said. "How did you live? Where are you from?"

"I'm from Washington, DC," I lied. "And I still lived with my parents back there in DC and I just didn't have to work."

She looked at me like she was trying to decide if I was telling the truth.

"But now I have to work," I said, trying to sound earnest. "I have to find me a job. And I need a Social Security card. Isn't that right?"

"Yes, it is," she said. "Hold on."

Then she handed me a pen and an application. I walked over to the counter in the middle of the room and filled it out, using the last address I'd had when I lived in DC. I figured when the card got there, I'd have to call Ulysses and ask him to send it to me somehow or I'd have to go down there to get it myself. I signed my name Bobby Love for the very first time.

"Oh, so you're still living in Washington, DC, Mr. Love?" the lady asked me when she looked at my application. "You want the card sent there?

"Yeah," I said. "Because I don't have an address here in New York yet, but I plan to get one."

She looked at me again, her eyes narrowed.

"Okay, Mr. Love," she said, looking down at my application. "Wait here." Then she went back to her desk. I started pacing around a bit and thinking how I would get the card from DC. Ulysses might not even live at that address anymore. I probably should have sent it to Raymond's house, but I didn't want Raymond mixed up with anything I was doing. Plus, I figured the cops were probably watching all of my siblings closely and I didn't want to tip them off.

"Mr. Love!" I turned around when I realized the lady was calling me. I wasn't used to my new name.

"Sorry," I said as I hustled back over to the window.

"Here," she said, and she pushed a brand-new Social Security card for Bobby Love across the counter to me. I was shocked.

I looked up at the woman and she was smiling a knowing smile.

"Thank you," I said, slightly in awe.

"Hey, we all need a little extra help sometimes," she said. And then she called out, "Next in line!"

Between the man giving me thirty dollars at the bus station and the lady at the Social Security office giving me a card on the spot, I felt like God was showing me that I was on the right path. By the same token, I told myself that if I got caught and sent back to prison, then that would be God's way of showing me that He didn't approve of what I was doing. This was when I really began to see that there was a greater power playing a part in my life and I had to pay attention.

I didn't get to use my Social Security card right away. For a few days I kept going back and forth to the Bowery and hitting the streets, trying to find a restaurant job. I stopped sleeping in those fleabag hotels because none of them had heat and I had discovered that sleeping on the subway trains was a lot warmer. And it was free.

About a week after arriving in the city, I was back on the Bowery early in the morning and noticed these blue flyers all around advertising jobs at a hotel in upstate New York. The flyers listed the name of one of the shelters in the area as the point of contact for more information.

I found that shelter and asked the man at the front desk about the jobs at the hotel.

"They're looking for dishwashers, housekeepers, maintenance workers, things like that," he told me.

"I could do a dishwashing gig," I said.

"Do you have any experience?" he asked.

"Yeah," I said, not daring to mention it was at a prison.

Escape

The man looked me up and down and made a decision. "I'll put you on the list. What's your name?"

"Bobby Love," I said.

"All right, Mr. Love," he said. "They're sending a bus to pick you guys up from here tonight at eight p.m. We'll provide you with a meal to take with you, but you better be here at eight or the bus leaves without you."

"I'll be here, man," I said. And I was. I was the first cat on that bus. I had eleven dollars left in my pocket.

There were about fifteen other guys on the bus with me. With traffic, we didn't arrive at the hotel until almost 10:30 p.m. Even so, the hotel manager made us sit through orientation that same night. They gave us our work schedules and showed us the boardinghouse where we'd be staying with the other staff, far away from the fancy hotel guests.

When they showed me my room, I was so happy to see a clean bed. I took my first shower since escaping, and right before I fell asleep, I thanked God for keeping watch over me.

The next morning I was put to work washing dishes. From my prison experience, I knew my way around an industrial kitchen, so nobody had any complaints about the new guy. I worked for three days straight and then I had four days off. When I wasn't working, I would get some snacks, watch television, and sleep. I went into the small town once or twice to buy myself a pair of jeans, underwear, and toiletries, but for the most part I stayed at the hotel. It felt like a good hideaway, and I didn't think anyone from the North Carolina prison system would be looking for me up there. I made sure to follow all the rules and never gave anyone cause to pay extra attention to me. I soon got into a steady routine, and working there gave me the confidence that I could work and live on the outside just fine. The only problem was, I was making far too little money to survive. Since they'd put me on the schedule to work just three days a week and they took room and board out of my check, I was only earning thirty-three dollars every two weeks. I made up my mind to stay through Christmas and then go back down to Manhattan.

I was back in New York City by the new year, 1978. I resumed my wandering around the city, sleeping on the trains and looking for another job.

One day I decided to venture down into the Financial District on Fulton Street. Right away I saw a bunch of employment agencies and I got really excited. The one with the biggest sign said, "Martinez Employment Agency." I walked right in.

"I don't have any more jobs today," a man called out before I even said anything.

"Really, man?" I said walking over to his desk. "You don't have anything?"

The man looked up. His nameplate said George Martinez. "What can you do?" he asked me.

"I can do anything in a kitchen. Bus tables, cook, wash dishes," I said, listing off all the skills I'd acquired in prison.

Mr. Martinez pulled out a clipboard and attached a few papers and then he handed me the clipboard. "Well, fill these out, then. Give me your name and everything like that. And you have to be here at eight o'clock in the morning. If I'm going to send you somewhere to bus tables for the day, you have to be here that early because the shift runs from ten a.m. to three p.m. for the lunch hour. You got that?"

"Yes, sir," I said.

"Okay. I'll see you tomorrow morning, then," he said.

The next day I was standing in front of Mr. Martinez at 8:00 a.m. with a clean white shirt and dark jeans. I remembered what my mama always said about looking presentable.

Mr. Martinez sent me to a restaurant right there in the Financial District called Guarino's. The hostess was an older white woman named Ana. She looked me over and told me what the job entailed. I had to bus the tables for the waiters, but only after the waiters gave me the signal. "We get a lot of people from the trading floor coming in so we have to be quick with no mistakes. Am I making myself clear?" she said.

"Yes, ma'am," I said.

Guarino's was a busy restaurant. They served burgers and steaks, plus some typical Italian dishes. Men in their buttoned-up suits started coming in at 11:00 a.m. and didn't stop until 2:00 p.m. At three o'clock I was done and I was sweating. I hadn't stopped moving the entire time. I'd barely had a moment to breathe, but I liked the quick pace because it made the time go by faster. Before I left, I asked Ana if I could return the next day to work again.

She gave me an encouraging smile. "You certainly did a good job today, Mr. Love. I'll call Mr. Martinez and tell him we want you back so you can come straight here."

"Thank you, Ana," I said. "I appreciate that. And I'll be here right on time tomorrow at nine a.m."

She smiled back at me. "Okay, we'll see you then."

Working at Guarino's, I'd earn twenty dollars a day, but they would take out $2.50 for Mr. Martinez. It wasn't a lot of money, but it was a start, and it was an honest dollar. Ana would arrange for the chef to make me a cheeseburger when I was done working, and she liked to chat with me while I was eating. We made small talk, but I never revealed too much about myself, especially the fact that I was homeless.

At night I would sleep in the subway station up at 181st Street in Manhattan because it was so warm in that station. Of course, the trains would wake me up as they roared through, but other than that, it was preferable to trying to find a safe place on the streets, especially during the winter.

I didn't want Ana to know my situation, but I did ask if I could work full-time for the restaurant. She denied my request because, she said, the restaurant didn't make enough money to hire full-time bus-boys.

"That's why we always get help from Martinez," Ana explained. "Otherwise, you know I'd try to help you out," she said.

That meant I would have to find another job making more money because living in the subways was not my idea of making it in the city.

The way I finally found a place to live is a funny story. Mr. Martinez sent me to another restaurant for an evening busboy position. While I was there, I met this cat who invited me back to his place in Staten Island to smoke a joint and play cards. His name was Floyd. Since I didn't need to rush back to my corner at the Washington Heights subway station, I took him up on his offer. It turned out, Floyd lived in a rooming house on Staten Island. It was nothing fancy, but I had no cause to judge. I even asked Floyd if he thought there were other rooms available once he told me he only paid twenty-five dollars a week for rent. With my salary at Guarino's I could afford that.

"Naw, this place is full," Floyd said, "but I'll ask my landlady next time I see her."

"Thanks, man," I said. "I appreciate that."

"Where you staying now?" Floyd asked.

I shrugged. "You know, here and there."

Later that night after we finished playing cards, Floyd told me he was going to go stay with his girlfriend for a few days.

"Why don't you stay here while you look for a place?" he said.

"Really, man?" I said.

"Yeah, no reason the place should be empty while you're looking," Floyd said, handing me the keys. "I'll be back on Tuesday." And he left.

Floyd didn't come back on Tuesday. Or Wednesday. Or Thursday.

I was still staying in his room when someone knocked on the door on Friday morning.

It was the landlady. "Who are you?" she said when I opened the door.

"My name is Bobby," I said.

"Where's Floyd? He owes me his rent money," she said with a sour look on her face.

"He said he was staying with his girlfriend," I told the lady.

"Well, who told you *you* could stay here?" the woman demanded.

I didn't know what to say. So I just stood there.

"Who is going to pay the rent?" she asked, her voice getting shrill. "Somebody owes me twenty-five dollars."

I went and got my wallet and pulled out twenty-five dollars from my savings. I handed it to her.

"So, you're going to stay here?" she said.

"Yeah, if I can," I said.

She sniffed. "As long as I get my twenty-five dollars every Friday."

"Not a problem," I said, smiling.

And that's how I got my first apartment in New York. I never saw Floyd again.

The weather turned warm as spring turned into summer and I was still working at Guarino's. I had proven myself to be a dependable worker, always showing up on time and never missing a single day of work.

One day after my shift was done and I was eating my burger, Ana came over to talk.

"You know the Guarino brothers supply food for the cafeteria at the Hertz corporate headquarters in midtown," she said.

"You mean Hertz the car rental company?" I asked.

"Yeah, them," Ana said. "The Guarinos have a commercial kitchen down here where they make sandwiches, and then someone drives them up to the Hertz building. They need someone to help out, but you'd have to be at the kitchen by six in the morning. Are you interested?"

I shrugged. "How much do they pay?" I asked.

"They'll pay you a hundred and fifty dollars a week, off the books."

I smiled. "I'm there. Just tell me where I need to be."

From making sandwiches, I eventually ended up working at the Hertz cafeteria. Just like at Guarino's, I was busing tables, emptying the garbage, and cleaning. I was still living in my room out on Staten Island, which meant I had to take the Staten Island Ferry and then catch a subway to get to work. But I was never late, not a single day. Between my two jobs I was making $175 a week, still off the books, and able to save a good deal of money in just the few months I had been working there. Which was why I said no when a woman from the human resources department at Hertz came to offer me a job with the company.

Apparently this woman had been watching me for a while and had spoken to my supervisor, Doug, who confirmed that I was a conscientious worker.

"Would you like a better job?" she asked me after introducing herself one day when my shift was over. Her name was Mrs. Pearson.

"Excuse me?" I said.

"Mr. Love, we have an opening down in our warehouse, and after speaking with Doug, I think you might be a good fit," she said.

"Is that so?"

"Have you ever done mailings or worked in shipping and receiving?" she asked me.

I shook my head. "No, not really."

"Well, would you like to come down to see our warehouse?" she said. "We would train you for the job."

"No, thank you," I said as politely as I could. "I'm not interested."

She gave me a polite smile, said okay, and left and went back to her office.

I did appreciate the offer, and I was pleased that people thought I was a good worker, but I was afraid of what could happen if I applied for a corporate job. First, I'd have to fill out an application. And I knew they would investigate everything I put on there. How would I account for the six years I was in prison? I didn't want all that worry. I was perfectly happy staying where I was, working in the cafeteria and getting paid off the books.

But Mrs. Pearson was persistent. She came back the next day.

She started telling me more information about the job.

"You'll have very good benefits, and you will get paid every two weeks," she said. "And, Mr. Love, you'll make more money than you're making here. I guarantee it."

"Thank you," I said again. "But I'm not interested."

She just smiled and said "Okay," but I could tell she wasn't done with me.

When she left, my boss, Doug, came over to me.

"Hey, Bobby, can I talk to you?" he started.

Oh boy, I thought. *Now he's going to try to convince me to take the job.* And sure enough, that's what he did.

"Listen, Bobby, Mrs. Pearson really wants to give you this job," he said. "It's not a hard job. You'd be working in the shipping department. They've got a big warehouse down there on Twenty-seventh Street on the West Side."

I didn't say anything. Doug kept talking.

"It'd be a good look for you," he said. "You know, you're going to get benefits, and one day if you have a family, you're going to need that. You should take it, Bobby."

I shook my head. Here I was, finally able to make a decent living, nobody was searching for me, and these people wanted me to risk it all.

Doug gave it one more shot. "Listen, Mrs. Pearson asked me if you could come down there on Monday, just to check things out. I told her I could get someone to cover for you Monday, if you want to do it."

I wanted to tell Doug and Mrs. Pearson to leave me alone, but I could see they were just going to keep asking me. So I agreed to go check out the warehouse on Monday.

Doug clapped me on the back. "Good for you, Bobby," he said, beaming. "You don't want to pass up a good opportunity when it comes your way."

On Monday I showed up at the warehouse, and Mrs. Pearson and another man were waiting for me. They gave me a tour of their facility and showed me where I'd be working and what I'd be doing. I stayed there the whole day observing and shadowing some of the other guys. Like Doug said, it seemed like easy work.

At the end of the day, Mrs. Pearson came to collect me and looked at me expectantly.

"So, Mr. Love, have we convinced you to take the job?"

"I need to think about it," I said.

She frowned. "Mr. Love, we need to have your answer before the end of the week. We have placed an ad in the newspaper and need to start interviewing other people for the position if you're not going to take it."

"Okay," I said, unwilling to allow her to force me to make a decision I would later regret. "I'll let you know." And then I left. All the way home on the bus, subway, and ferry, I tried to decide what to do. They were giving me this job. All I had to do was show up. But the fear of being found out and getting sent back to prison prevented me from making that call. In my mind, I was tormented with images of Mrs. Pearson looking into my background and finding out that Bobby Love didn't exist.

But by Thursday morning, I'd started thinking differently. I reminded myself that I was the guy with the big imagination who didn't make moves based on fear. When there was a good opportunity, I went with it. This job offer was a good opportunity—and it was all aboveboard. Plus, I had to admit a few hard truths to myself. I didn't want to bus tables for the rest of my life. No woman wanted to go out with a busboy, as I had recently discovered when trying to talk to some of the ladies at Hertz. And I knew there was no real way to get ahead working a job under the table.

I called Mrs. Pearson on Friday and told her I'd take the job. When I had to fill out the paperwork, I just left certain things blank and prayed that it wouldn't matter. Under "previous employment," the only thing I wrote, other than my current position in the Hertz cafeteria, was my work at Guarino's. I started at the warehouse the following Monday.

Once I was working at Hertz, I began to feel like my life was truly falling into place. I was feeling better than I had ever felt in my life. I now had enough money to live like a responsible adult. I bought myself some decent clothes, and some new sheets and towels for my room in Staten Island. I could afford to start enjoying all that New York had to offer a young man looking to sow his wild oats before settling down to start a family. I'd go up to Harlem on the weekends, where I became a regular fixture at the clubs. I easily met women and liked taking them out and showing them a good time.

Meanwhile, I was still working at Guarino's occasionally, filling in a shift here and there. During one of those shifts, I saw Ana for the first time in a long while. She told me I looked like life was treating me well.

"Thanks, Ana," I said, happy to see her again.

"How about we go out for a drink after your shift?" Ana asked me.

"Okay," I said, giving her a sly grin. Ana had always kept things professional, but she was being kind of flirtatious. I wondered if having a steady job suddenly made me more attractive to her.

Later over drinks, I told Ana how well things were going at Hertz. "They're sending me to Xerox school, because they want to move me out of shipping."

"Are they?" Ana said. "They must really like what you're doing."

I shrugged. "I guess so. They're going to have me working up in their main building on Madison Avenue. I'm going to be doing all the copying and stuff up there."

Ana drained her drink. "Good for you, Bobby Love. I knew from the minute I laid eyes on you, you were going to do well here in New York. I could just tell."

"Really, you thought that?" I said. "How'd you know?"

"I could just tell you were something special," she said, looking me in the eye. "I mean, you're a good-looking man. You're hardworking. You're the whole package."

Ana was Italian, at least five years older than me, but now there was no doubt that she was flirting with me.

By the end of the evening, Ana had really inflated my ego and made me feel like I could do anything I wanted to do in New York. I had been feeling the same way lately, but the fact that Ana was saying it too gave me an extra shot of confidence. I don't know why I did it, but I shared with her one of my secret dreams.

"Ana, I want to be a model," I said, telling her all about how much I loved fashion and how, when I was little, reading *Jet* magazines with my sister, I had dreams of walking the runway for some big-time designer, traveling and seeing the world. I knew that's how the actor Richard Roundtree, who played Shaft, got his start, and I wanted to do the same.

"So, go for it." Ana smiled at me. "What are you waiting for?"

I don't know if it was the buzz from the beer, or the fact that this attractive older white woman was telling me I had what it took to be a model, but I decided that I was going to do it.

Two days later I signed up at the Barbizon modeling school. I'd seen commercials for them all the time on TV. It was a serious money investment, but I looked at it as investing in myself. I would go to class in the evenings during the week and then for four hours on Saturdays. I really started to feel myself, once I got my portfolio put together. I was literally living my dream. But then my fears of being discovered caught up with me. I was enjoying my life so much, I forgot I was a wanted man. If I became a successful model, my pictures would be everywhere, and I'd surely get caught. The thought was sobering and put a damper on my dreams, but I still finished the course and actually booked a few local modeling gigs. That was as close as I got to being the next Richard Roundtree.

As time went on, I stopped worrying so much about getting caught, but God always found a way to remind me to stay alert.

I had gone on a few dates with this pretty woman I'd met while out clubbing in Harlem. Her name was Denise. She had cinnamon-brown skin, long legs, and she wore her hair in a bob, like a lot of women were wearing in the early 1980s. The relationship hadn't gone beyond a couple of dates, and I'd done nothing more than kiss her on the cheek, but one night after leaving a club we were sitting in her car. I was hoping she was going to invite me over to her apartment. But she was hesitating.

"What's the matter, Denise?" I asked, as I slid over closer to her in the front seat.

"Don't push up on me, Bobby Love," she said in a way that made me move back and give her a look.

"I thought we were cool," I said. "Did I do something to offend you?"

"No, you didn't do anything," she said, real matter-of-fact.

"So what's the problem, then?" I asked with a smile.

"The problem is I put your name into my system to check you out, and nothing comes up but your driver's license."

My heart started to race. "What do you mean you put my name in your system?"

"I just wanted to find out if you were hiding anything."

"I thought you said you were a teacher," I said.

"Bobby, I work for the FBI," she admitted.

I felt the contents of my stomach rise to my throat. I had gotten a New York State driver's license, but I'd had to pay a guy at the DMV to overlook my suspicious-looking birth certificate, which I had forged to read "Bobby Love." If Denise found out about that, then she would definitely find out about my past.

"Really?" I said, trying to appear unfazed by her admission.

"Yeah," she said. "A lot of guys get intimidated when I tell them I'm an FBI agent, so I don't always share that right off. Are you okay with it?"

"Yeah, I'm good," I said, playing it cool, even though I wanted nothing more than to get out of that car and as far away from Denise as possible. If she hadn't found out anything about my past yet, it would only be a matter of time.

"Well, okay, then. I gotta get home because we're working on a big case," Denise said.

I didn't need to hear another word. I opened the door of the car and said my goodbyes, promising to call her in a few days. I had to force myself to walk away from her car instead of run, which is what I really wanted to do. Needless to say, I never called Denise again and stayed away from the club where we'd first met.

Another time, not too long after fleeing from Denise, I was walking down Eighth Avenue with a co-worker from Hertz. As usual, there were throngs of people on the sidewalk. But I noticed a guy walking toward me who looked familiar. Almost like someone I'd gone to school with in Greensboro. Sure enough, as we got closer, he yelled out, "Cotton Foot!"

It was Morris Carter. He was a grade behind me in school and we played basketball together sometimes. He looked the same except he was wearing a uniform and was carrying a bunch of packages.

I swallowed the lump of fear in my throat and prayed he wouldn't say anything about prison or use my real name in front of my co-worker.

"How's it going, man?" I asked Morris when we were standing face-to-face.

"Good, man," he said, smiling. "I can't believe we're bumping into each other like this, though, in New York!"

"Yeah, it's crazy, man," I said, trying not to lose my cool. "You good?"

"I'm surviving," he said, nodding toward the load of packages he was carrying.

An awkward silence followed because I was trying not to hold a conversation with my past. Morris got the hint. "I gotta run, man, but it was so good seeing you," he said. "Let's catch up, Cotton Foot."

"Yeah," I said. "Let's do that."

After he was out of earshot, my co-worker turned to me. "Why'd he call you Cotton Foot?"

I was so relieved that that was the only question he had, I told him the whole story about the rusty nail, the copper penny, and the fatback that cured me.

Then there was the time I was hanging around 42nd Street. It was a Friday night and the peep shows, strip clubs, and movie theaters were in full swing. Tourists and locals alike were all around the area, taking in the spectacle. Bright colorful lights bathed the whole scene in an unnatural neon glow. I was enjoying myself. I was still high after smoking a joint and was trying to decide what show I might want to see. As I stood in front of this one theater, a white man with red hair bumped into me. Right away I pegged him as a tourist because he had an orange backpack on, and he was obviously intoxicated.

I didn't think anything about it, but then he bumped into me again, stumbling to the point where he almost fell over. I righted him up and asked, "Are you okay, man?"

He mumbled something in return and continued to wobble around the area. I ignored him and went back to reading the sign in front of the theater to see what this show had to offer. And then once again, the guy with the red hair came stumbling back my way. I didn't know what he was trying to do or who he was with, but he came closer and closer to me, seemingly so drunk he could barely stand up straight. When he got right up close to me, he turned his back to me and I saw that he had a bunch of twenty-dollar bills sticking out of his backpack. Someone was going to steal them if he wasn't careful, and I yelled at him that he should close his pack.

"Yo, man, somebody's going to take your money!" I said to him, right before he crashed into me again, this time almost knocking me over. I was annoyed, but I helped him up one more time. The thief in me couldn't help but reach for a few of those twenties as I did so. As soon as I started to put the bills in my pocket I heard, "Police, stop! Put your hands up!"

The two twenties in my hand fluttered to the ground as I raised my hands above my head and I had to bite my lip to keep from crying. Had I just ruined everything for forty bucks? A police officer came out of nowhere and slapped a pair of handcuffs on me and then led me to a waiting police car across the street. Rather than whip me off to the police station, the cops left me sitting there while they pulled this same sting operation on some other dummies like me. That little red-haired tourist was actually an undercover cop. The police apparently did this regularly to fill their quotas of arrests for the night.

I spent the night in jail but I didn't sleep a wink. Instead, I paced my cell nonstop, waiting for my time in front of a judge. I got to meet with a lawyer first and I told him what had happened. He found the whole thing ridiculous and told me that he would try to get me a light sentence. I was devastated, angry with myself, and a nervous wreck. Bobby Love could not do time.

When we entered the courtroom, the judge asked the lawyer to explain my crime. When the judge heard what happened, he asked the arresting officer to approach the bench with my lawyer.

"Is the lawyer's version of events true?" the judge asked. "Your guy bumped into Mr. Love three times, and the first two times he tried to help him and the last time he took the money that was falling out of the backpack?"

The officer looked sheepish but he answered clearly, "Yes, sir, that's pretty much how it happened."

The judge rolled his eyes and shook his head like he couldn't believe he had to listen to such a stupid case.

"Mr. Love," he addressed me directly. "You're free to go."

"Really?" I said.

The judge looked at me. "You wanna stay here longer?"

"No, sir," I said, grinning.

The tension in my shoulders eased. I released the breath I'd been holding. I wanted to jump and shout, but I just thanked the judge and waited for the bailiff to escort me out of the courtroom.

Once I hit the cool air of the New York morning, I let out a little whoop and then I thanked God, over and over, my entire journey back to Staten Island. I knew what I had just experienced was God's grace. It couldn't have been anything else. I did not want to squander the second, and now third, chances I'd had at living freely. These brushes with my past made me realize I had to remain ever vigilant. And I knew that I had to suppress completely, once and for all, the thief in me. I didn't beat myself up about what I'd done. I just told myself that I had to do better. And as with everything else I had accomplished in my life, I knew I could do it if I put my mind to it. I knew I could leave Walter Miller in the past and build the future I wanted for myself, as Bobby Love.

chapter seven

Our Love Story

CHERYL

"You've been through a lot, Cheryl, but you deserve to be happy. You're young and you have your whole life ahead of you. Yes, you lost the baby, but life will go on. You'll go on, Cheryl. You're only nineteen years old."

I was talking to myself in the mirror. I was still mourning the loss of the baby I carried for almost five months. My blood pressure had spiked to dangerous levels and the baby died. And I was still heartbroken over my ex-boyfriend Deon. I really thought we were going to be together forever.

But I knew it was time to move forward with my life. I kept going to the library, just like Mommy used to, to take out self-help books so I could figure out how to better myself and reclaim my life.

My friend Deena told me I should start exercising to feel better, so I turned on Richard Simmons every morning and worked out before I ate breakfast. And it was working. I was feeling a little better every day. I tried not to think about the past, and instead I started thinking about the future, about what I wanted. What would make *me* happy? I told myself I was done thinking about boys and relationships, and instead I was just going to focus on being the best person I could be.

Because I had thought I was going to be a single parent, I'd dropped out of community college, thinking I should focus full-time on getting a job and saving money. Now I wanted to go back to school, but I felt bad asking Daddy for the money. I decided I should start acting like an adult and get a real job and make my own money, like Deena. I couldn't just sit at home and keep taking care of my brothers.

Once I made up my mind that I was going to find a real job, I hit the streets and started looking. Initially, the only opportunities I could find were retail jobs — first at a clothing store and then at a grocery store. I worked a few weeks at both places, but neither job lasted very long. The clothing store went out of business, and the grocery store manager fired me so he could hire a relative. I kept looking.

One day my godfather's wife, Mrs. Thompson, caught me in the elevator of our apartment building.

"How are you doing, Cheryl?" she asked. "What are you up to? Are you still in school?"

"I'm hoping to go back to school," I said. "But I need to get some money saved first, so I'm trying to find a job."

"Well, I can ask down at the hospital if they're hiring. They always need people."

"Thank you, Mrs. Thompson," I said, smiling, as the elevator reached her floor and she walked out.

"Don't thank me yet," she said. "Let's see what they say."

The next day Mrs. Thompson knocked on our apartment door. She barely waited for me to open it before she announced, "I got you an interview at the hospital!"

"You did?" I practically shouted.

"Yes I did," she said, beaming. "You gotta go over there Monday at two p.m. and ask for Ms. Carrington. She's real strict, but you'll do fine. She knows me and I put in a good word for you."

"Oh, thank you, Mrs. Thompson!" I said, wrapping my arms around her in a grateful hug.

She patted me on the back. "You're welcome, Cheryl. I know you're going to make me proud."

The Baptist Medical Center sat right behind the Pink Houses. The name had changed, but it was the hospital I was born in and the hospital my mother died in. It only took me ten minutes to walk there from our apartment, so I was right on time for my interview on Monday afternoon.

I was told to wait in the little waiting room outside Ms. Carrington's office, so I sat down and tried not to sweat through my extra layers of deodorant. I had on a denim skirt that went below my knees and a pink blouse. I thought I looked responsible and professional.

I only had to wait for about five minutes before Ms. Carrington called me into her office. I sat in the chair across from her desk and found myself sitting up straight and praying I wouldn't say the wrong thing in front of this woman. Even though she was Black and seemed to be about the same age as my father, there was nothing soft or familiar about Ms. Carrington. Her mostly gray hair was pulled into a severe bun at the back of her head, and she never cracked a smile the whole time I sat in her office.

Ms. Carrington shuffled through some papers and then said, "I hear you want to work here?"

I cleared my throat before answering. "Yes, ma'am," I said. "I heard there was an opening in the kitchen."

"Yes. We're hiring a new dietary aide. Have you ever done this type of work before?"

"No," I said, hoping this wasn't going to be the end of the interview.

"Well, how do you know you're going to be able to do the job then, Ms. Williams?"

I tried to think of something to say that could make up for the fact that, one, I had never been a dietary aide, and two, I didn't even know what a dietary aide did. But I ended up just telling the truth. "Well,"

I said, earnestly, "I pick up things really quickly, and I'll watch and learn what needs to be done."

Ms. Carrington didn't look up, but she made some noises that sounded like she approved of what I said. I watched as she wrote some things down on her paper and then she stood up and walked to the door. "Someone will get back with you soon, okay?" she said.

"All right," I said. It was such a short interview I figured there was no way I was going to get the job.

As I walked back home, I tried not to let my disappointment get the best of me. *There are always other jobs, Cheryl,* I told myself. That night Mrs. Thompson popped up to our apartment to see how the interview went. I told her what happened and she laughed at my discouraged tone.

"You're going to get the job, Cheryl. Ms. Carrington is just like that. She thinks she's still in the military and she doesn't know the meaning of the word 'smile.'"

I had to chuckle at that because that woman did seem so serious. But I wasn't so confident that I was going to get the job.

Every day for the rest of the week, Mrs. Thompson would come to assure me that I was going to get the job. And every day I'd stare at the phone, waiting for it to ring. It finally did on Friday afternoon. Ms. Carrington called me herself to tell me that I got the job.

"You start on Monday. Your shift begins at four p.m., but you better get here at three thirty so we can get you your uniform and your physical taken care of."

"Yes, ma'am," I said. "And thank you, Ms. Carrington," I added.

"No need to thank me," she said. "Just show up on time and do your work."

Once I got my white coat, plastic gloves, and hairnet, I was taken into the kitchen. The Baptist Medical Center consisted of both a hospital and a nursing home, and the kitchen churned out food for both facilities. Needless to say, it was a huge, bustling operation, and the

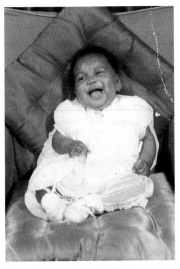

Cheryl as a newborn in 1963.

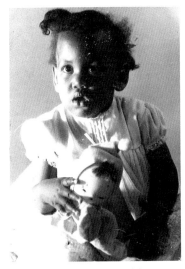

Cheryl at age two, ready to take on the world.

Bobby, at right, age one, with his sister Jean (standing) and a cousin.

Bobby, age three, on the right again, with two cousins.

Cheryl, age fourteen, talking on the phone, probably to one of her besties, Carla or Deena.

Bobby's eighth-grade school photo from Gillespie Park Junior High School.

Bobby with an Afro, age fifteen, at Morrison Training School (for juveniles) when his older brother Raymond and sister Jean visited, along with two nephews.

Cheryl graduating from Columbia High School in Decatur, Georgia, in 1981. She needed a small break from Brooklyn.

Bobby and Cheryl were a beautiful young couple, with eyes only for each other. Cheryl was pregnant with their first child here.

The Loves love dressing to impress. Especially at church. This was Easter Sunday in 1985.

Bobby happily greeting his wife . . .

. . . and the two of them grinning broadly afterwards.

Cheryl was really excited that some of her best girlfriends could attend her wedding celebration in the community room at the Pink Houses, where she grew up. Among the group is Cheryl's beloved godmother, Katherine (directly behind her), and two godsisters, Anna (far right) and Muriel (third from left).

Bobby played it cool at the wedding with his groomsmen. But he was thrilled.

Cheryl's father gives her away. She was happy that he approved of the union.

After the wedding, the Loves were ready to begin the next phase of their life together.

Their first child — a daughter, Jasmine — was just a few weeks old here.

Then came Jessica. Here is Cheryl with Jasmine, age five, and Jessica, age three.

Sisters Jasmine and Jessica have always been close. Oh, how they begged for a little brother!

The Love family was four strong for a while.

The girls were Bobby and Cheryl's entire world.

Bobby was so proud to be able to take the girls to Disney World and fulfill every kid's dream.

News of two more babies was a surprise but a blessing. Bobby and Cheryl enjoyed celebrating their expanding family.

Jordan and Justin's arrival finally gave their big sisters what they had been asking for. And Bobby was more excited to have sons than he anticipated.

Finally, their family of six was complete.

Jordan and Justin, at eleven years old, really enjoyed the beach and were doted on by the whole family.

And the girls are doing well. Cheryl was so proud when Jasmine graduated from junior high school.

The Loves.

sounds of clanking pots and pans and people laughing and talking assaulted my ears when I first walked in the room. I saw mostly Black and Latino men and women working. The women were doing food prep and the men did the dishwashing and heavy lifting.

My job as a dietary aide was to assemble the meal trays according to the color-coded system. Yellow meant a diabetic meal, so those trays got the low-sugar foods. Blue meant high blood pressure, so that meant a low-salt meal. Green was for a liquid diet. Sometimes there was a special request for a cold plate with just a salad or a cold sandwich. Once a tray was complete, I would add it to the wagons that would be wheeled up to the patients' floor, where I would be responsible for distributing the meals to the patients. I had to announce myself to the patients and simply leave the food, but as I got more comfortable with the job, I would sometimes talk to the patients and maybe try to cheer them up.

It didn't take me very long to learn how to be a good dietary aide. And pretty soon, the faces in the kitchen started to look familiar too. It turned out many of the people who worked there also lived in the Pink Houses. Even though I wasn't a nurse, I began to feel like I was living the life I was supposed to be living. I was helping people, I liked the people I worked with — even though most of them were much older than me — and I loved having money in my pocket.

Initially I worked the afternoon shift, from 4:00 to 8:00 p.m. Soon they offered me some eight-hour weekend shifts as well. I was happy to take them. With my new income, I opened my first bank account, and I could contribute to our household needs as well. Even though Daddy continued to give me money to buy the groceries, I used some of my own money too. And I always made sure to give my brothers Don and Scott some money if I didn't make dinner so they could get something to eat. By the time I turned twenty, I could honestly say I loved the way my life looked.

Since I didn't start work until 4:00 p.m., during the daytime I could go shoe shopping — my favorite pastime — or hang out with my friend Carla, who was in college and often had free time during the day. I'd get dinner ready or do the grocery shopping, and I'd still have time to watch my favorite story, *General Hospital,* before walking over to Baptist Medical.

One day when I came in to work, I heard a man singing over by the dishwashers who was so loud I could hear him warbling over the usual riot of noises.

"Who is that?" I asked my friend Janet as I pulled on my gloves and got ready to get to work.

"Oh, that's a new guy," Janet said. "His name is Bobby."

"Well, Bobby sure is loud," I said, peering through the dish rack to see who this tall, dark drink of water thought he was. All I could see was that he had deep-chocolate-colored skin, which contrasted nicely with his white dishwasher's uniform. And I noticed he wore his cap sideways so it looked like a little sailboat atop his head. *Clearly this man likes attention,* I thought, and then I promptly forgot about him.

A couple of weeks later, I was up on the patients' floor delivering trays when I entered a man's room to bring him his dinner. He was an older white man, and I was supposed to give him a low-salt meal. I grabbed the tray with the blue sticker and came into the room with my usual smile and greeting.

"Hello, my name is Cheryl and I have your dinner here. Would you like to eat it now or shall I just leave it for you for later?"

The man mumbled something, but I wasn't clear what he said, so I asked him to repeat himself.

He turned over in his bed and looked at me and bellowed, "I said, you dumb bitch, that I don't want any of that nasty slop you call food! Get it out of here and you get out of here!"

Just then the loud guy from the kitchen stuck his head in the room.

"Hey, what's going on in here? I heard all this yelling in the hall-way."

The man in the bed was now sitting up and he was pointing at me. "I told this bitch to get this food out of my face. I don't want it."

By this time I was too afraid to go near the man and retrieve the tray.

Bobby wasn't afraid though. He told me I could leave, which I was grateful for. I scampered out of the room but hovered in the doorway to see what was going to happen.

Bobby grabbed the tray from the man's table and then said, "You don't ever talk to that woman again, you hear me? She was just doing her job. If you don't like the food, you don't have to eat it. But don't take it out on the women who are here to serve you."

And then he stomped out of the room.

"Thank you," I said. "You didn't have to do that."

Bobby shrugged. "Someone needs to teach these guys some manners," he said.

Later, when I told my friends down in the kitchen what happened and what Bobby had done, they looked impressed.

But then Janet asked, "What room was that?"

I told her and watched her eyes grow wide. "Oh, Cheryl, that man in there is one of those mafia guys."

"Oh no! Really?" I moaned. It was a known fact that Baptist Medical was the preferred hospital for New York City's mafia. We would get gunshot victims in the hospital who would be treated, but there would be no records of them ever having been there. I had heard plenty of rumors, but it had never affected my work. Until now. I suddenly felt very guilty about what I had gotten this Bobby character involved in. I was so scared for him that I went home that night and prayed. I sat on my father's bed with the Bible next to me, saying, "Lord, please let that man Bobby be okay. Please keep him safe, Lord. Don't let the mafia get him for taking up for me like that."

That night I didn't sleep well. And I couldn't calm down until I got to work the next day and saw Bobby, looking sharp as ever in his crisp white uniform, seeming unbothered. I went right up to him and thanked him again for what he had done. And then I asked if he knew that that guy was mixed up with the mafia.

"I ain't worried about that guy," he said to me. "Besides, he's gone. They discharged him this morning."

I felt some relief at that. "Thank goodness," I said aloud, but inside I was thinking, *This guy must be really brave or really stupid.*

After that I started paying more attention to Bobby. He was always in the center of everything, telling stories and making people laugh. I liked being around when he was telling jokes at the lunch table where we would all sit on break. He seemed much older than me, so I wasn't thinking of him in a romantic way, just as another coworker who was fun to be around.

One day as I was coming back from the city from another shoe-shopping expedition, I heard a voice calling me as I exited the subway near the Pink Houses.

"Hey, Cheryl, wait up!"

I turned to find out who was calling me, and it was Bobby Love from work.

I don't know why, but I checked my outfit to make I sure I was looking cute, because this was the first time Bobby was seeing me outside of my uniform and hairnet.

I was wearing yellow shorts that showed off my legs and a hot-pink shirt. I knew I looked pretty good. And I could tell when Bobby caught up with me that he appreciated what he saw. But he didn't say anything about how I was looking. He just asked if he could walk with me. I said yes.

"Are you going to work?" I asked him.

"Yeah," he said. "I think I was on your train."

"Oh, I was in the city just doing some shopping," I said, holding up my bag from the shoe store. "Do you live in the city?"

"Yeah, I live up in Harlem," Bobby said. "I just moved up there not too long ago."

It was a short walk from the train to the Pink Houses, but it was enough time for Bobby to tell me that he had recently taken a test at work and was being promoted from dishwasher to cook. And that they were sending him to cooking school in the evenings.

"That's great," I said. "Do you like to cook?"

"I do," Bobby said. "My mother was a great cook."

"Mine was too," I said wistfully, always amazed that even after all this time, talking about Mommy could still bring a lump to my throat.

"Did your mother pass?" Bobby asked.

"Yeah," I said. "When I was nine."

"My mother died too," Bobby said. He didn't elaborate. I didn't ask for details.

And for a little while, we walked in silence.

"Well, this is where I go in," I said to Bobby.

"Okay," Bobby said. "I'll see you at work in a little while."

"Okay," I said, smiling. "See you then."

Something shifted between Bobby and me after that. I noticed him noticing me. And I made excuses to linger even when my shift was over if Bobby was still working. A few weeks after that, Bobby asked me out on a date. Even though we'd been kind of checking each other out, I wasn't sure Bobby Love was really my type. For starters, he was twelve years older than me, and he seemed really worldly and extroverted. I didn't know if I could keep up with someone like him. Also, I didn't want to date somebody I worked with. I turned down the date.

But he asked me again. He wanted to take me to see this hot new movie that everybody was talking about that Prince was in called *Pur-*

ple Rain. I loved Prince, and a movie seemed innocent enough. I said okay.

The night of our date, I tried to find the most mature outfit I could put together. I chose a purple dress that highlighted my cleavage, since I thought that was definitely my best asset. I put on some strappy high-heeled shoes, and I was ready to go. When Bobby picked me up, we took the subway into the city and we talked the whole way there. He was so easy to talk to, I found myself sharing my whole life story. I told him about my plans to be a nurse and my secret fantasies to be an actress.

"My dad and I always used to watch Carol Burnett together," I told him. "And I'd love to be a comedian like her on TV or on Broadway."

Bobby smiled but didn't laugh at me. He told me that he could tell I could do whatever I put my mind to. We were talking so much we almost missed our stop.

The movie was great, but I was looking forward to just having the time to talk to Bobby some more. Going out with him was far more satisfying than going out with the boys my age. Bobby really listened to me and asked me questions and gave me advice on the things I was struggling with. I even told him about my miscarriage and how scared I had been when it happened. He just listened and told me he was sure I'd have healthy kids someday.

By the time we got back to the Pink Houses, Bobby insisted he was going to accompany me all the way up to my apartment. But he didn't try to get fresh with me.

"I just wanted to make sure you got home safe," he said at my door. And then he kissed me on my cheek and went home to Harlem.

The next day at work, I was sure everyone was going to be able to tell that Bobby and I had gone out on a date. Unlike Bobby, I wasn't trying to be the center of attention, and I certainly didn't want my co-workers to know my business. As far as I was concerned, my romantic life was not something anyone should know about at work. So

I didn't say anything to my friends at work about the date, and Bobby didn't either.

But we continued to see each other.

I enjoyed our time together and felt like I was always learning something new with him. Bobby seemed to know something about everything. He read the newspaper every day, and I started to do the same thing so I would have something to say about the day's events which he always had an opinion on. We went to the movies and concerts, and sometimes we just walked around the city, checking out different neighborhoods and shopping at all of the little boutiques. Bobby loved looking good and he had a real eye for fashion. He liked to buy me clothes and jewelry as gifts. At first I was surprised that a man could pick out women's clothes so well, but everything he bought me — a leather skirt, a pair of earrings — was perfect.

The only thing that bothered me about Bobby was that he never wanted to spend time at his place in Harlem. He told me it was because he was embarrassed about the little room he rented from another guy, and he barely had any furniture due to the fact that he'd been robbed when he lived up in the Bronx.

Even though Bobby had given me no reason to believe he was lying — I had seen his place once or twice and it was kind of sparse — I kept thinking maybe he was keeping another girl up there and he just didn't want me to know. I was still cautious after my previous experience with Deon.

So one Sunday afternoon I just showed up at his apartment without telling him I was coming. Rather than catching him in the act of I don't know what, all I found was Bobby ironing his uniforms for work the next day. It was exactly what he'd told me he'd be doing.

I felt so ashamed for not believing Bobby, but I also felt relieved that I hadn't found what I dreaded. After that, I really let myself start falling in love with him. I realized that Bobby Love didn't lie and that was everything to me. If he said he was going to do something, he was going to do it. I knew I could trust him. He even came down from Harlem one Sunday morning and went to church with Daddy, my brothers, and me. Afterwards, he treated my whole family to dinner. Although Daddy was worried at first because Bobby was so much older than me, after that he gave our relationship his stamp of approval.

Bobby and I had been dating for only a few months when I realized I was pregnant. I was angry with myself for allowing this to happen again. Considering this was the second time I'd been in this situation, I was afraid to tell my father. And even though Bobby and I were definitely together, I didn't know what he would do when I told him a baby was coming. My expectation was that he would dump me and I'd be on my own taking care of the child. It wasn't what I'd hoped or planned for, but I'd seen enough girls in the Pink Houses raising their children alone. I already had a job, so I knew I'd be able to handle things. And even though I knew my father would be so disappointed in me, I also knew he'd never kick me out of the apartment. I'd always have a place to live.

Still, the fear I felt on the day I decided to tell Bobby the news was so heavy on my heart, I almost couldn't bear it. But I couldn't delay things another moment. I waited until there were few people around the kitchen that day at work, and I asked Bobby if we could talk in private. We slipped down to the break room, and I started to cry before I could even get one word out.

"What's wrong, Cheryl?" Bobby said, his voice laced with concern.

"Bobby, I'm pregnant," I said through my tears.

Bobby didn't say anything. and I was afraid to look up to see what emotion I might read on his face.

"Why are you crying?" Bobby said quietly.

"Because this wasn't supposed to happen," I said. "But if you want to break up, just say it now. I'll be okay." I tried to put on a brave face, even though the tears continued to fall. But I meant what I said. I would figure out how to take care of this baby with or without Bobby.

"Cheryl," Bobby said, lifting my chin so I would look him in the eye. "I'm not going to break up with you."

"You're not?" I said.

"No," he said. "We'll figure something out. Together."

"Really?" I said.

"Yeah, really," he said. "Now clean yourself up or else everybody's going to know something's going on between us. And with you boo-hooing like this, they're going to think I did something to you."

I laughed at that, because he was absolutely right. I went into the bathroom and splashed cold water on my face.

I looked in the mirror and tried to give myself another pep talk.

"You're going to be okay, Cheryl. You're going to be okay."

BOBBY

When Cheryl told me she was pregnant, I was surprised but not shocked. I knew how babies were made. Still, it wasn't something I was prepared for. I really liked Cheryl and I could tell she was the type of woman who I'd want to be with long-term. She was kind and sweet and she took good care of her family. I liked the fact that she went to church, and obviously she had a strong moral character. She was really different from the girls I was used to hanging out with from the clubs. Cheryl knew how to go out and have fun, but she wasn't getting drunk, smoking, or popping pills like a lot of other women I saw. She seemed pure to me, and everything in my soul told me I should be trying to protect this woman and keep her safe.

When I went home that night after she told me, I took stock of my situation. According to my own life plan, I was a few years late on my married-by-thirty goal. Even though I hadn't officially announced to anyone that I was off the market, since I'd been seeing Cheryl, I hadn't been with anyone else and hadn't wanted to be either. I knew what I felt in my heart, but I wasn't sure if I could trust those feelings. I really wanted to talk this over with someone I trusted, and the first person who came to mind was my sister Jean.

I had waited nearly four years after escaping from prison before I called Jean and let her know that I was okay. I was too afraid that her phones might be tapped or that the cops would be monitoring her home. I was afraid I might mess up and say something that would give away that I was living in New York.

When I finally did call, she was so relieved to hear my voice, I felt bad for causing her so much grief. But she didn't yell at me. Her main concern was that I was safe. I kept the call short because I was still nervous, but Jean told me that nobody had called her or asked about me since 1978. "Nobody around here is thinking about you, Buddy," she told me in a way that only a big sister could. After talking to Jean, I called my brother Raymond. He too wanted to make sure I was safe and that I wasn't doing anything that would get me in trouble. "I'm good, Raymond," I told him. "I'm doing good."

As time passed, I'd call Jean on a semi-regular basis just to check in. But now I decided to call her because I needed her to tell me what to do about Cheryl.

"Jean, my girlfriend is going to have a baby," I told her after we said our hellos.

"Are you sure it's your baby?" Jean asked.

"Damn, Jean," I said. "Of course I'm sure. Cheryl's not like that."

"Calm down, Buddy," Jean said. "I don't know what kind of girl you've found up there in New York. Where did you meet her?"

Jean was suspicious of anything and everything in New York. She firmly believed that nothing good could ever prosper in a city as crowded and dirty as New York. Apparently that included the people.

"Cheryl is good people," I assured my sister. "We work together at the hospital. She works in the kitchen as a dietary aide."

"So what are you going to do?" Jean asked me.

"That's what I'm calling you for," I said, getting exasperated. "I want to know what you think."

"Buddy," Jean said, sighing. "You've always done whatever you've wanted to do no matter what anybody tells you. So I don't know why you're asking me what you should do."

"I just wanted to hear what you had to say," I said.

"Look, Buddy, all I'm going to tell you is that if the child is yours, you have to do the right thing and take care of it. Whatever happens between you and the girl is your business, but that child is already family."

After I hung up with Jean, I started to think about what she'd said. "That child is already family." It was my responsibility to take care of my family. Of my child. Just thinking about it that way actually made me excited. I loved kids and always wanted my own. Even when I was back in junior high school in Greensboro, I'd take my niece and nephew into town for ice cream and tell everyone they were my children.

Considering my current situation, I wasn't sure what was going to happen between Cheryl and me, but I knew I was going to be the best father I could to my child.

The next day after work, I went over to Cheryl's apartment and told her that she shouldn't worry about a thing, that I was going to provide for her and the baby. And that the two of us would make it work. Cheryl looked so relieved. She smiled at me and showed me those dimples and I just knew I was doing the right thing.

After that, I started acting like a man who was going to have a family. I officially told all the girls I used to hang with that I was off the market. And I began looking for an apartment where Cheryl and I could live together. Instead of going to concerts and movies, we shopped for baby furniture and apartments, and I would go with Cheryl to doctor appointments as well. I think that's when I truly started to realize that Cheryl was the woman I wanted to spend my life with. It was easy being with her. It was easy talking to her. She just had a way of making me feel good about myself, and she did the same thing for anyone she was around. She just made people smile.

One day after work, Cheryl told me I should come over to her house for dinner, so after I changed out of my uniform, I went over to the Pink Houses. I used to avoid the Pink Houses when I'd walk to work because I'd heard so many rumors about drug deals and shootings in New York City's housing projects, but now I associated the Pink Houses with Cheryl and her family. I knew some bad stuff went on there, but I knew there were good people living there too.

Cheryl met me at the door with a sweet kiss and the smell of spaghetti and sausages wafting in the air behind her. She was just barely showing then, and I put my hand on her belly and said, "Hi, baby." I really hoped it was a boy, but I knew I would be happy as long as the child was healthy.

Cheryl opened the door wide and told me to come and make myself comfortable. Unlike most times I came over after work, Cheryl's father was seated in the living room watching TV. Cheryl scampered back to the kitchen because she had to finish dinner.

"Hello, Mr. Williams," I said, as I sat down in the chair next to the couch.

"Hello, Bobby," he said, without pulling his eyes from the TV.

"Are Don and Scott here?" I asked, trying to make friendly conversation.

"No, they're out with their friends," he said, still not looking at me.

Then he finally stopped looking at the television and turned toward me and said, "So, what are y'all going to do?"

"What do you mean, sir?" I asked.

"I mean what are you going to do about the baby," he said tersely.

"We're going to take care of the baby," I said. "Maybe we'll get married . . . ," I started, but Cheryl's father interrupted me.

"What do you mean 'maybe' you'll get married?" he said. "Y'all done messed around and made a baby, y'all should be together to take care of the baby and raise the baby right."

I knew Mr. Williams had every right to be angry with me, but I was a grown man and did not like being told what to do. Because Cheryl was in the next room cooking, and because I didn't want to cause a scene, I simply nodded my head and said, "Yes, sir."

Seemingly satisfied, Mr. Williams went back to watching TV and I went in the kitchen to see if Cheryl needed any help. I didn't tell her what her father had said to me.

A few weeks later, I came to my own decision about marriage. I told Cheryl to wear something fancy because I was taking her to a restaurant in Greenwich Village. It was an Italian restaurant that I had read about in the *New York Daily News*. They had given it a good review for the food, plus they commented on the romantic atmosphere, so I figured it would be a nice place to do the deed. I waited until we were halfway through our meals — Cheryl had ordered the spaghetti with Bolognese sauce and I ordered a steak — and I said calmly, "Cheryl, I love you, I love our baby, and I'd like you to marry me."

"Shouldn't you be on your knees or something?" Cheryl teased, but she was smiling. I knew she was happy.

"There's not enough space for me in here to get on my knees," I said, "but I still want to know if you'll marry me."

"Yes," Cheryl squealed. "Yes, I'll marry you."

I didn't realize it, but I'd been holding my breath, waiting for Cheryl to answer me. And now that she had, everything felt right. No, we hadn't planned on having a baby like this, and things were happening fast and out of order, but I was falling in love with Cheryl more every day. I felt really lucky that after everything I had done in my life, God saw fit to bring a radiant light like Cheryl into my world. The more time I spent with her, the better I felt. And I missed her when I was away from her. I knew this was real love.

I didn't have an engagement ring for Cheryl, but I promised her she would have a wedding ring when the time came.

"I don't care about all that," she said. "I'm just so excited we're getting married."

"Where do you want to do it?" I asked.

For a moment a cloud passed over Cheryl's face. She looked at me and said, "We can't get married at our church because I'm pregnant and they don't allow girls who get pregnant out of wedlock to get married there."

I sucked my teeth and shook my head. I had some words for those self-righteous church folks who acted like they never sinned. But I kept my thoughts to myself because I knew Cheryl's father was a deacon at the church, and if they didn't have a problem with those rules, who was I to judge? Instead I offered another alternative.

"Let's get married in Jamaica," I said, thinking how nice it would be to get married on a tropical island surrounded by Black people. I also wouldn't have to explain why none of my family was in attendance if we got married on an island in the Caribbean. I could just say they couldn't afford the plane fare.

But Cheryl nixed that idea right away.

"I'm not getting married in Jamaica," she said, frowning. "I want all my friends and family to be at our wedding, Bobby, so I can't be going somewhere where half the people wouldn't be able to get to."

"Okay, Cheryl," I said, knowing it had really only been a fantasy. "We'll do it your way."

As it turned out, we got married in the community room of the Pink Houses. Cheryl's godmother and godsisters decorated the place with fresh flowers and white linen on the tables and it all looked beautiful.

Besides the fact that a man's wedding day is one of the most emotional days of his life, I had extra things to worry about because I had invited Jean and Raymond to come to the celebration. I knew I wanted them there to be a part of my wedding day, but I also worried about having them become a part of my new life. Speaking to them on the phone, I was able to keep Walter Miller and Bobby Love separate. But I was building a new family, and I wanted my old family to be a part of it. I didn't want to choose one family over the other. Somehow I had to figure out how to merge the two.

When I called Jean and told her that Cheryl and I were getting married, I asked her if she would come to the wedding, but I also warned her that she would have to keep my secret. "I could get you a hotel and you could stay here for a couple of days in New York," I suggested. "But you have to remember to only call me Buddy or Bobby."

"You know I'm not staying in New York," Jean said, refusing my offer of a hotel. "And I'm not going to call you Bobby. I'll call you Buddy, just like I have for the last thirty years." Jean said she would call Raymond to see if she could ride up to New York for the wedding with him and his wife, Marie. I thought that was a great idea. I hadn't been in contact with my other brothers and sisters for so many years that I didn't think it was appropriate to reach out now and invite them to my wedding. I asked Jean what she thought, and she agreed. "When they come by the house, I'll tell them you got married," Jean assured me.

Even though I would have liked Jean and Raymond to stick around for a few days, the fact that they were going to zip in and out of New York for the wedding meant I wouldn't have to spend a lot of time worrying that they might slip and say something to Cheryl or one of her family members about my past. I couldn't afford to let that happen when all my dreams were finally coming true.

On the day of the wedding, when Scott ran up to tell me my family had arrived and they were waiting for me down in the community room, my heart started racing. Before I went down to see them, I looked at myself in the mirror and asked God, "How do I look?" I laughed at my own nerves and decided I looked good enough to get married.

Even though it was just Jean, Raymond, and Marie, I was so excited to see my family after all these years. I had been down to Washington, DC, once in 1982 and had seen Raymond briefly then, but I hadn't seen Jean since I was an inmate in prison.

"You look good, Buddy," Raymond said after he hugged me.

I spun around so he could admire my tuxedo and my two-tone patent leather shoes.

"Yeah, Buddy, you look good," Jean echoed. "I can't believe we're actually here at your wedding. I never thought I'd see the day."

I laughed. "Well, I'm so glad you guys made it. It wouldn't have been the same without you."

I showed my family to their seats on the groom's side of the room. I knew it was going to look awkward with all of Cheryl's friends and family crowded on one side, while my side was mostly empty. The only other people I invited to the wedding were two friends I'd made when I was working at Hertz — a cat named Carlton and another guy named Randy. Cheryl knew that most of my people were in North Carolina, so I simply told her that the rest of them couldn't afford to come up. She was so excited about all the wedding preparations and the baby, she hardly paid attention to the fact that most of my family wasn't there.

We had the ceremony first, and the minister from Cheryl's church officiated. Then we had a catered dinner afterwards. The ceremony went off without a hitch. And Cheryl looked beautiful in her white dress that her godmother made for her. There was so much material on her body, you could barely tell she was pregnant. Of course, everybody knew she was expecting, so it wasn't like we were trying to keep the baby a secret. Even Reverend Cooper seemed joyful after he performed the ceremony and didn't try to shame us for putting the cart before the horse. He just shook my hand and hugged Cheryl and wished us both good luck and good health.

It wasn't until the ceremony was over that I could finally introduce Cheryl to Jean and Raymond. Since the room was full of Cheryl's friends and family, Jean and Raymond stood close together in a corner, looking mildly uncomfortable. I didn't blame them. I grabbed Cheryl and took her over to meet my family.

"Jean and Raymond, this is Cheryl," I announced proudly.

Cheryl flashed those dimples and hugged the two of them. "It's so nice to meet you both. Bobby has told me so much about you. I'm so glad you were able to come for the wedding."

Jean looked Cheryl up and down and said, "Buddy, she's not that young. You had me worried."

"Jean!" I cringed. "Why you gotta say things like that?"

"I'm not saying anything's wrong. You guys seem like a perfect couple," she said. "It was a real nice ceremony, Cheryl. Real nice."

"Thank you," Cheryl said. Then she turned those dimples on me. "I can't believe we're married, Bobby."

Raymond raised an eyebrow. "Yeah, Buddy, I never thought I'd see the day."

"Are you all going to stay for dinner?" Cheryl asked. "The food is really good and there's plenty of it."

"Yeah, we can stay," Raymond said.

"But we can't stay too long," Jean interrupted. "Because I want to be heading back south before it gets dark."

Jean never held her tongue, but Cheryl was too giddy to take offense. I could tell she wanted to get back to her friends, who were still squealing about Cheryl's ring and her dress.

Cheryl excused herself. "I gotta go back over there and take more pictures." Before she turned to go, though, she said to Jean and Raymond, "It was so nice meeting y'all."

Once Cheryl was out of earshot, Jean remarked, "She seems nice."

And I could tell she meant it. And that meant a lot to me, because since Mama died, Jean had become the de facto head of our family, even though she wasn't the oldest. If she gave Cheryl her stamp of approval, then I was satisfied.

Our wedding was in March, and our daughter Jasmine was born in July. She had all five fingers and all five toes, exactly where they were supposed to be. When the nurse handed me my daughter to hold for the very first time, I just looked at her and whispered with tears in my eyes, "I am going to be the best dad you could ever have. I will always be there for you, and that's a promise."

That same day she was born, I called my family and some friends and announced, "We have a baby girl and she is perfect and beautiful." I was so proud, I even called my supervisor at the hospital and told her that Jasmine had made her arrival.

And just as I had suspected, Cheryl was an excellent mother as soon as that baby came out. As a couple, we decided that Cheryl would stop working so she could stay home and take care of the baby. I worked as many hours as possible to support our new little family, but I couldn't wait to get home to be with my little girl. Someone gave us a baby carrier at our shower, so after work, I would put Jasmine on my chest and go walking with her all around Brooklyn. I always got smiles from the ladies in the neighborhood when they saw me with Jasmine, but I only had eyes for one girl and that was my daughter.

I wanted to move our new family of three into our own apartment, but Cheryl convinced me that we should stay in her father's apartment in the Pink Houses so we wouldn't have to worry so much about money.

"My father sleeps at Estelle's house every night, so we can stay here and share the rent," she argued. Cheryl also liked the fact that her godmother lived on the fourth floor, her godfather and Mrs. Thompson lived on the second floor, and her godsisters lived on the fifth floor. In other words, she was surrounded by people who loved her and could help her with whatever she might need. I still bristled at the idea of living in the projects, and the Pink Houses were getting more and more dangerous as the crack epidemic made its way through the city. But Cheryl had grown up there, and she saw the glass half-full. She still saw familiar faces, families, and good people all around her. If she had to avoid the elevator or the front of the building at certain times of the day because of drug activity, she said she didn't mind. The occasional sound of gunshots just meant to keep away from the windows.

I begrudgingly agreed to stay put because the arrangement gave us time to focus on our family without stressing about money. All told, we ended up living in the Pink Houses for almost seven years. We decided to have another child along the way. Our daughter Jessica was born two years after Jasmine. Whereas Jasmine had been the most easygoing child, Jessica was the type of baby who would cry if she wasn't in Cheryl's or my arms. So in the end, I was happy that we'd decided to stay with Cheryl's family because we received a lot of help and support with the girls, and with my salary, I could buy all the diapers, formula, medicine, and clothing that we needed. I even saved enough money to take our little family on vacations, including a weeklong trip to Disney World in Florida. We weren't flush with cash or anything, but I knew how to make things happen. I dibbled and dabbled in playing the numbers. I bought lottery tickets, and sometimes I'd run my own sports pools that folks could bet on at work. I wanted to give my girls and my wife everything I didn't have growing up, most importantly a loving and caring husband and father.

But then it happened. I came home from work one day and Cheryl told me with tears in her eyes that they had found a young woman from the fourth floor of our building, murdered, chopped up in pieces, and thrown down the incinerator. Cheryl was devastated, and now she was finally ready to admit, the Pink Houses couldn't be home anymore.

chapter eight

Real Life

BOBBY

In 1992, when we finally left the Pink Houses to move into our own apartment as a little family of four, everything was good. The Baptist Medical Center had been shut down after years of mismanagement and dogged by rumors about the mafia. I had found a new job cooking in the kitchen at a hospital in the Bronx. It was smaller than Baptist Medical had been, but I was still turning out massive quantities of food for both the patients and the entire staff. It didn't take long for my reputation as a good cook to grow there, to the point where people would come to the cafeteria specifically asking if Bobby was on duty. My signature dish was fried chicken. On the days I made fried chicken, we'd usually run out before the day was over.

Once I was comfortable working up there, I found out about a nurse's aide position at a nursing home in the Pelham Bay area of the Bronx. After taking and passing the nurse's aide test, I was offered a part-time job there. So I worked both jobs, starting my day at 4:00 a.m. because I had to take the subway from Brooklyn all the way up to the Bronx and my shift at the hospital started at 6:00 a.m. When I was done at the hospital at 2:00 p.m., I would then hurry over to the nursing home for my 3:00 p.m. to 11:00 p.m. shift.

I didn't mind working hard for my family. I wanted to take good care of them. And if that meant working two jobs to pay for clothes, food, vacations, and dinner out, then I was happy to do so. I'd work three jobs if I had to, just like my mother used to do for us. I wasn't the type of guy who defined himself by his job title or the company he worked for. I looked at all work the same: How much would I get paid for doing it, how could I excel once I was there, and was I being respected by my co-workers and superiors? I left Hertz because I didn't believe they were paying me fairly for the work I was doing, but I found another job soon after, doing the same type of work and getting better compensation. When that company went bankrupt, I didn't panic, and eventually I ended up at Baptist Medical working in another kitchen. I became a union rep at Baptist Medical, too, and learned about workers' rights and how to argue for fair pay. I used that knowledge at every subsequent job I ever had. My commitment to doing honest work was sincere, but it was still all a hustle in my mind. The difference was it was a legal one now. And that was all for the better, because I needed to keep the money flowing for my family. I was ready, willing, and able to exhaust all my skills to make that happen.

One of our biggest expenses was Jasmine and Jessica's school tuition. After seeing those rowdy kids on the playground at the public school in our neighborhood, Cheryl and I decided we weren't sending our girls to a place like that. So when we walked by a small Catholic school not too far from where we were living and saw the kids at recess, playing games, being orderly, and not shouting, we decided we wanted our girls to go there. Tuition for both girls to attend was nearly five hundred dollars a month, but I thought it was worth it.

By now Cheryl was working too, but my salary was the one that paid most of the bills. And even though I was gone for most of the day and night, on my two days off, usually Mondays and Tuesdays, I would spend as much time as I could with the girls. I'd take them to the park, or shopping for clothes and things. Sometimes we'd go to the movies, too. I admit I wasn't as hands-on as I would have liked with the girls, not with my work schedule, so Cheryl took up a lot of the slack. She was an excellent, attentive mother. I knew she was raising them right, including taking them to church every Sunday, just like her mother had done with her. Cheryl took them to the same church she had been attending her whole life. Because I had to work most Sundays, I hardly ever went to church with them, which provided a convenient excuse for me. Deep down, despite my belief in God and my thankfulness for His guidance and mercy, I didn't feel comfortable carrying my secret into His house, especially in front of Cheryl's family. It felt hypocritical, and I wasn't ready to deal with those feelings. So when Cheryl would ask me to go to church with the family, if I wasn't working, I'd make up an excuse not to go. She always looked disappointed, but she didn't press the issue, and I convinced myself that everything else I was doing for our family made up for my short-comings in this one area.

Otherwise, life was really good. The only thing I couldn't give my girls, which they asked me for, was a little brother. "Daddy, we want a little brother," Jessica would tell me when she was around five years old and Jasmine was seven. The two of them would pester Cheryl and me for a baby brother, and we would just smile and tell them that that train had left the station.

Even though Cheryl and I weren't opposed to having another child, we soon realized that two children were enough for us to han-dle. As the years passed, the girls stopped asking for a new sibling and instead started asking for a puppy. I had no interest in adding a dog to our family, but I was happy that the question of more children had been laid to rest. I was perfectly content with my two girls.

Then came one night in the fall of 1997. Cheryl and I were getting ready for bed.

"Bobby, I feel funny," Cheryl said to me.

I had to get up early for work the next day, so I wasn't paying a lot of attention to what she was saying or how she was saying it. Instead, I started pulling the covers up over me in the bed and was about to turn out the light on my nightstand.

"Bobby," Cheryl said again, this time tapping me on the shoulder and forcing me to turn around to look at her. "Listen. I'm feeling funny in my stomach like I did when I was pregnant with Jessica and Jasmine."

Now she had my full attention, but only because I thought she was crazy. "Cheryl, you're not pregnant," I said. "It's been ten years since Jess was born. We've been doing the same thing all these years and now you think you're pregnant?"

Cheryl rolled her eyes and then reminded me of the night a few weeks before when we hadn't been so careful.

Still, I shrugged it off. To make Cheryl feel better I said, "If you think you might be pregnant, go to the clinic and take a test."

"Okay," Cheryl said, and I turned out the light.

"But I know my body," she whispered in the dark. "You'll see."

Cheryl made an appointment for the following week. The appointment was for the early evening so she could go in after work. I wasn't really thinking about it, but I did want to make sure she wasn't sick or anything. When I got home that night, Cheryl was waiting for me practically at the front door.

I hadn't even taken off my coat when she said, "I'm pregnant, Bobby."

"Really?" I said.

Cheryl nodded. "And they also think it might be twins."

I dropped my keys on the floor. "What do you mean they think it might be twins?"

"They think they saw two heartbeats," Cheryl said.

"Well if they weren't sure, have them do it again."

"You want me to take the test again?" Cheryl said. "The nurse was pretty sure she saw two babies."

"I have insurance," I said. "I don't care how much it costs. We can't have a maybe. Please take the test again."

The next day when I came home, Cheryl was grinning and holding out a sonogram picture with two big red circles around two beating hearts.

"That's Baby A and Baby B," Cheryl showed me.

I'm not the type of person who gets real showy with his feelings. I like to keep things cool. So when Cheryl told me she was having twins, I'm sure I said all the right things a father should say. But I have to admit, I felt a mixture of emotions. Even though we were hanging in there, money was tight. I had lost my job at the nursing home, so I was only working at the hospital in the Bronx. Just the thought of starting over with two new babies when the girls were almost teenagers felt daunting. Cheryl was only thirty-four years old, but I was almost fifty — and I was going to be a dad again? That night I didn't wait until I was in bed to say my usual prayers of thanks. I had a real conversation with God because I didn't know how this was going to work out. I opened my mouth and said, "God, you got to help me with this. I don't know what to do."

When I woke up the next morning, I just decided I had to take it one day at a time. It was my job to make sure that Cheryl stayed healthy and that the babies were born healthy. As a husband and father, I knew that's what I was supposed to do. And so I focused on that and waited to see what the future had in store for us.

"Bobby, you're taking too many days off. It's like every week you got to have a day off," my boss Linda said to me one day after calling me into her office. It was early January and Cheryl was five months pregnant, but I hadn't told anybody. Not even my boss. I had been taking days off from work so I could go with Cheryl to all of her doctor's appointments. I hadn't told anyone because it wasn't any of their business, but also, I guess I was still in a state of disbelief about it myself. Now I had to say something.

"Linda, my wife is pregnant," I said.

"Oh," Linda said with a look of surprise.

"Yeah, and she's pregnant with twins."

"Oh, wow!" she said. "That's really something, isn't it?"

"Yeah," I said. "It wasn't exactly planned, but I really need to go with my wife because she's at risk for some complications with her blood pressure."

"Well," Linda said, "I feel for you and your situation with your wife, but just be aware that you can't keep taking days off."

I rubbed my hand over my now bald head and sighed. "Linda, I really don't want to lose my job. I need this job, especially with two more babies on the way. But I have to be there for my wife. What if something happened to her on the subway or walking up a bunch of steps? What if the doctor has to do some test and she needs help getting home? I would never forgive myself if I wasn't there. So you do what you have to do, but I'm going to do what I have to do for my wife and our children."

Now it was Linda's turn to sigh. "I understand," she said tersely. And then she dismissed me from her office.

After that conversation, Linda didn't comment on how often I was taking days off, even though I continued to do so at a regular pace. It seemed like every week Cheryl's doctor needed to check something else. Her blood pressure. Her sugar levels. Even though I held no love for the job I was doing, now that I had been transferred out of the kitchen to the housekeeping staff because the hospital had changed ownership and the kitchen was shuttered, I was still grateful that I had a job that came with decent insurance, because Cheryl wasn't going to be able to work much longer at her medical billing job. The thought of how much money we were going to need to care for two more kids weighed heavily on my mind. I knew I would have to find another part-time job, but for now there really wasn't time to look, so keeping my job was critical.

One night I was working the late shift at the hospital and I was called to the front desk because I had a phone call. Cheryl very rarely called me at work unless it was an emergency. As I trotted over to the phone at the nurses' station, I said a silent prayer that whatever news Cheryl had to share, it wasn't bad. But it wasn't Cheryl on the other end of the line. It was Jessica.

"Daddy!" her little voice pierced my ear. "Mommy is going to have two boys! We're going to have two brothers, Daddy!"

"Oh my God," I said, laughing and grinning like a child. Finding out the sex of the babies left me elated. All that time I had been telling myself that making sure Cheryl was healthy and that the babies came out healthy was all I cared about. I had given up the idea of having a son years before and had made peace with it. But hearing that I was now going to have two sons filled me with a sudden joy. Unexpectedly, my mind flashed back to a childhood fantasy of having a twin brother, where the two of us would grow up to be professional athletes together. I felt like God was giving me a replay on my own childhood, but from a father's perspective. I felt so blessed.

"Jessica, you didn't have to call me at work to tell me that," I said, still standing there at the nurses' station with a grin on my face.

"I know, Daddy. But I knew you'd be happy," she said. "Mommy said I could tell you."

"Okay," I said. "Well, thank you for telling me, then."

"You're welcome," she said. "And Daddy," she added. "Have fun at your work."

"You go to bed, Jessica," I said, laughing. "And tell your sister I said good night."

And then we hung up.

▼

Cheryl was due at the end of May in 1998. But by the beginning of May, she was done.

"Bobby!" Cheryl cried. "I'm going to tell the doctor that I want these babies out of me. I can't do this anymore."

"But your due date isn't until the end of the month, Cheryl," I pointed out.

"I don't care. They have to come out," she said.

I felt for Cheryl. I knew she was uncomfortable. I knew she couldn't sleep properly or go to the bathroom, or even eat what, when, or how she wanted to. I was exhausted for her. So when she told the doctor that she wanted the babies out of her body, I didn't try to argue or convince her that she should wait for them to come out on their own time. The doctor agreed. She told Cheryl to hold on for a week and then she'd schedule an induction.

Our twins, Jordan and Justin, were born on May 18. Jordan came out first. Justin was breech and needed some coaxing. But both boys had all five fingers and all five toes exactly where they were supposed to be.

"You have two healthy boys," the doctor announced.

I felt such an overwhelming relief and joy. I felt like I had been holding my breath for nine months straight.

"Oh my God, oh my God. Two boys," I kept repeating like I had lost the power of coherent speech. I was so grateful. I kissed Cheryl on the forehead and thanked her for all the pain and suffering bringing our boys into the world had required.

"You did it, Cheryl," I said.

"*We* did it, Bobby," she corrected me.

The first two years with the twins passed by in a blur. Diaper changes, endless feedings, and lots of walks around the neighborhood. I bought a double stroller for the boys, and Cheryl and the girls would take turns walking them around to keep them happy. The cost of diapers and formula was no joke. I was lucky to find a part-time nurse's aide job with an organization called IAD — Institute for Adults with Disabilities. But I worked the overnight shift, which meant I often left Cheryl at home with the babies at night. Jasmine was only thirteen, but she helped her mother a lot with the twins during those early years. I fully admit that Cheryl and the girls raised the boys when they were babies. Between my job at the hospital and the part-time work at IAD, I was often a ghost in my own home, but I always told Cheryl that if I didn't work so much, we wouldn't be able to eat, have nice clothes, and go on the family trips that we still managed to take. It was a sacrifice in some ways that I worked so much, but it was worth it to be able to provide for my family. I often reminded Cheryl that at least with me working so much, she should feel good knowing that I wasn't out in the streets like a lot of other cats, messing up, drinking, and on drugs. Not since Jasmine caught me trying to sneak a smoke in the back bedroom at the Pink Houses when she was a toddler, and I'd whacked my head on the windowsill, had I picked up any reefer. And while I might enjoy an occasional beer, my drink of choice now was any caffeinated soda, like Mountain Dew or Pepsi, to keep me awake while I worked all day and night.

When the boys were three years old, I promised Cheryl a big surprise, because I knew how hard she was working, not just at her new job but also with the children. I knew she understood why I worked so much, but she still deserved a break.

"We're going to Disney World again," I announced one Sunday after everyone came home from church. Cheryl and I had taken the girls to the Florida theme park when they were small. I wanted our boys to be able to go too.

"Bobby, what?" Cheryl said, looking at me like I had sprouted a second head. "We can't afford that."

"Cheryl," I said calmly. "If I say we can afford it, we can afford it. I've been saving the money, plus my numbers hit."

"Are you sure?" Cheryl said, still looking dubious.

"I mean, if you want me to throw all these tickets and stuff away . . ." I said.

The kids jumped in then. "No, we want to go! We want to go!" Jessica and Jasmine had been talking about taking the boys to Disney since they'd been born. The girls remembered how wonderful their own experience had been.

"Okay," Cheryl said, looking at the kids going crazy, dancing around the living room of our apartment. "If you say so, Bobby."

"I got this, Cheryl," I said. And I did.

The other reason I wanted to go to Disney World again is that I wanted to take the boys down to meet my family. I knew if we were driving to Florida, we could make a pit stop in Greensboro, just as we'd done with the girls when they were little. Over the years, I'd gone back to Greensboro a few times. I knew it was risky and even reckless, but I couldn't stand to be away from my people forever. The first time I went back, more than ten years had passed since I'd escaped from prison. I kept a very low profile on those trips at first, and I'd get nervous whenever a police car would pass by me on the road. But as the years went on, it got easier to relax, and I felt bolder about making the trips. I didn't think anybody was looking for me at that point. And I felt protected by the people around me down there. My brothers and sisters all knew about my past and were aware of the double life I was leading. I knew they'd keep my secret. They loved me as much as I loved them. It was only when I was down in Greensboro, surrounded by my siblings, that I felt like I could fully unwind and be Buddy again.

So Cheryl, the kids, and I drove down to Florida, and on the way, my family gathered at Jean's house and met the twins. They were polite to Cheryl and loved on the kids, but I could tell some of them felt awkward around Cheryl. They didn't want to give anything away that might make her suspicious about who I really was. One of my cousins would always pull me aside and tell me I should tell Cheryl the truth, but I wasn't going to risk what I'd created. I was fine keeping my worlds separate. And for the most part, my sisters and brothers were fine with it too.

After the pit stop, Cheryl, the kids, and I got back on the road and had a wonderful time at Disney World. And when we came back home, life went on.

When it was time for the boys to start kindergarten, Cheryl and I decided to do the same for them as we'd done for the girls. We found a private Christian school for them to attend. We had moved to a bigger apartment in a different neighborhood in Brooklyn, and I had finally made the decision to quit working at the hospital. I had given them fourteen years, but through all of the management changes and getting moved around from cooking in the kitchen to cleaning up the blood and guts in the operating rooms, with my salary going down and my hours going up, I just decided it wasn't worth it. And the money I could make working full-time plus overtime hours at IAD meant I didn't have to really worry about a dip in our finances.

By the time the boys were five, I had been working steadily as a counselor for IAD with developmentally delayed adults. I had to learn how to deal with adults who often couldn't do basic things like talk or eat or even use the bathroom without assistance. Some of my earliest experiences working for the organization had me wrestling with a 250-pound nonverbal man who had to be taken to the bathroom multiple times in the middle of the night or he'd wet the bed.

Sometimes I had to break up fights or simply sit with a client — we were told we had to call them clients, not patients — while he ate to make sure he didn't steal the food off the plate of the person sitting next to him. It took me a while to understand how to do my job, but I soon got really good at it, and IAD assigned me to a new facility in the Bronx where the men were delayed and struggling with substance abuse. These men literally had nothing. Even the clothes they wore were donated. But they now had this group home to live in, and it was our job to help them care for the house and themselves so they could be functioning members of society. I sympathized with them, and even though they didn't know my story, I felt like I was in a good position to show them how they could survive in the world, even if they were starting with nothing.

So I would help them cook, shop for food, and keep house. Sometimes we would take them on field trips to help stimulate their minds and get them excited about life. There were about eight young men in the house, and they all got to know me and like me — some of them even called me Pops. And in turn, I did my best to share with them the life skills I'd acquired over the years.

One time IAD even arranged for us to take the men on a trip to Florida. One of their board members had a house in Orlando, and she allowed us to take the guys down there. It was great to see the look on their faces, flying in an airplane, walking on the beach. Even when people stared at us or told us they didn't want our group to come into their restaurants or establishments, I wouldn't let it bother me. In fact, we took the guys into a pizza restaurant one time for lunch, and when the manager tried to tell us that we couldn't stay, making up some lame excuse, I told him that the law said he had to seat us. He eventually did, and this woman came up to me afterwards and told me I had done a noble deed. I didn't think it was a "noble deed." I was just doing my job. I knew these guys had feelings like anyone else, despite their disabilities, and they deserved to be treated like human beings.

This was something I'd learned in prison. You have to treat all people like you want to be treated, not like you think they deserve because of their background or because of something in their past.

Still, working with these men was really difficult and emotionally draining. In addition, the commute from Brooklyn to the Bronx was exhausting. So when my boss asked me if I wanted to transfer to a new group home that was being opened that would shorten my commute time, I said yes.

One of my co-workers at the new house was a younger woman named Shannon. In both looks and temperament, she reminded me of one of my cousins from Greensboro. Shannon had two kids and a boyfriend who was always up to no good, according to her. I always arrived at the house about an hour early so I could eat breakfast and not have to rush. Shannon liked to get there early too, and the two of us would talk. Actually, Shannon would do most of the talking and I'd do most of the listening, and sometimes offer some words of advice. After a while, Shannon got more and more comfortable with me and started sharing more intimate details about her sexual exploits and what she was doing to get back at her cheating boyfriend.

One day I finally just told Shannon that all of her messing around wasn't going to solve any problems. I told her that her behavior was just going to make things worse. She didn't like what I had to say and she stopped talking to me in the mornings.

A couple of weeks later my boss, Mr. David, called me and told me I needed to come to his office. "There's been a complaint about you, Bobby, and we need to get this sorted out," he said over the phone.

When I got to his office, he informed me that Shannon had made a sexual harassment claim against me. She told my boss that I had said some slanderous things about her character. Mr. David looked down at his paper and said, "She said you said she was 'promiscuous.'"

I rolled my eyes. "Mr. David, she was telling me all these things about her personal life every day," I explained. "I wasn't harassing her.

I was just responding to what she was telling me. I was trying to give her some advice."

"I hear you, Bobby," Mr. David said, "but I have to turn this in to management, and they'll probably have a hearing and then let you know what's going to happen. But I just wanted you to hear it from me first."

"Thank you," I said. "I appreciate that."

By the following week I had been suspended from my job. A few weeks later I was fired. When I heard the news, my emotions ricocheted from anger to disappointment to sadness. I couldn't believe that after all my years working for IAD, and the dedication I showed to helping our clients, I was being thrown out like a piece of garbage. I felt like a failure and like I'd let my family down. I hadn't felt this way since I was being hauled off to the Morrison Training School and my mother gave up on me without a fight.

I tried to put on a brave face when I told Cheryl what happened. I didn't want her to think that I wouldn't be able to pay my share of the bills. But more importantly, I didn't want her to think less of me.

"You got fired for what?" Cheryl asked after I gave her every detail. "That doesn't make any sense."

"I know, but she said I called her 'promiscuous,'" I said, repeating the word from the official report.

Cheryl shook her head like she couldn't believe my foolishness. "You don't talk to women like that, Bobby. That's none of your business."

I tried to explain more, but Cheryl didn't want to talk about it. She said I should have known better than to get into other people's personal business on the job. Especially when it's of a sexual nature. She didn't understand what I was thinking. What Cheryl did want to talk about was what I was going to do for money.

"I'll go down to the unemployment office and apply for unemployment, and I'll start looking for a new job right away," I said, trying to assure my wife.

But when I went down to the unemployment office, they told me I couldn't collect unemployment because I had been fired *with cause.* That surprised me and scared me a little bit. We didn't have any savings, and Cheryl's salary as a nutrition coordinator would cover the rent, but not much more.

I took my job search seriously, but my usual sense that everything would be all right wasn't there. I couldn't muster up any enthusiasm to find the next hustle. Being fired from a job where I had given my all wasn't something I'd experienced before. I'd been let go from jobs for reasons that had nothing to do with my performance, but this was different. This firing hit like a sucker punch. I wasn't expecting it at all, and for some reason, I couldn't mentally recover from the blow.

I applied for a position as a janitor at a restaurant but was turned away because I wore a suit to the interview. The lady interviewing me thought I was too uppity for the job. Then a friend of Cheryl's told me about another job opening at an organization similar to IAD. I'd be doing the same kinds of tasks, working with developmentally delayed adults. She told me I was a shoo-in for the position. The company headquarters were up in the Bronx, so I slid into my suit again and headed out early in the morning on the day of my interview. But when I got to the front of the building, I couldn't make myself even walk through the door. Something in me was just too tired to start over again. I was fifty-eight years old, and the weight of all that I was carrying just couldn't be managed anymore.

I very rarely thought about prison during that time, but I had trained myself to keep my emotions hidden, lest I reveal something that might give me away. I didn't have friends I could share my burdens with, and even Cheryl wasn't privy to my deepest thoughts and fears. I only had myself. I had organized my life that way on purpose. I was in charge, so I would be the only one to blame if things went wrong. Well, things had now gone very wrong, and I could only blame myself.

I went home and told Cheryl that I didn't go to the interview.

"Why not, Bobby?" she asked with concern.

"Because I'm tired, Cheryl," I said, sitting down on the couch. "I'm just tired."

CHERYL

The dream woke me up again. In the dream I was begging Bobby to talk to me. "Just tell me the truth, Bobby!" I kept crying. But when Bobby opened his mouth to speak, a long, thick white rope, like the kind you would use to anchor a ship, came pouring out of his mouth. And he just stood there trying to talk, but all he could do was pull that rope out of his body. And as he pulled, I just watched as the rope piled up on the ground at his feet, waiting for him to say something.

I shook my body under the covers and tried to clear my head. That dream had been invading my sleep for years, and I knew it meant something because I always had it after Bobby and I argued. The arguments were always the same. I'd beg Bobby to open up to me and share what was on his heart and he'd tell me there was nothing wrong. I'd walk away in a huff, then at night I'd have the dream.

Knowing I wasn't going to fall back to sleep, I slipped out of bed and made my way to the kitchen. I figured I might as well enjoy a small bit of quiet and calm before the kids got up and everyone started getting ready for the day. I got my tea, but instead of turning on the radio like I usually did, I sat down at the little table and prayed. *Dear God, please help our family. Help us get closer. Help us get the knowledge and understanding to better understand each other. Please, God, open up my husband's heart so that he will understand that I am here to be his wife and his friend. Please protect us all, God, and bless us with your mighty favor. Amen.*

When I opened my eyes, I looked around our tiny kitchen and thanked God for that too. Our apartment wasn't that big, but at least we were finally in a stable home. It'd been five years with Bobby out of full-time work, getting evicted from one place after another, even having to go to that shelter up in the Bronx for one night. It was humiliating and painful for our family. Especially for the kids. Jasmine was so mad at Bobby for letting our finances get so bad, I think that was the night she decided she was moving out for good. "You're always telling us we have to take care of our business, Daddy," she'd said. "And look at you now."

That was one of our lowest moments, but it didn't break us. And even though I hated to see our eldest daughter leave home, I was happy she had a safe place to land: with her fiancé, Rich. They seemed so happy together, and now, four years later, Jasmine was expecting her first child. Just thinking of Jasmine becoming a mother and me becoming a grandmother made me smile as I sipped my tea.

On the outside, I knew our family looked like we were doing okay, but we weren't. I was the only one with a steady paycheck, while Bobby juggled side hustles, the occasional lottery win, and borrowing money from family members. But even when we couldn't pay the rent, we always made sure the kids had what they needed for school and their extracurricular activities. Bobby insisted on that. He didn't want our children to suffer because of his failings. That's why, even though he wasn't working, Bobby poured more time into doing things with the boys. He started coaching Jordan's football team and Justin's baseball team and did so for years. When the twins were in middle school, Bobby was the parent who would pick them up after school and go to all of the parent-teacher conferences when they were scheduled during the daytime and I couldn't get off work. Bobby did most of the cooking and shopping too. I knew I had a good husband. So what was I praying about? Why was I asking for God to intervene in my marriage?

It wasn't only that we were barely making it financially, living check to check, or that Bobby had fallen from a ladder and had broken his femur bone and now walked with a slight limp. It was that after all these years, I still felt like my husband was keeping a part of himself away from me.

The kids said Daddy just liked being alone. My family members thought Bobby was just a solitary type. My friend Deena called him arrogant. And I knew he was all of those things, but I didn't understand why he had to close himself off to me. His wife! Earlier in our marriage, I thought maybe Bobby was hiding something, like another woman or even another family, but I never saw any evidence that he was cheating, and he would always assure me that he was committed to me and to our children. Plus, Bobby was always working two jobs, so there was no way he would have time to cheat. But now that he wasn't working, save for a few odd jobs here and there, he still wasn't any better at opening up or telling me what he was feeling or thinking. In fact, after he got fired, I think he closed himself off even more. But my anguish didn't start with Bobby's lack of employment. It was deeper than that.

My friends thought I was crazy when I'd try to explain what I felt was wrong with our marriage, because I couldn't put it into words right. I couldn't say, "My husband refuses to have his picture taken and doesn't have any friends," and expect sympathy. Those were just some of his quirks I'd gotten used to, but it was all part of the reason I felt so frustrated.

"Does he beat you?" one friend asked.

"No," I'd say.

"Is he cheating on you?" another one would ask.

"No."

"Does he help out around the house and with the kids?"

"Always," I'd answer truthfully. "He's always been a good dad to the kids."

"Then what are you complaining about?" they'd say, exasperated.

But I was the one exasperated, because I couldn't pin down what the problem actually was other than the fact that, after almost thirty years of marriage, I felt like my husband still didn't trust me. I felt like he was hiding something from me, but I didn't have any solid proof other than a gut feeling and my recurring dream. This dream that had woken me up yet again. I sighed because I knew I wasn't going to figure out any answers at 6:00 in the morning. So I gulped down the rest of my tea and went to wake up the boys.

A few days later I was at my desk at work. After making the dramatic decision to join AmeriCorps at age thirty-seven, after working random office jobs for years, I had found a career that I loved, working for a social service agency as a nutrition coordinator. I worked for the organization during my AmeriCorps volunteer year, and my boss said she wasn't willing to let me go when my year of service was up. It was my job to help women and families navigate the food stamp and Medicaid system and help them get on their feet after falling on hard times. I really liked helping these women, and I loved my co-workers. After being there for close to eleven years, I felt we were almost like a family. I could also walk to work from our apartment, which was an added benefit.

The phone rang. "Hello, this is Cheryl. May I help you?"

It was Jasmine on the other end of the line. "Oh, hi, Jas," I said, trying to block out the noise from around the office, people talking and the constant buzz of phones ringing. "How ya doing?"

"I'm okay, Mommy," she said, and then she said something else, but there was so much noise around me I really didn't hear what she was saying. That morning I was in charge of taking all the incoming calls to the office, so I made some kind of positive response and tried to hurry Jasmine off the phone.

"Well, I'm at the hospital now," Jasmine said. "I just wanted you to know."

"Okay, honey. Well, I'll talk to you later, okay? I'm on front desk, so I can't talk right now. Call me later when you're done with your appointment."

And then I hung up.

Ten seconds later, the phone rang. It was Jasmine again.

"Mommy, did you hear what I said?" Jasmine yelled into my ear. She knew I hadn't really been listening. "I'm in the hospital and I'm having the baby now!"

"Oh, my goodness! Lord have mercy!" I hollered. "Jasmine, I'm on my way, baby!" And then I sprang into action. I stood up and announced, "Listen, y'all! I got to go, I'm sorry. I know I have appointments, but my daughter's in the hospital. She's going to have my first grandbaby!"

The room erupted into applause, and people were cheering and congratulating me. My supervisor, Ramona, told me she'd handle my appointments as I gathered my things and headed for the door. Before I walked outside, I called Bobby to share the good news and to tell him to meet me at the subway entrance so we could ride up to the hospital together.

"They don't need us to go up there, Cheryl," Bobby protested.

If I could have reached through the phone and snatched him up, I would have. Instead I said, "Listen, you better be at that station when I get there, Bobby. This is our first grandchild."

"Okay, Cheryl. I'll be there," Bobby said.

I refused to let his attitude ruin this moment for me, but it seemed to be his perpetual state these days. Ever since he'd gotten fired from IAD, Bobby had slipped into a funk that we couldn't shake him out of.

Bobby didn't really have any friends that I could ask to help cheer him up. He liked to hang out with my brother Scott, but Scott and his wife had moved down to Atlanta, so that wasn't an option. Bobby had finally started going to church more often, now that he couldn't use work as an excuse, but it hadn't made him open up to me at all. I think the only time I saw Bobby really happy and open was when he was with his family in North Carolina. I had gone down there with him two or three times, and the difference was clear. When Bobby was with his siblings, he just seemed to light up and let go. Those were rare occasions that I witnessed.

Bobby had traveled to Greensboro a couple of times without me as well over the years. He would make excuses about why he preferred for me not to go with him. He would tell me that his family was always acting crazy and he didn't want me to see that. It felt like he wanted to keep his New York family separate from his Greensboro family, so after a while, I just stopped asking him to take me with him when he went down there.

When Bobby and I got to the hospital, we only had to wait about two hours before our grandson, Levi, was born. He was round and brown like his father, and Jasmine looked so happy and proud. There is something magical about seeing your firstborn become a mother. Even Bobby couldn't stop smiling, looking at that little boy. I was glad I made him come with me, and we both laughed and talked like we used to on the way home that night, remembering the night Jasmine was born and how I had been such a mess, screaming and hollering, forgetting all of my breathing techniques that we'd learned in our birthing classes.

"You did all right, Cheryl," Bobby said, smiling at the memory. "I mean, look at how well Jasmine turned out."

"Yeah," I said, remembering those early days we were together when our future had looked so bright. "I think I was a lot calmer with Jessica."

"You were," Bobby said. "You had motherhood in the bag by then."

When we got home, Bobby and I had a simple dinner and went to bed. Before I went to sleep, though, I thanked God for a blessed day.

A few months later, instead of celebrating a new life, we learned that Bobby's brother Leroy had died. Even though Leroy was ten years older than Bobby, the few times Bobby mentioned this brother, it was with fond memories. Bobby didn't talk about his childhood that much, but I knew he loved his brothers and sisters, so I was prepared to help him get through this loss. I was already calculating how many days I could take off work in order to go down to North Carolina with Bobby for the funeral. I was also trying to figure out whom I could get to stay with the boys, since Jessica worked nights. Because they were in high school, I didn't want the twins to miss any classes. But then Bobby told me he didn't want me to come.

"What do you mean, you don't want me to come?" I said.

"It's a funeral, Cheryl," Bobby said. "Why would you want to come down there? I'm going to be helping out with everything, running around doing this and that. You wouldn't have anything to do."

"But I'm your wife, Bobby. I'm supposed to be there for you. And for your family."

Bobby brushed off my concern. "Cheryl, you don't need to bother. I can handle everything. I'll be fine. You stay here with the boys."

I know I should have been used to this by now, Bobby keeping me away from Greensboro, away from his family, but it still hurt that he didn't want me to come with him. I already figured his family didn't like me that much. The few times I had been down there, they were polite and kind, but they always seemed a little standoffish with me. I got the distinct impression that there was something about me they didn't approve of. But I didn't understand what it was. Even when I called him Bobby, they exchanged funny looks with each other. I figured they wanted me to call him Buddy like they all did, but it just felt too weird to me.

"Okay, Bobby," I said quietly. "If you don't want me to come to the funeral, I won't come."

"It's not that I don't want you to come, Cheryl." Bobby tried to make it sound better. "I just don't need you to come. Besides, why should we spend any extra money on a bus ticket for you too?"

I couldn't argue with that. Bobby was still waiting on the settlement money his lawyer had promised he'd get from his accident falling off the ladder and breaking his leg. He had hired one of those lawyers off the TV that promised fast money if you were the victim of an accident. Well, that accident had happened in 2012. It was now 2014, and we hadn't seen a penny. In fact, Bobby had had to take out a loan against the settlement just to pay the rent and some money we owed for other bills. He didn't have to tell me twice that it made no sense for me to go to the funeral with him. From a financial standpoint, I had to agree. So instead of going down to Greensboro with Bobby, I just ended up helping him pack and made him a bag lunch to take with him on the bus.

While Bobby was down in North Carolina, I called my sister. I tried to act like I was just calling for one of our usual sister chats and to check on my father, who had recently moved down to Atlanta. Daddy had been living alone since he and Estelle separated for good in 2000, but he was growing increasingly forgetful and was worrying all of us kids. He now lived with my brother who had also moved down south, but Sis would check on him when she could. She caught me up on the latest about Daddy, but she could tell right away that I wanted to talk about something else.

"What's the matter, Cheryl?" she said.

"I don't know, Sis," I started. "It's Bobby."

"Oh, Lord," she said. "What's he done now? Do you need money or something?"

"It's not that," I said.

"So what is it?" Sis asked.

I told her that Bobby was at his brother's funeral and he hadn't wanted me to come.

"Do you think that's normal?" I asked. "I mean, I'm his wife. Shouldn't I be at the funeral with my husband?"

"Cheryl," Sis started. "You know Bobby is his own person and he does things his way. He thinks that he's in charge and you're just supposed to do what he says."

My big sister thought Bobby married me because I was so much younger than him and that meant he could boss me around, but that wasn't what concerned me. "Sis, I can stand up for myself," I said. "Bobby thinks he's the boss, but I do what I want to do too. Remember when I used my AmeriCorps money to take acting classes? Bobby didn't want me to do that, but I did it because it was something I'd wanted to do since I was in the fifth grade."

Sis laughed at the memory. "Yeah, you were the oldest one in that class, too — fifty years old, trying to be an actress."

"Hey," I said, laughing myself. "Those classes really help me with my job now when I have to make presentations. And they were fun."

"Yeah, but did Bobby come to your final performance, or did Daddy? Who was there to support you?"

"Daddy," I said, sighing. "Daddy has always been there for me and the kids." And that was the problem. My father had been such a kind, loving man to my mother and to me, it was hard for me to be with Bobby and not see the same kind of openness and affection I'd seen between my parents.

"Cheryl, you told me once that you were ready to walk out of the marriage, but you stayed. Why did you stay?"

I thought back to that time before the twins were born, when I was so frustrated that Bobby would shut down and never share his true thoughts and feelings with me. But after praying on it and then having a dream where my mother appeared to me to tell me everything would be okay, I decided to stay. The twins were born soon after that, and things did seem to get better. But then once he lost his job, everything that had been bad just seemed to get worse.

I said all that to my sister. "I just don't know what to do, Sis."

"I think you need to pray on it again, Cheryl," my sister said. "Ask God to show you the path you're supposed to take. But remember, Cheryl, what you want matters too. You are smart and your opinion counts in all things."

"Thanks, Sis," I said, and I meant it.

Talking to my sister always made me feel better. Without her, my godmother, and my godsisters, there's no way I would have been able to deal with all of the challenges in my marriage and not lose my mind. My family and my church family really kept me grounded and lifted up through all these years, but even their love and wise words weren't always enough. I was reaching what felt like a breaking point.

By the time New Year's Eve rolled around at the end of 2014, I was no closer to knowing what I wanted from Bobby, from our marriage, or anything. I just knew I needed something different in the new year. I felt like a dam had been built around our relationship, but the water behind it was steadily building up and was about to crash through the walls.

"Honey, do you want to come to watchnight service with me and the kids?" I asked Bobby, already knowing he was going to say no, yet still hoping for a miraculous yes.

"Nah, Cheryl," Bobby said. "You guys go on without me."

Jasmine was going to church with her husband and his family, so it was me, Jessica, and the twins who got dressed up and took a cab to the church that night.

As the minister preached his sermon, telling us all to lay down our burdens from the past year and to set our sights on the year to come, I started to cry and I couldn't stop. Jessica kept looking at me like I was crazy, but I just couldn't control the emotion that was pouring out of me. It was like that dam broke, right there during the final minutes of 2014, and I could not stem the flow of tears.

That night I went to sleep feeling so drained, but also knowing that 2015 was going to bring a world of difference to our lives. I didn't know what was coming, but I knew some kind of change was on its way. It had to be, because I couldn't live the way we were living anymore. I couldn't live with a husband who couldn't open up to me and share his full heart and true soul.

Only a few weeks later, in mid-January of 2015, as I was sitting in the kitchen sipping my morning tea, a violent knock on the door brought the change I had asked for.

chapter nine

No More Secrets

CHERYL

Bobby's lawyer's name was Erica Valdez. She was an attractive woman who I guessed had to be in her mid-forties. My memories are fuzzy about everything that went on that day when we first met her, the day after Bobby was arrested. Whether she wore a skirt or pants. Whether Jasmine and I were in her office for a few minutes or an hour. Everything that she said about Bobby was a blur, except when she said they were going to send Bobby back to North Carolina for a crime he'd committed more than forty years before. That they were going to make him finish serving his sentence.

I just couldn't believe it. I decided then and there that Ms. Erica Valdez must be crazy or she must have her facts wrong. How could they send Bobby to prison for a crime that happened so long ago? He wasn't a criminal. He was a sixty-four-year-old diabetic grandpa who walked with a limp. Of course I didn't say any of this to Ms. Valdez. I just nodded my head as she went over Bobby's case. But when Jasmine and I got home, I opened my mouth and shared my thoughts. Without holding back.

"This just doesn't make sense," I said, pacing around the living room. Jessica and the twins agreed with me as we tried to figure out what we could do to get Bobby out of jail. There had to be something.

"Mommy, look at this." Jasmine called me over to the dining room table, where she was sitting with Jordan's laptop computer.

I walked over and stood behind her chair. "What? What is it?"

Jasmine had pulled up her father's arrest records online. "Mommy, it says that Daddy's real name is Walter Curtis Miller."

I collapsed into the chair next to Jasmine and repeated the name. "Walter Miller!" Of course. That's why his siblings had the last name Miller and Bobby didn't. I remembered asking him about that the first time we'd been down to Greensboro, and he'd told me that since his siblings were half-siblings, they had a different last name. I didn't question it at the time because I had no reason to doubt, but it was all coming together now.

"Mommy, there's more here." Jasmine interrupted my thoughts. "It says that Daddy robbed more than one credit union and he did other robberies too," she said.

I leaned over and scanned the records Jasmine had found.

"Wow, Dad really was a gangster," Justin said.

"Shut up, Justin," Jordan said to his brother.

I couldn't say anything. I had assumed Bobby had robbed one place, but now I could see that he had been a real criminal, and suddenly so many things Bobby had told me started to fall into place like the pieces of a jigsaw puzzle. Getting shot. Why he wanted me to stay away from North Carolina. Bits and pieces of his life in Washington, DC, that had sounded scandalous. Maybe all these years Bobby had been trying to tell me about his life but I had brushed him off. Whenever he started a story that had to do with him partying or living hard, I'd say, "Oh, please, I don't want to hear that stuff. That's nothing you should be bragging about." And then he would shut down. Now I wondered if Bobby had been wanting to tell me who he really was all these years and I had pushed him away.

Unfortunately I didn't have much time to figure it all out because Ms. Valdez called me the next day to tell me her strategy for Bobby and what she wanted me to do. "Look, Mrs. Love," she started. "Bobby doesn't want to be sent back to North Carolina, so I'm going to see if we can keep him here in New York, but I'm not going to lie. It is very unlikely that's going to happen. His crimes were committed in North Carolina, and he escaped from their state prison, so that's where he has to serve his time."

"I see," I said, even though I really didn't.

Ms. Valdez went on. "So I'm going to file as many motions as I can to see what I can do on that front, but I'd like you to talk to the media to try to get Bobby's story out there in the world. The more people who know about it the better. When the public is on your side, it can't hurt, but it can certainly help."

"What do you want me to say to the media?" I asked, already wary.

"Look, this is just an incredible story. You don't have to focus on what your husband did in the past. You just need to tell people that he was a good father and a good husband. A member of the community and all that. Just tell the truth. Basically, you need people to know that he has been a law-abiding citizen for all these years."

"Okay," I said, even though the thought of talking to the media about my husband's secret criminal past filled me with unspeakable dread. Old warnings from my father to keep our personal business out of the streets flashed across my mind.

Clearly Ms. Valdez heard my hesitation. "Mrs. Love, this is going to help your husband, I promise you."

I sighed. "Fine. I'll do it. But how am I supposed to get the media to talk to me?"

"Don't worry about that." Erica laughed. "They will find you. Trust me."

Sure enough, the very next day, a woman from the *New York Daily News* called me while I was at work and asked if I was willing to be interviewed about Bobby's story.

So far I hadn't told anyone about what was going on in my life, so I lowered the volume of my voice and made sure nobody was in earshot of my conversation.

"I can talk," I said quietly into the phone. "But not now."

"How about next week, Wednesday at six p.m.?" the woman asked. "After you finish work?"

"That would be fine," I said, trying to hurry off the call.

We agreed that the woman would come to the apartment, and then I hung up and tried not to look as nervous and agitated as I felt.

I didn't want people all up in my business. I didn't want people to ask me questions about Bobby, especially because I didn't have any answers myself. I had just found out that the man I had lived with for almost thirty years wasn't who he said he was, so who was I to be answering questions?

The thing was, after talking with the reporter, I knew I wouldn't be able to hide much longer. The reporter seemed like a nice woman, and she told me the same thing the lawyer did, that this article was definitely going to make people aware of this "incredible story." I prayed that they were right, but that meant that I would no longer be able to keep things private. The journalist said she was going to interview some other people too, including Bobby, so I had about two weeks before my business would be in the streets for good. I started making a list of all the people I needed to tell about Bobby's past before they found out from the Internet like I did.

When I was done, the list included my father, my siblings, and my two best friends, Carla and Deena. Of course I had to tell my godmother and godsisters as well. I would have to tell the people at work, and I would have to tell the bishop from our church and his wife. Telling the folks at church was the part I dreaded the most. How would I hold my head up once the congregation knew that my husband had been a criminal and he had been lying to me our whole marriage?

Jasmine came down from Harlem to go with me when I went to talk with the bishop, whom we affectionately call Bishop, and Bishop's wife, known as the first lady. It was a Saturday, so neither one of us had to work. Bobby had been in jail for two days and at that point, it was still a secret from most everyone. Just the night before, I'd finally told my father and my sister and brothers. Everyone was shocked when they heard the news, but they all had something to say about it too. Daddy, of course, told me if I needed anything to call him and that he was there for the kids and me. Sis wanted to know if I wanted to come stay down in Atlanta with her while Bobby was in jail, but I told her no. I wanted to stay in New York and be close to him. My brother Scott was really sad to hear the news, but he also said he wasn't surprised. "I always felt there was something Bobby was hiding," he said. "I didn't think it would be all this, but yeah, Cheryl, I always knew there was something."

Once my family knew, I had someone besides my kids to share the burden with, even though the burden I felt as Bobby's wife was mine alone to carry. It was me he had lied to all those years. And it was me who had never put the pieces together. And it was me who had to decide if I could stay with a man who had deceived me and who had committed these crimes, even if they were in the past.

At the church, Jasmine waited in the sanctuary while I went in to speak with Bishop to tell him what happened. His wife sat in the room with us. Because we all knew each other quite well, it wasn't as painful to share my story as I had feared, but I was in tears by the time I was done. The first lady handed me a box of tissues, and Bishop told me to dry my eyes.

"Cheryl," he said. "You have nothing to be ashamed of. I am thankful you told us what happened so we can support you, the kids, and Brother Bobby in any way that we can."

"Thank you," I said through my tears, adding, "I know this article is going to come out in the newspaper soon, so I wanted you to hear it from me before you read about it somewhere else."

"We appreciate that," Bishop said. "And again, you shouldn't have to shoulder this burden alone, Cheryl, so it's good that you let us know. And please tell us if we can do anything to help speed up Bobby's release from jail. Of course we will pray for him and for your family."

"Thank you," I said again.

Then Bishop looked over at his wife and she nodded at him.

"I'm going to excuse myself and let you ladies talk for a minute," he said. "Sister, you're going to be okay. Stay strong in your faith and remember, you are not alone."

"Thank you, Bishop," I said and watched him walk out of his office door.

The first lady then moved over to sit in the chair next to me. "Cheryl, what else is on your heart? I can see you're struggling."

The tears started up again as I tried to put my emotions into words. "I just don't know how I should feel. Bobby lied to me this whole time we were married. And I know people are going to say I was so dumb for not knowing anything. And if I stay with him, people are going to think I'm stupid for that too."

The first lady handed me more tissues. She reached for my hand and squeezed it. "Cheryl, why are you thinking about other people? Who are you married to?"

"Bobby," I said.

"And do other people decide what happens in your marriage with Bobby?"

"No," I said, wiping my eyes.

"Well, then, you should stop worrying about other people as you try to decide what you want to do, given your current situation."

"But I don't know what to do," I wailed.

"Let me ask you something," she started. "Do you love your husband?"

"Yes," I said without hesitation. "I love Bobby. But that's not even his real name. His real name is Walter Miller." Those words, Bobby's real name, sounded foreign on my tongue.

"But who have you lived with for these thirty years? Who is Bobby Love to you?"

I thought about my answer. Yes, Bobby did all those things all those years ago. But over the course of our lives together, he had tried his best to be a good father, a good provider, and a good husband. His worst habits were playing the numbers and being a horrible manager of our money. But who was I to judge? I had horrible money management skills too. Bobby wasn't perfect, but neither was I. Bobby was a human being with flaws. I loved him with his flaws, and I loved the family we built together, with both our flaws. I'd always known that my husband's heart was large and that something was getting in the way of him showing it to me fully. Now I knew why.

I answered the first lady's question. "Bobby is my husband and I love him."

"Well, then." She smiled. "You know what to do, then."

"I do?" I said.

"Yes. You need to ignore the busybodies in your business and anybody who tries to make you feel guilty for staying true to yourself and the love you have for your husband. I have gotten to know Bobby these last several months since he's been working at our house and when he was helping to clean up the church after Hurricane Sandy. I know him to be a good man, Cheryl. Apparently he has a past, yes. But it seems to me he's been working hard over these thirty years to make up for that past."

I wiped at my eyes and nodded. "You're right. Bobby practically worked himself to death over the years for us. And now I just wonder if he was trying to make amends in some way."

The first lady stood up. "That's something you'll have to talk to Bobby about. But Cheryl, you are a strong woman who I know walks with the Lord. You lean on Him. You lean on Him when you feel weak or when you feel alone or when you feel angry. And know that I am always here for you too."

"Thank you," I said, feeling truly grateful. And as I gathered up my coat and scarf and prepared to leave, I realized I felt lighter than I had when I'd arrived. Talking to the first lady had helped me clarify my thoughts, and I felt like a burden had been lifted. One thing I now knew I had to do, something I knew I could do, was keep loving my husband.

The next day, we were finally able to get over to Rikers Island to see Bobby. Jessica and the twins came with me. We took the subway to Queens and then got the Q100 bus, which would take us all the way to the visitors' center at the prison. Visiting hours on Sunday only lasted until 4:00 p.m., so we were sure to get there at 2:00 on the dot. I was a bundle of emotions — nervous, scared, and worried. I had heard all of the horror stories about Rikers Island and didn't know what I was going to find or what condition Bobby was going to be in, even though it had only been a few days since he'd been taken away. As we crossed the bridge leading to the island, I prayed silently, grasping Jessica's hand, asking God to protect us and to protect my husband.

I don't think anything could have prepared me to see Bobby in prison for the first time. Before we were led into the visiting room, the kids and I were searched and sniffed three times by dogs. That alone spooked me, and I couldn't imagine what Bobby must have gone through when he was brought here. The visitors' room had sterile white walls, with bars on the windows and a worn gray linoleum floor. Flimsy gray plastic tables and chairs were scattered about where people could sit. The smell in the room reminded me of the gymnasium from my high school in Queens, a combination of musty sweat and industrial-strength disinfectants. I saw Jessica's eyes grow wide as she took in the scene, and I knew I had to be strong for the kids.

"Come on over here." I gestured to a cluster of plastic chairs near a window.

We all sat down and then waited, as we'd been instructed, for Bobby.

We didn't have to wait long. Jessica saw him first. "Daddy!"

Bobby walked over to us, dressed in a baggy one-piece jumpsuit. His face was a mixture of sadness, joy, and shame.

The five of us hugged, and almost immediately Bobby started to cry. I had never seen him so vulnerable and grieved.

"Oh, honey, hush," I soothed, leading him to his chair and fighting my own tears.

But Bobby couldn't stop crying, and he kept repeating over and over again, "I'm so sorry. I'm so sorry."

"Daddy, you don't have to cry," Jordan said. "It's okay. We're okay. We're not mad at you."

"Yeah, Dad," Justin tried to joke. "We always knew you were a gangster!"

We all looked at Justin then and burst out laughing. It was what we needed to get through the horrible moment.

I pulled some tissue out of my purse and handed it to Bobby and watched him wipe his eyes and blow his nose. He took some deep breaths and then turned to me.

"Cheryl, if you want to leave me, I'll understand. You have to do what you think is right, but please don't keep me away from my children."

And then he started to cry again.

I had never seen Bobby like this and it scared me. "Bobby," I said, grabbing his chin and forcing him to look at me. "I'm not going anywhere and I'm not thinking anything like that. I'm not leaving you."

"I should have told you," Bobby said, refusing to look me in the eye. "I should have told all of you."

"Why didn't you tell me, Bobby?" I cried. "You could have told me."

Bobby hung his head down and whispered, "I was so ashamed of what I had done, Cheryl. And I was afraid if you found out, you'd leave me." He looked up at me then and said, "I never wanted you or the kids to know about my past. I wanted to take this secret with me to my grave."

Bobby stayed in jail on Rikers Island for nearly six months while he waited for his sentencing and Erica fought extradition to North Carolina. The kids and I went to visit him every single week. Without fail. Sometimes it was the girls and me. Sometimes it was the boys and me. Sometimes I went by myself. But I made sure we got there for visiting hours so Bobby could see us. I was deeply worried about his mental health. People told me that men would go crazy out there in those tiny cells at Rikers. I'd heard about men throwing their own feces and urine at the guards. I knew Bobby was strong-willed, but I didn't know how anybody could handle one day, much less six months, in a place like Rikers. And at his age.

At first I was embarrassed, having to go visit my husband in jail.

But I had to take myself out of the equation. My embarrassment didn't matter. What mattered was that I had to keep our family together. I simply accepted that this was what our family looked like *for the moment*. But I kept telling myself and the kids, "It's going to get better. Bobby is going to get out of jail and we're going to have a wonderful life together."

I had to continuously recite this mantra to myself because I was tested all the time. Once Bobby's story came out in the news, I felt like everybody knew who I was and wanted to ask me how it was possible I never knew my husband was a former criminal and a wanted man. Even at church, folks would pretend they were interested in my well-being, but really they just wanted to press me to see if I had noticed any clues about Bobby's past. I didn't stop going to church, but after a while I stopped staying for the fellowship hour after the service. Even at work, people treated me differently. The room would go quiet when I entered, as if people were talking about me all the time. Finally I just had to announce one day, "If you have questions, you can ask me. You don't have to stop talking to me."

One day, one of those tabloid TV news shows just showed up outside our apartment building with their cameras rolling. I refused to go downstairs to talk to them and simply waited for them to go away, which they eventually did, but I was so embarrassed because everybody in the neighborhood knew why they were there. I never wanted attention like this, so in response I slowly drew my circle of friends and family tighter and smaller. Pretty soon I felt like it was just me and the kids against the world.

Thankfully the kids all decided to handle themselves like angels and were there to support me and take care of me every step of the way. Jasmine and Jessica called me during the day just to make sure I was okay, or sometimes to ask if I wanted to do something fun like go to a movie after work. I would often go up to Harlem and spend the night with Jasmine's family, just for a change of scenery. The twins kept up with school, both continued to make good grades, and Jordan continued playing football with the same intensity he always did. He was hoping to secure a football scholarship for college, and those dreams were not deferred because of Bobby's situation. Initially I was worried that the boys might be suffering and not telling me, but even their school counselor, who knew what was going on, contacted me and told me that both Justin and Jordan were showing no signs of distress. For that I was so grateful, and I just felt like my children had built a cocoon around me to make sure I didn't fall apart.

In addition to dealing with the new public scrutiny of my life, without Bobby at home, managing our finances fell squarely on me. Even when he wasn't working, Bobby still managed the money, stretching our dollars and making decisions about what bills to pay and which ones to hold off on until he could figure something out. We had fallen behind on the rent and loan payments, and now I had to be the one to negotiate with the landlord for more time to pay and call on friends and family to borrow the money we needed. Sometimes I felt like I wasn't going to be able to deal with everything, but I didn't really have a choice. If I didn't do it, who would? I had to remind myself constantly that God only gives us what we can handle. If God was laying these burdens on my back, I had to assume He thought I could handle them. So I did.

Even though our lives were challenging with Bobby gone, when I went to visit him at Rikers, I didn't want to trouble him with what was going on in the outside world. When we visited, I spent all of my time trying to keep his spirits up, reminding him that we all loved him and that we were all praying for his release. Figuring out how to pay an overdue utility bill paled in comparison to the life Bobby was living in a six-by-eight-foot cell. Every time we stepped foot in that jail, I could feel the degradation of the place. Bobby always tried to put on a brave face, but I knew he needed to see our smiles and feel our positive energy to keep him motivated.

Luckily, Bobby had been placed in the infirmary because of his diabetes, so at least he wasn't housed with the general population. Even so, he told me if any nonsense between inmates started to pop up, he would tell the guard to lock him in his cell so he'd be protected. I still worried about him all the time. I worried about his diabetes getting out of control. I worried about him getting into some kind of fight with another inmate. I worried that the vertigo he suffered from might act up and he'd fall and hurt himself. I worried he'd get sick from the food or because some other inmate might have something contagious.

For his part, Bobby never complained when we came to visit. He mentioned that the regulation prison sneakers hurt his feet, but other than that, whenever we were at the jail with him, Bobby kept his mood upbeat. Sometimes he would have us laughing about the things he saw going on around him. Bobby even managed to get himself a job at Rikers. The way he explained it, he had become something of a hall monitor, tasked with walking the hall of the infirmary where he was housed and making sure all the other inmates were okay and that nobody was breaking any rules or hurting themselves. "They're paying me twenty-eight dollars a week to do this," he told us with a grin, "and I get to stay out of my cell all day instead of being locked up, because I'm on duty." This was so typical for Bobby, figuring out how to make something good out of the worst situation.

Bobby never let us end a visit without giving the kids his attention. He'd talk to the boys about their schoolwork and grill Jordan about football. He would ask Jasmine about Levi, and he always told Jessica to keep an eye on me — since she still lived at home and we joked that she always would. The last thing he always said was that he knew that God would help him get out. He seemed steadfast in his belief that he would be released sooner rather than later, and we were all hoping, against all odds, that he wouldn't have to go back to North Carolina. I'd never heard Bobby speak so fervently about God and I just hoped his predictions would come true.

But it didn't work out that way. When the phone call came early on a Thursday morning in June, it was Erica Valdez who gave me the news.

"They're sending Bobby to North Carolina," she said. "I just got word and I wanted you to know."

I sighed. "When will he be sent down there?" I asked.

"Today," she said. "They're having the extradition hearing this morning."

I almost dropped the phone. "Today? Why so soon? Can we see him one more time?"

"Mrs. Love, this is how it works," Erica explained. "You can go to the court hearing, but you can't really talk to him, and you won't be able to hug him or anything. Some people actually prefer not to go for that reason."

"What time do we have to be there?" I asked, my mind already made up. If they were going to send Bobby to North Carolina, I didn't know when I'd be able to see him again. And I didn't know what kind of conditions he was going to be living in once he got down there. He needed to see us as much as we needed to see him.

Erica told me where I needed to be, and when I hung up the phone, I texted the twins, who had already left for school, to tell them to meet me at the courthouse in Manhattan. I texted Jasmine and Jessica as well. There was no way we weren't going to say goodbye to Bobby.

I saw the boys as soon as I came out of the subway in lower Manhattan. The three of us rushed into the building and found out what courtroom Bobby would be in. There weren't that many people in the room, just us, the judge, Erica, and some guards and other random officers. Out of the corner of my eye, I also saw the newspaper reporter who had interviewed me from the *New York Daily News.* When they brought Bobby into the room, my heart just leapt into my throat, but I couldn't say anything, of course. Even though I'd seen Bobby every week, I still scanned his whole body for any changes in his appearance. The beard he'd been growing since he was arrested was now thick and bushy and covered the lower half of his face in a white cloud. He was wearing regulation gray sweatpants and a sweatshirt, and I could see the edge of a white undershirt around his neck. I could tell by the way he was walking that his feet hurt, and I was glad I'd brought his sneakers that he'd asked for. I was hoping to give them to someone who was going to be with him going down to North Carolina.

The whole procedure lasted less than thirty minutes. The judge made a show of looking over Bobby's paperwork, and then he explained that he was sending Bobby back to North Carolina to finish serving his sentence. The judge said Bobby would have to serve ten years. I nearly fainted when I heard that. Ten years! Bobby had been away from us for six months and it already felt like a lifetime. How in the world would we be able to handle ten more years like this? How would Bobby handle it?

Jordan nudged me out of my stupor. "Ma, come on, they're taking Dad out."

I got up out of my seat and followed the boys and the few other people out of the room.

"Mrs. Love." Erica tapped me on the shoulder. "Come out this way and you can see them take Bobby away."

The boys and I followed Erica out the door to the front of the building, where there was a white van waiting that was going to take Bobby down to North Carolina.

"Remember, he can't talk to you or hug you or anything," Erica said. "They've told him to look straight ahead and not make any eye contact with anyone. So he's not ignoring you, he's just following directions."

Sure enough, they led Bobby out of the courthouse in handcuffs, and even though he walked right next to the boys and me, he couldn't turn his head and say goodbye. Seeing Bobby like that, like an emotionless robot, nearly broke my heart in two. I knew he was hurting. But just because he couldn't say anything didn't mean we couldn't.

"We love you, Bobby!" I shouted, not caring that I was standing outside and causing a spectacle. "Don't forget that! We love you and we're here for you!"

The boys joined me. "Bye, Dad! We love you!"

I know Bobby heard us, but he just kept his head up and kept walking toward the car.

And then suddenly I heard a familiar cry, "Dadddddyyyyy!" It was Jessica. She had been furiously texting me saying she was trying to make it to the courthouse from work. She wanted to see her father before he was taken away. I told her where we were and encouraged her to hurry because they were not wasting any time getting Bobby out of New York. I watched my daughter sprint across the front of the building, hollering at the top of her lungs. "Daddy, wait! Don't go!"

That stopped Bobby. He couldn't ignore his baby girl, not even at the risk of being punished by the law. He turned his head and looked at Jessica and gave her a hint of a smile. I grabbed Jess before she tried to throw herself in Bobby's arms and really got him in trouble.

"Bye, Jessica," Bobby said. "Ya'll be good." And then they put him in the car.

We all just stood there waving, yelling our "I love yous" through our tears. And then Bobby was gone. I looked down and I noticed I still had his sneakers in my hand.

I had to wait an entire month before I heard from Bobby again. I assumed he was alive because nobody had called to tell me he was dead, but other than that I knew nothing about my husband. I tried to get information from Erica, but now that Bobby was in North Carolina, he was no longer her client. She assured me he would be getting a lawyer down there, but before Bobby was extradited, she sent his case down to an organization in North Carolina that helped advocate for people with excessive or unfair prison sentences. She told me that someone would be getting in touch with me from the organization as soon as they reviewed Bobby's case. I was happy to hear that, but it didn't stop the pain of not knowing or hearing anything for those four long weeks.

And that's when I had to have a "come-to-Jesus" meeting with myself. I had been going through the motions of living, going to work, being with the kids, even going to church. But sometimes I'd wake up in the middle of the night still in my clothes, having fallen asleep watching TV, and just wonder how I'd gotten there. My friends and family were all trying to help me cope, offering encouraging words, but I needed to do something or else I was going to go crazy. So I did the only thing I knew to do: I turned to the Bible. I got into the Word. I started to build a wall of faith around myself. Every morning I'd start my day listening to my favorite hymns, dancing around the kitchen, just letting the spirit wash over me. At night and on the weekends, I would watch my favorite ministers preach on TV. I had to deepen my faith and truly believe that God had a plan for Bobby and He would keep him protected. I had to believe in the power of prayer, and so I prayed faithfully every day and with all of my heart that Bobby would be released from prison. I just filled my spirit with the word of God and tuned out almost everything else. I had to be my own cheerleader, protector, and friend. I had to be strong for Bobby, for the kids, and for me, and the only way I could do that would be to truly lay it all in God's hands and believe in His power. Even though I'd been going to church for my entire life, and I never wavered in my belief in God, I had come to a point where my faith was truly called to the test.

When Bobby was finally able to call home, sometime in late July, I was so happy to hear from him, tears sprang to my eyes.

"Bobby!" I practically shouted into the phone. "Where are you?"

"Hey, Cheryl," Bobby said. "I'm sorry I haven't been able to call until now. They wouldn't let me."

"Are you okay?" I asked.

"Yeah, I'm fine. They just put me through all this testing and moving me around and all this."

"Well, where are you now?" I asked again.

"I'm out here in this place called Spruce Pine," Bobby said.

"Spruce Pine?" I said. "That sounds like a summer camp."

"Well, trust me, it's not," Bobby said. "I'm out in the middle of the woods, but it's no summer camp."

"Can we come visit?" I asked.

"Cheryl, I don't want you all to come down here," Bobby said. "This place is so far up in the mountains, I don't even know where we are and I don't know how you'd even get here. The roads up here are so narrow and treacherous, I'd be worried the whole time thinking about you trying to get someone to drive you here. It's not worth it for you to try to come. Besides, I know I'm not going to be here that long."

"How do you know that?" I asked.

"I just know," Bobby said. "I've rehabilitated myself. I've been a good citizen. I've paid my taxes. I've done everything I was supposed to do. Even my lawyer told me she didn't think I should be here."

"But has anyone told you since you've been down there that you weren't going to have to serve the ten years?" I asked.

"No," Bobby said. "But God has saved me so many times, Cheryl, I don't think He's going to stop now."

I smiled at that. It sounded like Bobby had had the same "come-to-Jesus meeting" that I did.

"Okay, Bobby. I'm praying every day that you're going to get out," I said.

"I'm going to get out, Cheryl," Bobby said. "And it will be sooner than you know."

From there Bobby asked me about the kids, and I quickly caught him up on everything that had happened in the last month. We couldn't talk that long, because Bobby said the inmates only got five minutes per call, so Bobby promised he'd call me again the next night at the same time. And he did.

Six thirty phone calls every night became our new normal. Everybody knew that I had to be home at 6:30 for Bobby's calls. I spoke to him every single day. Sometimes the ladies at work would ask if I wanted to join them for a happy hour drink or something, and I'd look at them like they were crazy.

"You guys know where I have to be at six thirty p.m. I have a date with my husband."

And they would laugh but never try to dissuade me from rushing home to talk to Bobby.

One day when I got home, there was an envelope in the mailbox addressed to me. It was from Bobby. I was like a giddy schoolgirl getting a note from her boyfriend. I tore it open before even getting up to our apartment and found a three-page handwritten letter. I kicked off my shoes and sat on the sofa and read the whole thing. In it Bobby poured his heart out, begging me to forgive him for all the mistakes he'd made over the years, for leaving me in the situation I was in now, and for lying to me about his past. Then he shared some of the passages in the Bible that he was reading over and over again that were really helping him endure prison.

I read the letter through twice, and when I was done, I pressed it to my chest and just wept. Bobby had really found God. I could tell. I knew he had been on a path even before this all started, but I could tell Bobby was truly getting into the Word and believing in God's grace. And he was telling me that he loved me in a way that showed his true heart. I ran back into Justin's room and found some paper and immediately wrote Bobby back. While I wrote, I listened to Bobby's and my favorite Earth, Wind & Fire album and was flooded with fond memories. In my letter I thanked Bobby for writing to me. I thanked him for sharing his heart. And I told him that I forgave him for everything. I also told him that I loved him.

It sounds crazy, but with Bobby in prison, we were communicating more than ever. I felt like I was falling in love all over again. We spoke every day on the phone and wrote letters to each other every week. My constant prayers for God to bring me and my husband closer together were finally being answered, just not in the way I'd hoped or expected.

In late August I heard from Bobby's lawyer from the organization in North Carolina. He introduced himself as Mr. Walker. He sounded young on the phone, but knowledgeable.

"I don't want to get your hopes up," he said, "but I think we have a good chance of getting Mr. Love out of prison. I need you to do a few things for me to help."

"Of course," I said. "What do you need me to do?"

"Well, my goal is to get Bobby out on parole. He's already proven for over thirty years that he can be a contributing member of society, so I want to argue that he should be able to continue to serve out his sentence on the outside. In order for him to go up for parole, I need a bunch of letters from people testifying to Bobby's good character. Could you collect a bunch of letters like that?"

"Yes, I think so," I said, already thinking of whom I could ask to write a letter on Bobby's behalf.

"Great," he said, and then he told me how many letters I should get and where and when I should send them once I had them all collected. He stressed that time was of the essence. He also reiterated that I shouldn't get my hopes up. "We almost never get a case where someone gets paroled on the first attempt, but we're going to try our hardest," he said.

As soon as I hung up the phone with the lawyer, I was ready to get to work. Now I had a purpose. Now I had something concrete to focus on to get Bobby out of jail, in addition to my constant prayers.

The first people I asked to write letters were Bishop and the first lady from our church. Not only had Bobby been attending church more frequently after he got fired from his job — he'd even started teaching adult Sunday school — but he had worked for the bishop and his wife in their house, too, cleaning and doing odd jobs. They knew him well and could say good things about him based on firsthand experience. Thankfully they agreed right away to write a letter.

I also asked Jordan to track down his old football coach, the one Bobby used to work with, so I could ask him to write a letter. I knew it would look good to see that Bobby had volunteered to coach the kids' football team for all those years.

I asked my father and my godsisters to write letters too, of course. When I had gone through all of the friends and family I could think of, I wasn't ready to stop. If the lawyer needed people to stand up for Bobby, I was going to go all the way. So I decided to write a letter to President Obama. I knew it was a long shot, but everything about Bobby's life was a long shot. Bobby was always telling me to try something if the opportunity was there, so I did it. I knew it couldn't hurt. I composed a letter telling President Obama everything about Bobby's story: how he'd started out with a life of crime but now he was a changed man, had raised four children, had a loving wife, and had rehabilitated himself and didn't deserve to be in prison. I asked him if there was anything he could do, could he please do it. I signed the letter with my name and sent it off to the White House. Inspired, I wrote a similar letter to the governor of North Carolina, pleading for clemency for Bobby.

I figured if the lawyer said these letters of support could help get Bobby out of jail, then a letter was a powerful tool. I prayed they would help Bobby's cause. In the end, I never received a response from the president nor the governor, but I still felt like everything I was doing made a difference in some way.

As summer turned into fall, life continued in Brooklyn for me and the kids. Both Jessica and Jasmine had followed in Bobby's footsteps and were working as medical counselors for an organization that served developmentally delayed adults. They both had a heart for helping people, and it didn't surprise me that they found careers in health care. The twins started their junior year of high school and began looking at colleges. I continued going to my job every day, and waited for letters from Bobby, instructions from the lawyer, and any sign or indication that this nightmare would soon be over. One evening as I was coming home from work, I swore I saw Bobby walking into the grocery store across the street from our apartment. It looked so much like him, I decided that had to be a sign that he was going to be home soon.

Two weeks later, my cell phone rang at work. I checked the number and saw that it was from Bobby's lawyer in North Carolina.

"Mrs. Love?" Mr. Walker said.

"Yes, this is Cheryl," I said.

"I have some great news. Bobby is coming up for parole!"

"What!" I shouted, then remembered I was at work in a room full of people. I lowered my voice. "Really? Are you serious? What happens now?"

Mr. Walker laughed. "I knew you'd be happy to hear this, but remember, the fact that he gets a parole hearing doesn't mean he's getting out. So please don't get too excited."

"Sorry, I'm already past excited," I said. "But I understand what you're saying."

"Okay," Mr. Walker said. "Now I have to ask, can you come down here and speak on Bobby's behalf? Just like with the letters, we need you and about three or four other people — just family is fine — to come and testify on Bobby's behalf."

"We have to come down to North Carolina?" I asked.

"Yes. Is that going to be a problem?"

"No," I said, shaking my head, even though I was already trying to calculate the cost of a plane ticket and how I'd scrape together the money. It didn't matter. I'd figure something out, and that's all the lawyer had to know. "We'll be there," I said.

"And one more thing, Mrs. Love," Mr. Walker said. "Bobby won't be at the parole hearing. You won't get a chance to see him unless you make a separate arrangement to go up to the prison, which is in another town altogether."

My heart sank. I was hoping to be able to see Bobby if we were going to be in the same state. But I couldn't dwell on that. I thanked the lawyer and hung up the phone.

Jessica flew with me down to Durham, North Carolina, where the parole hearing would be held. We were going to stay with my cousin Laverne, who lived there. My brother Scott was driving up from Atlanta and bringing my father with him, and Bobby's sister Jean was driving in from Greensboro.

On the day of the hearing, Laverne drove Jessica and me to the courthouse around 2:00 p.m. I had never been to a parole hearing before, but I decided to treat the occasion like I was going to church. I wore a nice dark-blue dress and a string of pearls. I'd gotten my hair done before we left New York. I remember Laverne telling me I looked so much like my mother when she saw me, which gave me a feeling of confidence for what we were about to do.

The courthouse was a nondescript one-story building, and we all met in the parking lot and walked in together. We had to go through a metal detector and then waited in the hallway until a gray-haired security guard came and told us to follow him into what looked like a conference room.

A tall young man with red hair met us at the door.

"Mrs. Love," he said to me. "I'm Mr. Walker."

"Oh, my goodness," I said, shaking his hand. "It's so nice to finally meet you in person."

"You too," he said. "Now, I don't want you to be nervous. Just answer the questions to the best of your ability and don't spare any details in sharing about Bobby's good qualities."

"No problem," I said. "I can do that."

We all assembled ourselves around the conference table, and then an older gentleman in a gray suit came into the room and introduced himself. He said his name was Mr. Anderson and he would be conducting the interviews for the proceedings. He sat at the head of the table and asked everyone to introduce themselves and explain their connection to Bobby. When we were done, he addressed me first.

"Mrs. Love," he said. "Tell me a little bit about Bobby and tell me why you think he should be let out of prison."

I took a deep breath. I had practiced what I wanted to say. I knew in my heart that I wanted Bobby back home with us. But all of a sudden my mind went blank. And then I wondered if what I was going to say would be enough. I tried to remember the notes I'd written the night before, but I couldn't get anything to register in my brain. Then a voice inside me said, "Cheryl, just speak from your heart." And so I opened my mouth and said, "I love my husband. I miss my husband, and I want him to come home."

"Go on," Mr. Anderson said.

I snuck a peek at Mr. Walker, who was nodding his head at me like he wanted me to say more.

"Okay, so, I know the things that Bobby did, what he did in the past wasn't right, but he rehabilitated himself without being in jail. He raised two sons and two daughters who are good kids. He teaches Sunday school at our church. He helps people who need help even though we don't have a lot of money. We aren't perfect, we don't have a big fancy house or anything, but we love each other and we love our children."

I continued to talk for about fifteen minutes. I talked about how hard Bobby worked. How he'd worked for almost fifteen years with developmentally disabled adults. How he worked two jobs for most of his life, and even how he saved up so we could take our kids to Disney World twice. I didn't sugarcoat things, and I mentioned how we'd struggled financially, but I said Bobby always took responsibility for his failings and did his best to support us.

By the time I was done talking, I had gone through at least half a box of tissues. Jessica, who was sitting next to me, was sniffling too.

When I was done talking, my father spoke, followed by Jessica and then Jean. Everybody shared their own examples and stories about Bobby. Jessica talked about her father being a great dad. My father said he'd watched Bobby develop into a loving and caring father and a son-in-law he could always count on. Jean talked about being so proud of Bobby for overcoming what she described as a difficult childhood.

"Our father died when Bobby was nine years old," she said. "And after that my mother did everything she could to keep Bobby out of the streets, but she couldn't handle all eight of us. Our little brother died of a drug overdose. Bobby's two oldest brothers were in trouble with the law when Bobby was still in middle school. Bobby started out on that path, but he turned his life around. On his own. He is a hardworking, law-abiding citizen, a good father, and a good husband to Cheryl."

Needless to say, there wasn't a dry eye in the room when we were all done talking. Well, the lawyers weren't crying, but all of us family were wiping our eyes. I didn't know if we had said enough to convince Mr. Anderson, but I felt the love in that room for Bobby all around me and it felt so good.

As we headed out of the room and started walking to the door, Bobby's lawyer, Mr. Walker, caught up with me.

"Mrs. Love, well done," he said. "You all did a great job."

"Thank you. What happens now?" I asked.

"Well, now we just have to wait and see," he said. "I wish I could give you a more concrete answer, but that's how these things work. I'd say we should hear something one way or the other within six weeks."

I smiled. "Once upon a time, six weeks would have sounded like a lifetime, but after all this, I can wait," I said.

Mr. Walker smiled back. "That's all we can do, right?" And then he excused himself, saying he had to go take care of some paperwork.

The rest of us gathered together in the parking lot and hugged on each other.

"I think we did a good job in there," Jean said to me.

"I think so too," I said.

"And Cheryl, I'm sorry if over these years you thought I wasn't being honest with you. I just —"

I cut her off. "Jean, please, you don't have to apologize for anything. We're family and that's all that matters."

She pulled me into another hug and we stood like that for a moment.

"Come on, you guys, we gotta get back on the road before it gets dark," Scott announced, breaking up the lovefest. He and my father were driving back to Atlanta, and Jessica and I had a flight back to New York in the morning.

"Thank you, everybody, for coming and doing this," I said one last time. "Let's keep praying that it works and Bobby can come home."

And that's what I kept saying to myself all the way back to New York.

BOBBY

On October 27, I knew my family was sitting in a conference room somewhere testifying on my behalf for my parole hearing. I was sitting in my cell, asking for my immediate release. But instead of asking my jailers, I was asking God, just as I had been every single day since arriving back in prison. Cheryl had given me a Bible back when I was at Rikers, and for the first time in my life, I really started to read it and tried to understand the meaning behind the passages. I dedicated myself to understanding God's word and His role in my life. Reading the Bible gave me great comfort, and I think that's when I finally began to understand what God can do. If someone can have a spiritual awakening, I'd say mine began at Mountain View Correctional Institution, way up in the mountains of North Carolina, near Asheville.

The actual town it sat in was called Spruce Pine. It sounded like a peaceful place, but it was just another prison made to warehouse criminals. The prison was built to hold around a thousand prisoners, but when I got there the inmate population seemed to be hitting maximum capacity. Cells meant for one person often had two. I was supposed to have a cell to myself, but many times I was given a roommate until space opened up somewhere else.

The majority of the guards at Mountain View were white, which was something I wasn't used to, and there were far more white prisoners than when I was in prison before. This was a medium security facility, and it was well locked down, with multiple watchtowers and double guards on duty everywhere. It never crossed my mind to try to escape. For one thing, not only was the security far more severe than I remembered, but also the prison itself sat in such a remote place, somebody would have to run for miles through the mountains before getting to safety.

But the biggest reason escape wasn't on my mind was because from day one I had a single mantra, and I would tell it to anyone and everyone who asked. "I'm going home." And I was going to do it lawfully this time. It was my prayer and my belief. I knew I had been rehabilitated and I knew I no longer belonged in prison. I was just waiting for everyone else to realize the same thing.

I had a counselor assigned to me who right away tried to get me to take a prison job.

"No thank you," I said.

"But if you take a job, it will help you take some time off your sentence," he said.

"What do you mean?" I asked for clarification.

"Well, you don't come up for parole for nine years," the counselor explained. "But if you work, then you might come up earlier because you're showing a good effort at rehabilitation."

"No thank you," I said again. "I've already been rehabilitated. I don't need a job. I'm going home."

"Miller, everyone wants to go home. That's why I'm telling you to take a job so you can get home sooner."

I kind of chuckled then. "I know you're trying to do your job, and I appreciate it, but I don't need to take a job. I know I'm going home, and it's not going to be in nine years."

The counselor looked at me like I was crazy, but I didn't care. I knew my time in that place was temporary, like I knew the sky was blue. I wasn't interested in figuring out how to work the system or play games of any sort. I was ready to submit to the will of God because I had come to realize that God had a plan for me. And it did not involve me spending the next decade of my life behind bars. I didn't claim to know what the plan was, but I thought the best way for me to use my time would be to study God's word and maybe figure it out.

During that first month, the counselor came back several times trying to get me to take on a prison job, but I kept telling him no, and he finally stopped asking. By then I'd established a pretty regular routine for myself. I woke up and went to breakfast, then I'd spend the majority of my day reading the Bible, writing letters to Cheryl, and praying in my cell. They had church service Monday nights, Tuesday nights, and Sunday mornings, and I went to every single one. From doing all of this reading, writing, prayer, and reflection, I truly realized how profoundly God had been working in my life. I now fully understood how God had kept me under His gaze of protection since I was a little boy. Given where I came from and where I had been, I should have been dead or living in the streets. Like my little brother Melvin, who had died from a drug overdose. The trajectory that I had been on for the first part of my life was a roadmap to destruction, and yet I had a beautiful, caring wife and family who loved me. I could look back on the last thirty-eight years and know I had touched many people's lives and made them better. Yes, there had been hard times, but even that to me was proof that God was always looking out for me, because I survived.

While I was trapped in that prison, I put all of my energy into understanding God's word and how He worked. All of the inmates knew that's what I was about. If they walked by my cell and saw me writing or reading, they knew not to bother me. The few times I did socialize with the other men, I found myself offering advice and just listening to their problems. I wasn't trying to make friends, but if people needed to talk, I was available to listen. I still regretted that I hadn't been able to have these kinds of talks with some of my younger family members who'd gotten in trouble with the law. So in some way, I was trying to make amends for that part of my past by helping the guys who really wanted to change their lives.

I lived my life in prison like a man on a mission. I did everything I could to stay out of trouble because I knew my lawyer was trying to get me released on parole. One evening I almost got written up for taking too long to finish my dinner. A guard told me I was supposed to get up and move out so the next group of inmates could come in to eat. I started to argue that I was just finishing my dessert and would be done in a moment, but I didn't want a piece of cake keeping me from getting back to my family. So I shoved that cake in my mouth and shuffled out of there.

I tried my hardest to stay positive and focused. I wasn't happy in prison, but I kept my focus on my faith in God, and He showed me that He was with me. The whole time I was in prison, my feet hurt because of the neuropathy I suffered on account of my diabetes. I wasn't allowed to have a cane, and so I was often shuffling with a limp through the long hallways of the building. One night I had a dream that God was just holding my feet. When I woke up the next morning, my feet didn't hurt, and I was filled with this feeling that God was with me. Another morning I woke up with the sun filtering through the window and hitting my bed. Normally the sun never hit my lower bunk, and again I took this as a sign that God was showing me that He was with me and I just had to keep the faith. There were certain passages in the Bible that I returned to again and again to help with this, like Philippians 4:19: *"And my God will meet all your needs according to the riches of His glory in Christ Jesus."* I knew my lawyer was working for me. I knew Cheryl was working for me. But it was God who I knew would truly meet all my needs and set me free.

So on October 27, when my family was pleading my case, I was doing my part too.

chapter ten

"I Am Bobby Love"

BOBBY

It was two weeks before Thanksgiving and I was sitting in my cell rereading my copy of Steve Harvey's biography that Cheryl had sent me. They announced my name over the PA system saying I needed to report to the gym. My counselor's office was in the gym, so I figured that was why I was being summoned.

When I got down there, another inmate was in the office with the counselor. He saw me outside his door and put his hand up indicating I should wait. As I stood outside his office, I tried to figure out what he wanted to talk to me about. I also started replaying my last few days in the prison and tried to recall any infractions I might have committed. I came up with nothing. But just because I didn't think I had done anything wrong, that didn't mean a guard or another inmate hadn't reported me for something. I remembered how the system worked.

Luckily, I didn't have to keep torturing myself trying to guess why I had been called, because the other guy walked out of the office and my counselor beckoned me in and told me to sit down. I sat in the chair across from his desk and waited for him to speak.

He shuffled through some papers on his desk and without looking up said, "Miller, you got to sign some papers because you made parole."

"What!" I said. "Really?"

"Yeah, it just came through," he said with about as much emotion as fish sticks on a Tuesday.

"Thank you, God!" I shouted, jumping out of my chair. "Can I hug you, man?" I asked gleefully. "I'm so happy."

"No," he said. "You may not hug me."

I sat back down and tried to contain my joy, but I couldn't stop grinning. Not only had my prayers been answered, but also, at that exact moment, I remembered that some of the other inmates had told me that my counselor used to be a guard and back then everybody called him Baloney Neck behind his back on account of the extra folds of flesh around his neck. Just that thought, on top of my indescribable joy, made me want to giggle like a schoolkid. Baloney Neck didn't want to hug me? I didn't care. I was going home!

"Do you know when I'll be able to leave?" I asked, barely able to contain myself.

He looked over some more papers and said, "No, not really. It's going to take a couple more weeks, maybe a month."

"Do you think I'll be home by Thanksgiving?" I asked hopefully.

"I doubt it," he said. "Things don't move that fast around here."

"Okay." I sighed, trying not to dwell on the fact that I would miss the holiday with my family. At least I knew I was going home. I signed all the papers where Baloney Neck had drawn an X and thanked him at least three more times before happily shuffling back to my cell.

When I got there, this young white kid, Kevin, who had temporarily been my cellmate, was waiting for me. He was from Asheboro and was serving an eighteen-month sentence for a robbery and dealing drugs. Even after he was moved to another cell, this kid liked to hang around me and tell me all about his problems with his ex-girlfriend and his baby girl. He was just a kid, so I tried to help him when I could.

"What was that meeting about?" Kevin asked me.

"I made parole," I blurted out, unable to keep the good news to myself.

"Really? How did that happen so fast?" he said.

"I told you, man, when you were in the cell with me. I don't belong here. I've been saying it every single day, and now I'm getting out."

He shook his head like he couldn't believe it. "Guys say they're getting out all the time, but they don't. You're lucky, man," he said.

"I'm not lucky. This is God's work," I corrected him. "But you better not tell anybody. I don't want these jokers knowing that I made parole."

"Why not? It's good news, isn't it?" the kid asked, proving to me how innocent he was. He truly had no idea how things worked in here.

I got up real close to Kevin then and looked around to make sure nobody was listening to us. "It *is* great and that's why you gotta keep it to yourself. There are guys in here that might try to sabotage me in some kind of way. They might try to plant something in my cell or something like that. They do things like that here. So keep it to yourself. Got it?"

"I got it," Kevin said and promised that he'd keep my secret. Since Kevin barely spoke to any of the other inmates, I didn't doubt his word.

I went into my cell then and thought about how I was going to tell Cheryl the good news. That night, when I made the call, before I could even say hello to Cheryl, she burst out with "Bobby, we did it! You made parole." Apparently, before I was notified, Cheryl had been called to ensure that upon release, I would have a safe and secure location to live. So while I didn't get to break the news, Cheryl and I spent the rest of our evening call replaying the moment we'd found out and then expressing our gratitude that this moment we'd been praying for had finally come.

Thanksgiving came and went and I didn't get to go home. I asked my counselor if I'd be home before Christmas, and once again, Baloney Neck told me it was possible but doubtful.

I didn't make it home for Christmas either.

Finally, on January third, they told me I was going home on January fifth.

Now it was impossible to keep the news to myself inside the prison. As soon as word got out that I was two days away from leaving, my cell became really popular. Guys kept coming by asking if they could have my stuff. My soap. My shampoo. My deodorant. My mattress. My books. Anything that wasn't nailed down, people wanted it. I kept my deodorant, my mattress, a few books, my letters from Cheryl, and my Bible, but I freely gave my other possessions away to my fellow inmates. If it was going to make their lives better, I wanted them to have it. I also took folks to the canteen and bought them sticky buns, noodles, gum, anything they wanted that I could afford with the funds I had in my account. I was feeling generous, knowing I was going home to my family and these guys had months and sometimes years left to spend behind these walls.

January fifth finally arrived, and a guard came to my cell early in the morning. I had no clothes to call my own, so the guard took me to the donation bin to find something I could wear home. There were slim pickings, and all I could find were some too-small dress pants and a pullover sweater. I picked out some high-top sneakers that I hoped would mask the fact that my pants didn't even cover my ankles. I was given two white laundry bags to pack my things, in which I put my books, my Bible, and my letters from Cheryl. I was ready to go.

Then the guard led me to the central office, where I was supposed to pick up my bus ticket and then be driven to the depot. But when we got to the office, the woman behind the counter looked at the ticket she was about to hand me and then she looked at the clock and announced to the guard, "He's going to miss this bus. Even if you leave right now, he's not going to make it."

I don't know who had made my travel arrangements, but apparently they couldn't tell time. Or somebody should have gotten me up earlier. I didn't know, but I was getting angrier by the minute while the guard and the lady tried to figure out what went wrong and who was going to fix it.

Even though I had survived for six months at Mountain View, now that I was set on leaving, I knew I wouldn't last even one minute more. I just stood there in agony and held my tongue, because if I opened my mouth, surely I would say something that would get me in trouble. Yes, I made parole, but I wasn't free yet.

The woman made some quick phone calls, and the guard found a computer no one was using and started typing something. In my head I tried reciting the Twenty-third Psalm to stay calm. *The Lord is my shepherd; I shall not want.* By the time I got to *"the valley of the shadow of death,"* the woman had an update.

"Okay, here's what we're going to do. The guard will drive you all the way to Durham, and you can get the bus there. We'll call the bus station in Durham and make sure you can get on there with your ticket. And the bus driver knows you are not allowed to get off the bus in Manhattan. They have to take you all the way to Brooklyn, where your wife will meet you and get you off the bus. Is that clear, Mr. Miller? You must be on that bus when it gets to Brooklyn."

"Yes, ma'am," I said, exhaling all of my anxiety. "Very clear."

The ride to Durham took four hours. The driver tried to make small talk with me, but I really had nothing I wanted to say to him, so we drove in silence. I said goodbye to those prison gates with a grateful heart, and I thanked God for helping me survive my time there. And then I started to imagine what it was going to be like back home with Cheryl and the kids. Back to the life I left behind. Eventually I fell asleep, dreaming about Brooklyn and the wonderful meal I was going to cook for my family when I got home.

The guard woke me up when we got to the bus station in Durham. "Okay, Miller, I'm going in to make sure everything is okay," he said. I mumbled "Okay" as I wondered if this would be the last time anybody called me Miller.

I sat up in the back seat and tried to get my bearings. When the guard came back, he gave me a new ticket and undid my handcuffs.

"Okay, Miller, here you go," he said. "I'm sorry about the mix-up."

"All right," I said.

"And Miller," he said before getting back into his car, "I don't want to see you in these parts ever again."

I smiled at that. "You won't. I promise."

He left and I was free.

I had four hours before my bus to New York left, so I found a pay phone and called my cousin who lived in the area. I asked him to come get me so he could take me shopping. Before sitting on a bus for eighteen hours, I wanted some clothes that fit me. I had cashed out my prison account and had enough money to buy what I needed.

Thankfully, my cousin agreed to come get me, and he took me to a department store in downtown Durham. My cousin had to run an errand, so he dropped me off and we arranged to meet two hours later.

It was great to walk around and feel like a normal person again, but it was also overwhelming. All the noise and the people after a year behind bars was a lot to take in. I wasn't twenty-seven anymore, looking for excitement and adventure. I was sixty-five years old and wanted to find a comfortable pair of pants. After wandering around the men's department and trying on a handful of items, I gave up on finding jeans that fit the way I wanted. Instead, I bought myself a warm winter coat, because I knew when I arrived in New York it would be cold. Shopping had always been one of my favorite pastimes, but now I just wanted to get out of that store and find my cousin.

I started to head toward the meeting spot we'd decided on, but I couldn't find my way. All of the exits looked the same. I walked past the shoe department what felt like a dozen times. I started to panic and worry that my cousin might think I'd left and now I was going to miss my bus back to Brooklyn. If that happened, that would be a violation of my parole and I'd be back behind bars before I even made it home. I could feel the sweat start to prickle in my armpits. *Think, Bobby,* I said to myself as I stood in the bright lights of the perfume department. *Figure something out.*

"Excuse me, Miss," I asked a woman behind one of the perfume counters. "Could I please borrow your cell phone to call my cousin? I was supposed to meet him somewhere around here, but I'm kind of lost."

The woman looked at me and shrugged. "Sure," she said and handed over her phone.

I called my cousin's cell phone and told him where I was. He said he'd been looking all over for me. I apologized and told him I'd gotten mixed up with every exit looking the same. A few minutes later I saw my cousin walking toward me, and with a sigh of relief, I followed him out to his car.

After my shopping adventure, I was happy to just sit at the bus station and wait for the bus. I couldn't help but think back to the day of my escape from prison what seemed like a lifetime ago. How nervous I was that I was going to get caught; how excited I was to get to New York; how many dreams I had for myself; how ready I was to bury Walter Miller and leave him behind.

Well, here I was again, making the very same trip. But for the last twelve months, Walter Miller had risen from the dead. I still carried tremendous guilt from that part of my life, but I knew that in the eyes of the law, Walter Miller had finally and officially paid his debts to society. That meant I was free to live my life out in the open, no more hiding my past. Walter Miller, Buddy, Cotton Foot, Bobby. I had answered to many different names in my lifetime, always thinking that a different name would make me a different person. But I've always been the same person. I've always been a hustler, a survivor, and a risk taker. I survived my childhood. I hustled through my adolescence and early adulthood. I took risks to escape incarceration. What changed was my motivation. I started out hustling for myself. I could see no further than my own wants and needs. But then I turned my instincts and skills toward helping my family to survive and thrive. The same hustle I employed to plan and execute a robbery, I used to plan and execute a trip to Disney World with four kids.

After this last stint in prison, it was clear to me that God had shifted my path so that I could be redeemed while fundamentally remaining my true self. If God doesn't make mistakes, then He did not err when He made me, but I still had to learn plenty of lessons on my journey. I had to learn the meaning of compassion and care, humility and sacrifice. I am positive God was guiding my steps when I jumped off that bus in 1977, and He helped me to see that I had something good to offer this world. And that something could just be me. The *real* me. My mother's lucky number seven. The boy who loved his family. The kid who loved fashion and music. The man who loved to cook. The gambler who always bet on himself.

By the time the bus pulled into the station, I couldn't wait to climb aboard and return to the life I had left behind. A life where I could now bring my whole self to the table.

CHERYL

"There he is!" I shouted, pointing to the lone figure on the bus. "There's Bobby!"

Jasmine, her husband, Rich, their little boy Levi, and Jordan and Justin all turned to look where I was pointing. The bus we had been waiting for, for the last thirty minutes, was finally pulling up to the Greyhound stop on Livingston Street in Downtown Brooklyn. We all ran to the corner where the bus was going to park, and we saw Bobby come stand near the driver as the bus was coming to a stop. He was the only one on board. As soon as the doors opened, he emerged from inside.

Bobby walked down the steps slowly with a big grin on his face, and we all just wrapped him up in the biggest hug, laughing through our tears of joy.

"Oh my goodness, Bobby, you look like Santa Claus with that beard," I exclaimed, and everyone laughed. It looked like Bobby hadn't shaved for the last six months. I didn't care. My husband was finally home. Our family was finally back together again.

"Are you hungry, Dad?" Jordan asked.

"I could eat something," Bobby said.

"Well, good," I said. "We're going to take you to the diner to celebrate."

Rich had a big SUV that we could all fit in, and we drove over to one of the diners nearby. Jessica, who had been working the night shift at her job, joined us at the restaurant, and when she saw her father, she couldn't stop laughing at Bobby's new look.

"Daddy," she said, as we were all eating pancakes, "you need to get rid of that beard."

After breakfast, we headed home. Rich drove and Bobby sat in the front seat next to him. We were all talking and laughing, and the kids were peppering Bobby with questions about everything that had happened to him over those last few weeks. From where I sat, I could tell Bobby was just overwhelmed by it all. He could barely keep up. I decided then to hold my tongue and save my questions and comments for when we were alone. He was back, and I knew he wasn't going anywhere, so there was no rush. I sat back in my seat and said quietly to myself, "Thank you, God, for bringing back my husband."

It wasn't until late that night, when Jasmine, Rich, and Levi had gone home to their apartment up in Harlem and Jessica and the twins had finally gone to bed, that Bobby and I were together at last. It almost felt like a first date, being alone with Bobby. We had been apart for a year and had to remember what it was like to be husband and wife. For a moment we just sat there on the couch without talking, listening to the faint sounds of WBLS radio in the background. I knew Bobby had to be exhausted and I didn't want to tax him too much, but I had one question that needed to be answered.

"Bobby," I started tentatively, and he turned to me. "Are we Millers or are we Loves? Are you Walter or are you Bobby?" I needed to know what to call this man. For the last year I'd seen the name Walter Miller more than Bobby Love. It was on all of the official documents I received, all of the important papers I'd filled out. When the parole officer had come to our apartment to make sure that Bobby would have a safe place to live, he had referred to him as Walter Miller throughout the visit until I started doing it too. Even though that name, that person — Walter Miller — was a stranger to me, I had to know from my husband himself who he really was.

Bobby reached for my hand and said, "We're Loves, Cheryl. And I'm Bobby."

"Okay," I said, but I probably didn't sound too convinced.

"Listen, Cheryl, you married Bobby Love. That's who I've been for these last forty years and that's who I'm going to be for the next forty years or however long God sees fit to have me on this earth."

"Okay, Bobby," I said with more conviction.

"And I'm going to change my name officially, too," Bobby added.

"You are?" I said. "Because I was thinking maybe we might have to go get married again or change our marriage certificate or . . ."

Bobby stopped me. "I don't want you to worry about any of that. This is something I need to do to fix what I did. I've spent all this time as Bobby Love, working, building a family with you, paying taxes, and I'm going to make it official. I don't want you or anyone else to doubt who I am. I am Bobby Love."

I trusted Bobby to do what he said he was going to do, and sure enough, in the following weeks, he started the process to legally become Bobby Love. He had to get a new birth certificate issued with the name Bobby Love and a host of other paperwork before it became official. That took care of the legal status of Bobby's identity, but we still had to work through what it meant for Bobby to be my husband as a man with no more secrets.

The day after he came home, Bobby sat me down and told me everything about his past. Even though Jasmine had found his arrest records and I had read some of the stories that had come out in the newspapers, I was clueless about all the things Bobby had done, from his time in the Morrison correctional facility to all of the things he'd done in Washington, DC, including getting shot by a police officer.

"Oh my God, you could have been killed," I said after hearing about that incident. To myself I thought, *This man must be in God's favor to come through a life like that unscathed.*

"I told you I was lucky," Bobby said with a smile.

I shook my head. "No, Bobby. God was protecting you."

Bobby quickly turned serious. "I know, Cheryl. And He's still protecting me."

"Why didn't you tell me any of this, Bobby?" I asked for probably the twenty-seventh time. "You should have told me. Keeping all of this inside and hiding it is too much for anybody to handle. It must have been eating you up inside."

Bobby hung his head and sighed. Then he looked up and said, "You would have made me turn myself in, Cheryl. You found a wallet on the ground full of cash and you took it to the police station. You most definitely would have made me turn myself in if I told you what I'd done."

Now it was my turn to smile. "You're right. I would have if you had told me all that."

We both laughed because we knew it was the truth. And it felt good that we could laugh together again.

That conversation lasted for another hour, and we revisited it again and again those first few weeks. Sometimes I would find myself angry with Bobby for keeping his secrets, but then I would have to remind myself that forgiveness without forgetting doesn't work. I could say I forgave Bobby, but if I kept dwelling on the wrongs he committed, then I would never be able to move on, and we'd never be able to grow as a couple. And I could see how hard Bobby was trying. He was talking more and sharing more, and he was far more affectionate with me than he ever had been before. I realized that I needed to be a better listener and not be so judgmental when Bobby talked about his flaws and mistakes.

I also saw how devoted Bobby was to his faith now. He had developed a meaningful and personal relationship with God while he was in prison. Whereas I used to have to beg him to pray with the kids and me, now he was praying with us and praying for us. Bobby was so eager to go to church on Sunday mornings, to teach Sunday school, and to help out with whatever work needed to be done that sometimes I would tell him to go ahead and I would meet him there because I was still working on my hair or something and didn't want to hold him up. I had always yearned to share my faith with my husband in a deep way, and now we did, and for that I was so very grateful.

Bobby had the same conversation with the boys that he had with me. He told them everything about his past and said they could ask him anything they wanted to. He really didn't want to have any secrets anymore with any member of our family.

We were so much stronger as a family after everything we had been through. I was proud of all four of our children, who had rallied around each other and me and not used their father's incarceration as an excuse to act crazy. Quite the opposite. Each and every one of them, in their own way, had stayed positive and remained focused on getting Bobby out.

But I knew it was me who had kept our family together. I think that's what God put me on this earth to do. Sometimes when I look back on Bobby's year in prison, I say to myself, "My God, I did this thing. I really did it. I took my marriage vows seriously, 'for better or for worse,' and I found the strength to do whatever was necessary to deal with whatever life put in front of me." There were so many obstacles, but with my faith in God guiding me and my love for our family empowering me, I found the strength to keep all of us together. I kept working and paying the bills. I had to find creative ways to keep money in our bank account. We celebrated holidays and birthdays despite the fact that Bobby was missing. And on top of all that, I was doing everything I could to help get Bobby out of prison and to emotionally support him while he was in there.

When I think about all of that, plus having all of my business plastered all over the news, I know a lot of people would have crumbled or maybe just walked away from the entire mess. But I didn't. I stayed and I fought for what was most important to me in this world. And I won. My prize was my family, together again and stronger than ever.

Are we perfect now? No. Do we still struggle with money? Sometimes. Do Bobby and I still argue? Of course. Do I still put my pants on one leg at a time? Every single day. But these are regular things that happen to regular people. And that's what we are. Regular people with a past. A past that doesn't define us, but it's one that has made us who we are today.

Acknowledgments

We want to thank God first, because without Him, none of this would have been possible. We also have to thank our children, Jasmine, Jessica, Jordan, and Justin, for being our continuous inspiration. We are grateful to our family members who have always been there for us; we wouldn't be where we are today without them. In addition to our blood family, we also want to thank our church family at Coney Island Cathedral of Deliverance, in particular Bishop Waylen Hobbs Jr. and First Lady Donna Hobbs.

We want to thank our wonderful editor Rakia Clark and the entire Houghton Mifflin Harcourt staff for making this process extremely welcoming. Also, we would like to thank our agent Brian DeFiore for connecting us to Houghton Mifflin Harcourt and for guiding us through this process during such a difficult time in the world. We are grateful for having Lori L. Tharps help us get our story on the page. We give a special thanks to Brandon Stanton from *Humans of New York* for bringing our story to the public and for being such an amazing man throughout this entire journey.

Finally, we would like to give a special shout-out to our son-in-law Richard Nelson for introducing us to our manager Jonathan Conyers, who believed our story was worth telling from day one. Jonathan brought all the wonderful people mentioned here together to create this opportunity for our family. We are forever grateful.